Endorsements

This is an honest, heartfelt, and heaven-calling look into the unbearable suffering caused by the death of a child. Can any suffering be deeper or more unthinkable? I've known the author and his family for many years. I had the privilege of speaking at his son's memorial service. I know firsthand the authenticity of his words and his life. This is a much-needed resource and offers real help to anyone suffering or seeking to help those who are.

—Rev. James Burgess, Senior Pastor
Fellowship Church
Dubai, UAE

Birthed in ongoing grief, this personal immersion in Scripture, theology, and experience will provide pastoral comfort to any in pain and anguish. Missionary-pastor-friend David Stevens takes the reader to the philosophical edge of a God limited by human choices and actions. And yet divine providence in both purpose and process finally prevails. Valuable exegeses of relevant Scriptures filled with powerful illustrations from history, geography, and literature will strengthen any soul. Read it slowly, humbly, and eagerly.

—Ramesh Richard Ph.D., Th.D.
President, RREACH and Professor,
Dallas Theological Seminary

David Stevens has chosen an age-old topic, perhaps the most thorny issue in the history of human relationship with the Judeo Christian God: How can a loving God tolerate rampant injustice in so many areas of our beautiful but savage world and still expect us to love and trust him? With solid biblical theology, the author carefully navigates the common and a few uncommon theological and psychological perspectives. This book can serve as devotional reading, or in pastoral or therapeutic counseling, especially for grieving parents.

—Dr. Lois Svoboda, M.D.
Physician and Marriage & Family Therapist

Travel with my friend, David Stevens, on a journey that is both emotional and philosophical, touching both raw human emotions and deep theological issues. This is not a typical grief story. It is ideologically deep and, at the same time, biblical and warmly encouraging.

—Jeff Townsend
Former pastor and currently National Director of Field Development, International Students, Inc.

David Stevens uses his gift of making Scripture come to life to lay the foundation of hope for anyone walking through the pain of loss. He shows how God's redemptive love gently leads us to the point of facing our real selves, guiding us towards deep happiness that glorifies God and satisfies our soul.

—Ray Sanford
Vice President, One Challenge

DISCOVERING GOD'S
PURPOSE IN YOUR PAIN

LIFE
WITH A
LIMP

DAVID E. STEVENS
FOREWORD BY PAUL LOUIS METZGER

PB ISBN: 979-8-9989086-0-6
ISBN E-Book: 979-8-9989086-1-3

Printed in the United States of America

To all who limp in this life while leaning into the next.

Contents

Acknowledgments

No one writes a book alone. Every author is shaped by those who have gone before or journey alongside in the present, speaking fresh insight into the writer's life. I am no exception. Beyond the inspired words of Scripture, I am deeply indebted to the writings of those cited in this book and who belong to the community of those who worship in pain.

Through their patience and prayers, my family members have participated in the writing of this book. My adult children, Rebecca Blumhardt, Mary Lynne McCulloch, and Justin Stevens, have inspired me with their persevering faith in the face of loss and doubt. My wife, Mary Alice, has been my closest companion in grief. As I have written, we have wept . . . and worshipped. Thank you for your honest, insightful feedback on every paragraph of this work.

A special thanks goes to my dear friend, Dr. Paul Metzger, who has written the Foreword to this book. Along with his wife and family, he also is limping by faith along the pathway of suffering. Your encouragment in my writing endeavors is deeply appreciated.

Finally, a special thanks to Ellen Bascuti, my meticulous copy editor who never lets a misplaced colon or misspelled word go unnoticed. Your experienced eye for detail and encouragement along the way contributed significantly to bringing this work to completion.

Foreword

by Paul Louis Metzger

Have you ever been on a guided tour of a city, museum, or nature excursion? The best guides are knowledgeable and authoritative, skillful in what and how they communicate, and personable. They are worth the price of the tour!

Now what if the tour guide is leading you on a tour of how to cope and find hope amid tragedy in life to gain resilience and experience growth? The best kind of guide would be well-informed and formed through the crucible of pain and suffering, clear and discerning in sharing the needed guidance for navigating the back and heartbreaking terrain, and empathic in their consideration of you.

So, it is with Dr. David Stevens and the guided tour book he wrote for you. In *Life with a Limp: Discovering God's Purpose in Your Pain*, Dr. Stevens provides biblical, pastoral, and personal reflections to instruct and comfort us as we journey through the night of pain and suffering into the daybreak of hope. It is one thing to experience pain on the path of life. It is quite another to walk with a limp that involves growing through suffering where we find our ultimate assurance and strength from Jesus. He is the God who triumphs through suffering for us. As your tour guide, David keeps his eye on Jesus as the north star as you go from chapter through chapter of the grieving process until the break of day. David relies on God's Word and Spirit as he provides direction so you can discover God's purpose in your pain for growth and healing.

As alluded to above, David knows suffering. He and his wife Mary Alice lost their oldest son Jonathan years ago. I cannot do justice to their story and so will defer to my dear friend to tell you what transpired. What I can tell you is that David's account of their loss and how he has walked through life with a limp and grown through pain and suffering deeply resonates and impacts me. My oldest child, Christopher, endured a catastrophic brain injury in January of last year. The probabilities of meaningful recovery are slim, though the possibilities are real. No matter the outcome, I have been learning to walk with a limp and grow through the suffering. I often falter and fall along the path. I am so thankful that I have a tour guide like my friend and brother David, whose *Life with a Limp* helps me to get back up and keep going and growing through pain.

My colleague David draws from decades of deep biblical meditation and instruction, countless hours of empathic pastoral listening and counsel, and lessons learned through agonizing trials in processing his own grief to bring you this spiritual treasure. I for one need guides who speak and live authoritatively in response to Scripture in pursuit of Jesus in dependence on God's Spirit and who share openly about their own struggles in caring for others. David is a sure guide to discover God's purpose amid anguish and heartbreak. You can trust him to provide biblical, pastoral, and personal counsel as you walk with a limp and grow as a person through your pain.

David and I met for lunch last summer when he and Mary Alice returned to the land of Lewis and Clark to visit friends and churches. They are world travelers who are often teaching and ministering in Europe, Africa, and the States. Last summer, he ministered to me on the banks of the Columbia River in Vancouver, Washington while meeting over lunch. As I processed my grief out loud, we discussed what it is like to walk through life with a limp.

David and I are both drawn to the biblical story of the Patriarch Jacob, the "heal grabber" who wrestled with God and prevailed. Jacob prevailed through loss, as the Angel of the Lord wrenched his hip so that he walked the rest of his life with a limp. David's account of Jacob's story plays a critical role in his book, as the title suggests. My prayer is that David's account will also play a critical role in our lives as we wrestle with God, not away from God, in the face of tragedy.

Like Jacob, I often try to go it alone, or put conditions on my relationship with God, even amid suffering. But as the Patriarch Jacob and the Apostle Paul eventually discovered, it is only when we are weak in total dependence on God's Son in the Spirit that we are strong. I need to rely on Jesus to bear my burden instead of trying to roll the heavy, large stone of trauma, bitterness, guilt, shame, and blame up a hill. After all, God rolled the stone of human depravity, despair, and death away when Jesus rose victoriously from the grave on Easter morning. Jesus invites all of us who are heavy laden to come to him and find rest. He is gentle and humble in heart. As we trust and obey him, he will lighten our load.

We should also learn to rely on others who can share the load of our daily experience with life-long pain and suffering that result from tragic loss. Those who endure tragedy and who wish to learn to walk through life with a limp and grow through grievous trials need to count on able tour guides and trailblazers. The perilous sojourn is unbearably lonely and too risky. We cannot go it alone.

My prayer for you and me is that we will lean into David Stevens' guidebook filled with biblical, spiritual, and deeply personal wisdom as we hobble through life. As David instructs us, only as we look to Jesus, our north star in the darkest hours of the night, will we find our wobbling feet, gain strength, and prevail. Only then will we make our way forward along the treacherous path in the aftermath of loss to daybreak.

Paul Louis Metzger, Ph.D.
Vancouver, Washington
Eastertide 2022

Introduction

He who limps is still walking.
—Stanisław Jerzy Lec

Life is painful. Pain marks our entry into this life, our journey through this life, and our departure from this life. As the poet, Francis Thompson, once wrote, "We are born in other's pain and perish in our own."[1]

Even our best years are filled with the nagging hunch that something is terribly wrong with everything. As a result, we all—to one degree or another—walk with a limp.

Maybe your limp is physical in nature. From the common cold to the ravages of cancer, no human frame is exempt from the capricious and seemingly meaningless onslaught of illness, disease, and ultimately death.

Many suffer from an emotional limp. Clinical depression is the leading cause of ill health and disability worldwide, affecting approximately 280 million people around the globe.[2] I personally belong to those statistics, having been treated at one point in my life by two perceptive psychiatrists whom God skillfully used to perform emotional surgery on my soul.

Closely linked to our emotional makeup is our way of thinking, reasoning, and viewing life. We are psychological beings through and through. Yet here, too, we experience the bruising inherent to life in a topsy-turvy world. Unhealthy thought patterns—often acquired in our younger, more impressionable years—become deeply ingrained in our soul, producing mental ruts later in life that propel us in destructive directions. Unhealthy perspectives inevitably lead to unhealthy lives lived with a limp.

Physical, emotional, and psychological pain often leads to spiritual pain—lingering doubts about the goodness of God or even his existence. Consequently, many limp along from day to day, void of inner peace or any real sense of identity or purpose.

Sometimes our pain is our own doing. We make choices that have their own destructive consequences. If you sow the wind, you'll reap the whirlwind. Often, however, our pain is simply the result of living in a fallen world and being inseparably linked to fallen humanity. The Apostle Paul tells us that "the whole creation has been groaning as in the pains of childbirth right up to the present time" (Romans 8:22). Since we are all inextricably associated with fallen creation, we groan also.

It's been said that philosophers and theologians are those who kick up dust and then complain they cannot see. Since I certainly don't want to be responsible for such a dust storm, my purpose in the following pages is not to address the plethora of philosophical and theological perspectives proposed through the centuries in response to the question of suffering. Space does not permit such an exposé. Furthermore, many excellent works have been penned on the subject and, to borrow the words of John the Evangelist, I suppose the whole world could not contain the books that could be written! My purpose is rather to recount my own grappling with one specific question: *How do we walk and grow through our suffering?*

Since the death of my firstborn son, I have wrestled intensely with God, seeking the answer to that question. Maybe you have also as you limp along through life. Thankfully, our Creator has not left us in the dark. Between paradise lost (Genesis 3) and paradise regained (Revelation 21-22), the Bible is replete with examples of those who walk through suffering. One of those is Jacob, the "God-wrestler," whose life begins with a strut, but ends with a limp—a limp that ultimately taught him to lean upon the One who alone could satisfy the deepest longings of his heart. As I see myself in Jacob and have better come to see the "Jacob" in me, I devote an entire chapter to this biblical character who limps and finally learns to grow through suffering. This is the theme of the Interlude entitled *Jacob at the Jabbok: Blessing from Brokenness* (Chapter 5).

The life of Jacob, who wrestled with God, points us to Jesus Christ, who is God—our God who suffers. The famed British preacher, C. H. Spurgeon (1834-1892) once remarked, "God had one Son without sin, but He never had a son without trial."[3] *That is why we must always allow our limp in life to lead us to contemplate the cross of Christ—God's final answer to evil and suffering.* This is the theme of Part 1, entitled: *Walking Through Suffering* (Chapters 1-4). The prophetic words of Psalm 22 will light the way, for there we discover six key principles that enlighten and comfort us as we limp through the night of suffering into the daybreak of hope.

While all walk through suffering, far fewer grow through suffering. This is the theme of Part 2, entitled: *Growing Through Suffering* (Chapters 6-10). Here we'll examine the insightful advice of a martyr, James, the half-brother of our Lord and author of the New Testament epistle that carries his name. This suffering saint tells us how to turn our trials into testimony as he points the way to discovering God's purpose in our pain, resulting in a different kind of happiness that will find its fullest expression in the promised world to come where tears will be no more.

Following the example of the biblical poets and prophets, the following chapters are a form of prayer, a quest carried out on the knees as much as in the head. Anselm's famous motto *fides quaerens intellectum* ("faith seeking understanding") summarizes well my objective. My prayer is that this reflection will also help others who are seeking to understand their own suffering in the light of God's infinite goodness and wise, loving sovereignty.

David E. Stevens
Tournon-sur-Rhône, France

Part 1 – Walking Through Suffering

CHAPTER 1

Out of the Depths

Then Jacob tore his clothes, put on sackcloth and mourned for his son many days.
—Genesis 37:34

Every one prays; but very few "cry." But of those who do "cry to God," the majority would say, "I owe it to the depths. I learned it there."
—James Vaughan[4]

As I pulled into the driveway, I was excited to be home. I was expectantly looking forward to some time with my wife and children after a typically long Sunday at church. I figured that we would all sit down, have supper together and interact on the events of the past week. After all, we had a lot to process as a family.

My mom had just passed through the doorway of death a few days before, and we were already making funeral plans necessitating a trip back east from Portland, Oregon. It had been a heart-rending week. Little did I know what I was about to hear.

My wife, Mary Alice, opened the front door and from the anguish in her voice and the tears in her eyes, I immediately knew that something terribly tragic had happened.

"Our Jonathan is with the Lord" were her first tear-soaked words.

At first I thought I had misunderstood. Maybe she meant something other than what I feared. Maybe she meant to say, "The Lord is with Jonathan." After all, I had just prayed God's protection and direction over Jonathan when we spoke with him two days before on the phone. Did she truly mean that our firstborn was dead? Could it be? Her words seemed surreal. Children are not supposed to die before their parents. Maybe this was all some kind of cruel joke or a terrible misunderstanding.

But it was not.

The poet and playwright T. S. Eliot once remarked, "Humankind cannot bear much reality."[5] For me, those words were never truer than the moment I learned of the death of Jonathan. I was numbed with paralyzing shock. An indescribable grief shot through my entire being like a bolt of lightning, leaving me in a sort of time warp. It was as if in seconds the entire life of my oldest son passed before my eyes and then came suddenly, tragically to an abrupt stop. Overwhelmed with an emotional agony that felt like lead weights pulling me to the earth, my legs gave way and I started to fall to the floor. Mary Alice, along with a fellow pastor from our church who had come to give comfort to our family, caught me and led me to the living room chair. Like the weeping prophet Jeremiah, my first word of lament was not *why* but *how*.

How *could* this happen? How *did* this happen?

Earlier that evening, Mary Alice received a phone call from the American Embassy in Seoul, South Korea. It was that dreaded kind of call no parent wants to receive. The news hit like a tidal wave. The man on the other end of the line identified himself as the chief of American Citizen Services. His words were piercing: "I'm sorry to inform you, but your son has died, and we believe it was from accidental carbon monoxide poisoning."

Jonathan had always had an adventurous spirit. As a young boy, it drove him to explore the outer limits of the island we had lived on in southern France, and later in life, to go back-packing on his own in South Korea, the country he had come to love. Though adventurous and initiative taking, he was also quietly disarming. His kind, sensitive spirit was often an open invitation for others to share their hidden secrets or emotional burdens that otherwise would go unvoiced. About a year before his death, Jonathan had enrolled in a study abroad program with Portland State University and left for South Korea, the "Land of the Morning Calm." And it was in that land in the early morning hours of November 28, 2004, that Jonathan quietly, softly entered the calm of his eternal home.

TERRIBLE IS THE MYSTERY OF DEATH

There is probably no greater pain and despair than what is experienced in the initial moments of an unexpected tragedy. It is numbing, debilitating, and overwhelming. Even as the initial shock gradually recedes, the ever-present sense of profound loss remains. Even now, more than fifteen years after his passing, an empty space remains at the table of our hearts that will never be filled this side of eternity. The pain of human loss is doggedly persistent and is reluctant to release its pernicious grip on our hearts.

The presence of death was not a new experience for me. I had previously lost my dad to leukaemia five years before, and only days before Jonathan's death, was preparing the message I would give at my mother's funeral. Long before that as a young man in my early twenties, I had worked in a funeral home. The job of retrieving the deceased at their home or hospital bed and transporting cold, motionless bodies into the embalming parlor placed me in intimate contact with the harsh realities of death. To avoid the eerie feeling I would at times carry on a pretend conversation with the deceased as I drove the hearse back to the funeral home! Later as a pastor, I presided over numerous funerals, often speaking confidently of our enduring hope as Christians. Of course, it is always easier to speak hopeful words of assurance to others who are lamenting their loss or pain rather than to oneself—just like Job's friends.[6] And it is certainly less painful to touch the cold corpse of someone you've never met than that of your own son.

A few days after receiving the news of our son's death, I left for Seoul, South Korea. I knew the trip would include much more than simply retrieving Jonathan's body and personal effects. Far more than a physical journey, it was an emotional and spiritual journey, a journey that would take me further into the quagmire of grief, pain, and sorrow. I kept telling myself that hope would be on the horizon, but for the moment, it was hidden by the clouds of utter confusion.

On the first day after my arrival in Seoul, I was taken to the police station located near the American Consulate. There I met with several of the officers who had investigated the incidents surrounding our son's death. Upon arrival, we all went into a dimly lit room and gathered around a cluttered conference table. The police showed me the pictures they had taken of Jonathan's body upon arriving at the hotel where he had died. The brutal shock of seeing his lifeless body spotted by the toxic effects of carbon monoxide was more than I could bear. I quickly turned down their offer to let me keep the photos. They also gave me Jonathan's personal effects, including the clothing he was wearing the night before he was found, his Bible, his calendar book, a Korean and Japanese grammar book, and a small backpack.

I then went to the morgue in downtown Seoul where Jonathan's body was being prepared for embalming. There I was introduced to the mortician who directed me into a crypt full of vaults that stored the dead. He opened one, rather mechanically pulled out the body of my son, and said via translation that I could have some time alone. There I stood, gazing at the lifeless body of my boy as if this was all a nightmarish dream. I spoke to him, longing for a response, and cherished the memory of the words we had exchanged on the phone only days before. My mind flashed back to the warm, soft touch when I held Jonathan (whose name means "gift of God") in my arms for the first time moments after his birth. And now, twenty-two years later, I'm hesitantly reaching out to touch that same body—motionless, cold, and hard. Had God taken back his gift?

At that moment, the full impact of my son's death invaded the depths of my being with all of its grim reality. Until then, I had been processing his death largely with my mind and emotions; the stark reality had not yet penetrated my soul. As the philosopher and theologian Nicholas Woltersorff writes in his *Lament for a Son*, "To fully persuade us of death's reality, of its grim finality, our eyes and hands must rub against death's cold, hard body, body against body, painfully. Knowing death with mind alone is less than fully knowing it."[7] With the intentional, delicate touch of his cold, inanimate body, I took one more step in accepting the fact that his departure was irreversible on this side of heaven.

The mystery that surrounds us in the tragic moments of life is both personal and philosophical. On a personal level one might ask, *How did this happen?* or *How can I survive this pain?* Eventually the more philosophical questions press in upon our minds: *Why did God let this happen?* or *How can I trust a God who would let my child die?* On the personal level, we feel. On the philosophical level, we think. However, both are essential in the process of encountering God in our suffering, for both are expressions of who we are as the image-bearers of our Creator.

The seventh century Christian monk and apologist John of Damascus wrote: "Truly terrible is the mystery of death. I lament at the sight of the beauty created for us in the image of God which lies now in the grave without shape, without glory, without consideration. What is this mystery that surrounds us? Why are we delivered up to decay? Why are we bound to death?"[8] It was and continues to be these questions—and so many others like them—that, *apart from the hope of the gospel,* relentlessly haunt the mind and plague the heart and plead for answers.

Yes, both the personal and philosophical questions are essential if we are to truly love God with all of our *heart* and *mind.* While both are essential, the personal normally precedes the philosophical; the question of "how?" normally precedes the question of "why?"

We must weep before we reason.

WEEPING IS PREFERRED TO WORKING

We must also weep before we work. Upon returning home to the States, I found myself caught up in a whirlwind of activity. There was work to be done—a trip back East for my mother's funeral, accounts to close, a coffin to choose, a burial plot to purchase, orders of service to decide for the two memorials. Each activity became in itself a cathartic expression of the painful, anguished cry of the human soul coming to grips with the reality of death. As a pastor, I was usually the one presiding at funerals, reminding others of the value of expressing grief. But now my entire family and I were sitting among the bereaved. Though we did our best, I wish now that I had wept better then.

Martin Luther writes in his commentary on Psalm 6:8 that "weeping is preferred to working and suffering exceeds all doing."[9] His statement seems to have followed the lead of some of the early church fathers like Ambrose in the fourth century. Writing of his own emotional limp over the death of his brother, Ambrose finds an example of healthy lament in Jesus' tears at the tomb of Lazarus. He writes: "We have not incurred any grievous sin by our tears. Not all weeping proceeds from unbelief or weakness. . . . The Lord also wept.

He wept for one not related to Him, I for my brother. He wept for all in weeping for one, I will weep for the all, in my brother."[10]

Unfortunately, such profound expressions of sorrow and grief have often been shunned and shamed in various cultures through the centuries. For many in the Greek and Roman world, any expression of grief reflected weakness and was considered to be primarily characteristic of women. Such a perspective entered the church through people like Augustine, who felt that it was sinful to voice suffering, unless it was a lament over one's sin. At one point, he briefly grieved the loss of his mother, Monica, only to grieve the fact that he had felt grief! Twelve centuries later, Calvin, strongly influenced by Augustine, still voiced the same perspective. He felt it was wrong to cry out "why" in the face of tragedy and loss, since as believers we already know (or should know) the answer. And following the death of his mother and best friend, he concluded that his profound grief was an indication of too much worldly affection.[11] Fortunately, Luther and the German reformers pointed the way for a more biblical approach to suffering. Recognizing that the medieval church had been too influenced by the pagan-like stoicism of the Greek and Roman philosophers, they came to place a renewed emphasis on Christ's loving presence in the midst of our suffering. But even so, they still seem to have missed the way in which the Scriptures give voice to the cry of the heart in times of trouble.[12]

Several years ago, I saw Mount Rushmore for the first time. Engraved in stone is the face of Teddy Roosevelt. TR, as they called him, had married the love of his life. Both had great talent and a vivaciousness of life that was contagious. They were elated when they discovered she was pregnant with their first child. But right before the birth, she became ill. At the same time, TR's mother became ill and died of typhoid. Then his wife died in childbirth. TR often wrote in his diary, but on that day all he wrote was an X—nothing else. The next day, he penned these nine words: "All the light has gone out of my life." He never mentioned his wife again. He tore pages from his diary that had been written concerning his wife, and he burned almost all the letters they had exchanged over the years. He counseled a friend who suffered a similar loss to do the same—to put it out of his mind and never mention it. "Just get over it" and move on with life was his approach.[13] But we must never do that. We must pursue the path of the biblical prophets and poets, not the path of the president.

THE KING DAVID BLUES

While the anguished cry of lament is found throughout the Scriptures, its poetical expression is best exemplified in the Psalms which are, in many respects, the prayer book of the Bible. I suspect the reason for this is because the Psalms speak not only *to* us, but also *for* us. In the Psalms, the Word of God *to us* becomes the Word of God *from us* as we pray it back to God. The Psalms are theology sung, not said; prayed, not preached.[14]

Not only do the Psalms speak for us, but they also speak for us "out of the depths." The expression comes from Psalm 130:1: "Out of the depths I cry to you, O Lord; O Lord, hear my voice. Let your ears be attentive to my cry for mercy." If there is any time that people have turned to the Psalms, it is when the bottom seems to be falling out of life. It is in our hour of deepest despair and adversity that the Psalms bring the necessary words for us to express our prayer to God.

Yes, when we read and pray the Psalms, we have the impression that someone has been reading our mail. Why? Because the Psalms express the full gamut of emotional, spiritual, and psychological experience. Could this explain why the Psalms are often neglected in our worship and even in our preaching? Many find it uncomfortable to be so blatantly transparent about their personal lives. In contrast, the writers of the Psalms, marked by a brutal authenticity of style that hides nothing from God or the community of worshipers, despairingly express their lamentation to God.

The quintessential expression of emotional agony is found in the psalms of lament, which outnumber all other types of psalms. Of the 150 Psalms, fifty-seven can be classified as laments. That's over a third of all the psalms! What is a "lament?" "The lament, at its heart, is giving voice to the suffering that accompanies deep loss, whatever that loss may be. Lament is not about suffering. Lament is not concerning suffering. Lament does not count the stages [of grief] and try to identify the stage in which one finds oneself. Lament is the language of suffering, the voicing of suffering."[15]

The language of lament is a language of disorientation. Intense suffering has a way of paralyzing our speech and stealing our words. The inspired psalms of lament, however, give expression to the aching heart, providing words to articulate the confusion and conflict that plague the soul in time of suffering. As such, these poetic prayers of lament draw the suffering soul into the orbit of God's compassionate concern and care.

If the psalms of lament teach us anything, it is that the pain of life must not be denied or lightly dismissed. I'll never forget arriving at the traditional Korean inn where Jonathan had taken his final breath. I was accompanied by a representative of the American Embassy, a local pastor, and a Korean police officer who had conducted the investigation into my son's death. As I approached the quaint, traditional inn, it became immediately evident why there were safety issues related to the maintenance of the building. Upon entering, an elderly Korean lady named Ms. Lee, who managed the small hotel, hesitantly approached. When she discovered that I was Jonathan's father, she collapsed to her knees and then lay prostrate on the floor at my feet, weeping uncontrollably for what seemed an eternity. It was as if her incessant, uncontrolled tears produced a ceaseless stream of lamentation before my very eyes.

Such expressive, emotional displays of grief and mourning are more in keeping with the examples we find in Scripture. For example, after Jacob died in the land of Egypt, we're told that the Egyptians wept for him for seventy days (Genesis 50:3). This is a remarkable statement, given that Jacob and his family were shepherds and as such despised by the Egyptians (Genesis 46:34). Then when Jacob's family came to his burial place, they "lamented loudly and bitterly; and there Joseph observed a seven-day period of mourning for his father" (Genesis 50:10). In stark contrast, we in the West have the pernicious tendency to inhibit the voice of suffering which, in fact, only serves to intensify it.

We must not waste our sorrows, but grow through them. The proper expression of lament is vital to such growth. David, the psalmist, says: "You keep track of all my sorrows. You have collected all my tears in your bottle. You have recorded each one in your book" (Psalm 56:8, NLT). According to an old Hebrew custom, those who mourn would collect their tears in a bottle as an indication of the depth of their sorrow. Archeologists have unearthed some of these small "tear bottles" deposited at the gravesite of loved ones. Over the years, I have left many figurative ones at the grave of my son, Jonathan.

If God takes our grief seriously (and He does!), so should we. I discovered early on that the more I tried to avoid, ignore, repress, or dismiss my pain over *my* son's death, the less I could deeply enter into God's pain over *his* Son's death. So talk about your loss, your suffering, your grief. Talk to God about your pain and express to him your troubled heart. Express to him your doubts. He understands. Allow the tears to flow. For it is only in our tears that we can even begin to identify with God's tears.

ON HELP AT DAYBREAK: PSALM 22

On my trip to South Korea to recover the body and personal effects of my son, I discovered the maxim that so well describes that country: "Land of the Morning Calm." Picturesque high mountains, clear waters and splendid tranquillity all contribute to the spellbinding natural beauty of the landscape accentuated particularly in the calm of the early morning hours.

But my heart was not calm. I cried out to God with the desperate words of one of the most well-known psalms of lament:

> My God, my God, why have you forsaken me?
>> Why are you so far from saving me,
>> so far from my cries of anguish?
> My God, I cry out by day, but you do not answer,
>> by night, but I find no rest. (Psalm 22:1-2)

I found it interesting that the superscription of this psalm, indicating its musical tone or style, is "The Doe of the Morning," which can also be translated, "On help at daybreak." (Spoiler: The significance of this for both the psalmist and our son will become evident in chapter 4.)

God says one thing to us in this well-known and much-loved psalm of lament—*In times of suffering, God hears and answers our cries for help according to his own perfect plan.* The psalmist David states it concisely in verse 24: "For he has not ignored or belittled the suffering of the needy. He has not turned his back on them, but has listened to their cries for help (Psalm 22:24, NLT). However, that truth is just as disturbing as it is reassuring. Even apart from those days and months immediately following the death of our son, there have been times in my life when I wonder if God truly hears my cries for help. Have there been similar occasions in yours?

Do you even now have the impression that God has turned His back on you?

In this psalm, David faces three problems. First, he has a problem with God. God seems so far away (vv. 1-5). Second, he has a problem with himself. He is depressed and feels as though he is near death (vv. 6-10). Finally, David has a problem with others who are vicious, abusive, and cruel (vv. 11-21). It is in these same three areas that you and I face the affliction of life, isn't it? Really, all of our troubles can be grouped under one of those categories: God, ourselves, or others.

Why is this important to identify? In any experience of suffering, it is crucial to search out its cause. I'll never forget meeting with a counsellor in the early days of a chemical depression that I experienced in my late thirties. On one occasion as she diagnosed my symptoms and potential root causes, she stated bluntly, "David, you've got to learn to kiss your monster on the nose." In other words, cut to the chase of your fears, anxiety, and inner turmoil by boldly and explicitly identifying the "monster"—that which you fear most. How thankful I am for those insightful and penetrating words that proved to be so helpful in identifying one of the root causes of my emotional limp.

Though no psychiatrist, C. H. Spurgeon, the well-known "Prince of Preachers" of the nineteenth century, stated it well: "To search out the cause of our sorrow is often the best surgery for grief. Self-ignorance is not bliss; in this case it is misery. The mist of ignorance magnifies the causes of our alarm; a clearer view will make monsters dwindle into trifles."[16] For the psalmist, there is no "mist of ignorance" that veils the source of his suffering. From the outset he unmistakably identifies his first problem as the perceived absence of God.

THE HIDDEN GOD
In the ensuing days and months following Jonathan's death, I often affirmed along with the French philosopher and

theologian, Blaise Pascal: *Vere tu es Deus absconditus*—truly you are a hidden God. His words are borrowed from Isaiah the prophet: "Truly you are a God who hides himself, O God and Savior of Israel" (Isaiah 45:15). It was a comfort to know that I was not alone.

The Scriptures are replete with a vocabulary of suffering that reflects the apparent hiddenness of God in times of suffering. As in Psalm 22, the psalmist elsewhere expresses the same anguish of soul in asking, "How long?" "My soul is in deep anguish. How long, Lord, how long?" (Psalm 6:3). Again in Psalm 13:2, "How long must I wrestle with my thoughts and day after day have sorrow in my heart? How long will my enemy triumph over me?" Brennan Manning once wrote in his *A Ragamuffin Memoir*: "It is better to live naked in truth than clothed in fantasy."[17] The truth of the matter is that there are times when God *seems* so far away! That was the psalmist David's experience in Psalm 22. In fact, he repeats that complaint three times in this psalm:

> Why are you so *far* from saving me, so *far* from my cries of anguish? (v. 1)

> Do not be *far* from me, for trouble is near (v. 11)

> But you, Lord, do not be *far* from me (v. 19)

Over the years, I've often heard the rhetorical question, "If you're not feeling close to God, guess who moved?" Of course, the presumed response to that question is, "You have!" But when we look at the laments of Scripture, we often discover it is not the sufferer who had moved, but God! Or has he? At the very least, it *feels* that He has moved—far, far away.

I recently attended the funeral service of a dear friend in France. For more than twenty years, he had battled severe depression that had ravaged his mind and depleted his body.

We corresponded briefly during the final years before his death. On one occasion he wrote: "Thank you, David, for your kind message. To respond in one word, I'm doing very poorly. I'm experiencing an existential depression that will not let go—fears, anxieties, battles, a test that has reached its limits. It's difficult to explain what I'm experiencing right now; it's complex. *The silence of God is tormenting me.*"

I knew my friend, and I knew that he wanted to be close to God. Now he is.

We tend to think that happy feelings are the sure sign of God's presence and blessing, whereas feelings of doubt, disappointment, and confusion indicate his absence. Yet the opposite is often the case. I have discovered it is in my times of bewilderment and struggle that God is most present, for it is often in the absence of feeling his nearness that faith grows the strongest. But even a faith that grows strong is not without doubt.

IN TWO MINDS

David's complaint reminds us that doubt in the Christian life is not to be avoided. The word "doubt" is a five-letter word. Unfortunately, many Christians have turned it into a four-letter word. That is contrary to the teaching of the Bible. Jude says, "Be merciful to those who doubt" (Jude 22). Doubt is a very real part of our life as believers. While life is full of misery and mystery, with God's help we can face it for what it is.

As we look at the Bible, we find many believers who doubted. The psalmist David expressed his doubts in no uncertain terms in his painful, poetic expression of Psalm 22. Though he complains about God's apparent silence, he hasn't given up. Three times in verses 1 and 2 he cries out, "*My* God … *my* God … *my* God." And this is not a flippant, irreverent, "Oh, my god!" No, David is clinging to his relationship with God as his last hope. The psalmist doubts, and yet clings to the assurance of his personal relationship with God. In spite of the fact that John the Baptist had foretold Christ's coming, baptised him, and then heard the voice from heaven saying, "This is my beloved Son, in whom I am well pleased," he doubted. From the dark hole of a dungeon, John sends word to Jesus, asking: "Are you really the one who is to come, or should we look for someone else?" Nevertheless, Jesus does not condemn John for his doubts, but rather commends him for his spiritual stature. Furthermore, Jesus reassures the doubting prophet by describing the messianic signs authenticating his ministry (Matthew 11:4-5, 11). As for the doubting disciples on the road to Emmaus, Jesus simply responds by giving the scriptural evidence for belief (Luke 24:13-35).

Doubt is not the opposite of faith, nor is it unbelief. It is rather the state of mind that hangs suspended between faith and unbelief. Jesus always distinguished between doubt and unbelief. Thomas came to Jesus, doubting his resurrection. Did Jesus lecture him about the virtues of blind faith and brand him a heretic? No, he respectfully, graciously, and tolerantly gave him the facts. In Mark 9:14-32, Jesus heals a demonized boy whose father says, "I believe, help me overcome my unbelief." Since Jesus never responded to outright unbelief, it's evident that this man's struggle was one of doubt, not incredulity.

Those who doubt say, "I'm struggling to believe." Those in unbelief say, "I won't believe." Doubters are honest; unbelievers are obstinate. Those in doubt are looking for light; those in unbelief are content with darkness.[18] The seeker of truth need not fear his own questions. After all, Jesus didn't. He cried out in his own birth language (Aramaic) on the cross, "*Eli, Eli, lema sabachthani?*" ("My God, my God, why have you forsaken me?" Matthew 27:46). Why did the translators leave the Aramaic expression? Because this was Jesus' birth language, which carried the greatest intensity of emotion. Furthermore, that desperate cry came from a heart overwhelmed by the evil laid upon him—your sin and mine. While you and I can never suffer as Jesus suffered, we do at times feel forsaken and alone. And at such times, we need to express our truest feelings and honest questions to God.

While doubt is *not* unbelief, it *is* a vital part of vibrant faith demonstrating the existence of truth. Augustine once said, "I doubt, therefore truth is."[19] Not everything is true, so not everything should be believed. If there were no absolute truth, then doubt wouldn't exist or serve a purpose. Our doubts also demonstrate the sincerity of truth. Since not everything is certain, we must strive to be more certain of what is true. Philosopher and author Os Guinness states it well: "Find out how seriously a believer takes his doubts and you have an index of how seriously a believer takes his faith."[20] Doubt keeps faith from being complacent. Doubt, if embraced properly, can flower into full-blown faith. Yes, David takes his doubts very seriously as he yearns for God's help in his mourning as described in Psalm 22.

HOPE IN OUR MOURNING

PASSIONATELY CRY TO GOD FOR HELP IN TIME OF NEED

When overwhelmed by God's perceived distance and our own perplexing doubts, we must follow the psalmist's example in pouring out our hearts in unrelenting prayer. The perplexing question of verse one—"My God, my God, why have you forsaken me?"—now becomes a passionate request. Though David complains about God's apparent silence, he hasn't given up.

> Every day I call to you, my God, but you do not answer. Every night you hear my voice, but I find no relief. (Psalm 22:2, NLT)

> Do not stay so far from me, for trouble is near, and no one else can help me. (Psalm 22:11, NLT)

O Lord, do not stay far away! You are my strength; come quickly to my aid! (Psalm 22:19, NLT)

He says at the end of verse 2: ". . . I find no relief." More literally, David complains, "I have no silence," or better "I am not silent." Ironically, God is silent, but David isn't! The psalmist is tenaciously clinging to his relationship with God as his last hope. This in itself is a sign of faith.

Trouble is near and God is far . . . or at least He *seems* far away. And this motivates David to pray incessantly and earnestly, as when he prayed for God to spare his first child born by Bathsheba (2 Samuel 12:16-23). When in trouble, we need to do the same. Jesus reminds us: "And will not God bring about justice for his chosen ones, who cry out to him day and night? Will he keep putting them off? I tell you, he will see that they get justice, and quickly" (Luke 18:7-8).

Lamentation of the soul is foundational to transformation of character. So, honestly express to God your deepest pain and despair. C. H. Spurgeon, who experienced deep depression himself, reminds us: "Prayer is never more real and acceptable than when it rises out of the worst places. Deep places beget deep devotion."[21] As did the poet David and the prophet Jeremiah, sit in his presence, naked and transparent, and pour out your heart like water to the Lord.

Cry aloud before the Lord,
O walls of beautiful Jerusalem!
Let your tears flow like a river
day and night.
Give yourselves no rest;
give your eyes no relief.
Rise during the night and cry out.
Pour out your hearts like water to the Lord.
(Lamentations 2:18-19, NLT)

Often when in the pain and suffering of life's journey, we don't know how to express to God the deepest groaning of the heart. We must remember that the Holy Spirit prays in us, for us, and through us with groans that words cannot express (Romans 8:26-27). Could it be that in the inspired laments of the biblical poets and prophets we have been given the very words that otherwise we have such difficulty expressing ourselves?

Finally, notice that in Psalm 22, David requests God's *nearness* more than his *deliverance* (vv. 11, 19). In our age of creature comforts and medical possibilities, we all too often want to be rescued *from* our pain rather than experience God's nearness *in* our pain. All too often, we want immediate healing, relief from financial pressure, or the resolution to some pressing problem more than we want God himself. However, God wants us to yearn most for his nearness *in* the difficulty more than deliverance *from* the difficulty.

RECALL GOD'S FAITHFUL CHARACTER

As we plead God's help in our mourning, our greatest need is a renewed vision of the Lord's faithful character. After only two verses describing the dark night of the soul (vv. 1-2), help at daybreak is on the horizon:

> Yet you are holy, enthroned on the praises of Israel. Our ancestors trusted in you, and you rescued them. They cried out to you and were saved. They trusted in you and were never disgraced. (Psalm 22:3-5, NLT)

With one small word ("yet"), David moves from complaint to confession, from a minor key to a major key, from low bass notes to high soprano, from sighing to singing. Here fear *begins* to give way to faith. In his trouble and feelings of distance from God, the psalmist refuses to give in to unbelief. Rather, he appeals to God's faithful character. The poet knows that to the degree our understanding of God's character is enlarged, to that degree the size of our problems diminish.

But how do I do this? How do I reconcile my experience of suffering with what the Scriptures tell me of God's faithful character? I'll explore this question further in Chapter Two. For now, however, the foundational principle is this: *Whatever we may encounter in life, we must settle in our minds that God is faithful and good, holy, and without sin.* That's what Moses says in his song just before his death: "He is the Rock, his works are perfect, and all his ways are just. A faithful God who does no wrong, upright and just is he" (Deuteronomy 32:4).

In support of this, David looks to the history of his people. He reflects on God's faithfulness to his forefathers and all he had done to deliver them from bondage and bring them into the Promised Land. As a result, Israel praised God, and these praises form a "throne" upon which God is sitting. It is the bedrock foundation of God's trustworthy character that enables the sufferer to not give up or give in.

In times of suffering, we often struggle not only with God's perceived distance and our own perplexing doubts, but also with feelings of isolation, depression, and rejection by others. In Psalm 22:6-8, David moves from his view of God to his view of himself. Not only does God seem far removed in the heavens, but David himself feels far down in the earth . . . *like a worm.* Being mocked for his futile cries to God, he feels almost subhuman:

> But I am a worm and not a man,
>> scorned by everyone, despised by the people.
> All who see me mock me;
>> they hurl insults, shaking their heads.
> "He trusts in the Lord," they say,
>> "let the Lord rescue him.
> Let him deliver him,
>> since he delights in him." (Psalm 22:6-8)

David begins with a note of contrast (*But* I am a worm...), which only highlights the felt dissonance between his experience and that of his forefathers (cf. vv. 3-5). It's difficult to avoid the conclusion that the author of this psalm is depressed. This is not just a "bad hair" day. This is a full-fledged, mind-bending, heart-wrenching, body-wracking, emotion-binding depression that results in some of the physiological symptoms David describes here. When in the throes of depression, that's how you feel—like a worm! A worm is not only insignificant, but also defenseless. You can really do very little for yourself. You can hardly pull yourself out of bed! And more than that, you feel paranoid about how others view you. Kathryn Green-McCrieght has described it this way: "Depression is not just sadness or sorrow. Depression is not just negative thinking. Depression is not just being 'down.' It's walking barefoot on broken glass; the weight of one's body grinds the glass in further with every movement. So, the weight of my very existence grinds the shards of grief deeper into my soul. When I am depressed, every thought, every breath, every conscious moment hurts."[22] I can think of no better description of my own chemical depression mentioned earlier. For months I felt as if I was merely existing among the walking dead. Torturous days of mental oppression coupled with sleepless nights filled with anxiety took its toll. Clinical depression has a way of feeding on itself, going from bad to worse and to what seems like the point of no return. Is this not what the psalmist describes in verses 14-15?

> I am poured out like water,
>   and all my bones are out of joint.
> My heart has turned to wax;
>   it has melted within me.
> My mouth is dried up like a potsherd,
>   and my tongue sticks to the roof of my mouth;
>   you lay me in the dust of death.

In Augustine's words, the psalmist is "deafened by the clanking chains of mortality."[23] He is drained physically (v. 15a) and emotionally (v. 14b) to the point of death (v. 15b). David clearly thought he would die as a result of his affliction. His enemies were so certain of David's imminent death that they were already invading his wardrobe in order to divide his clothes among themselves (v. 18).

In such a state, where is help found?

REMEMBER GOD'S UNFAILING ACCEPTANCE AND LOVE

When our emotional lights are frantically flashing on the dashboard of life, the first step is *not* to look inward but to look upward . . . upward at God's unconditional acceptance and unfailing love. With yet another contrastive "yet," the psalmist points the way to God's help at daybreak:

> Yet you brought me safely from my mother's womb and led me to trust you at my mother's breast. I was thrust into your arms at my birth. You have been my God from the moment I was born. (Psalm 22:9-10, NLT)

Over recent years, I've had the ecstatic joy of holding each of my grandchildren in their infancy. When an infant is at rest at his mother's breast, there is a sense of explicit trust, absolute dependence, and protective care. Elsewhere David says, "You knit me together in my mother's womb" (Psalm 139:13). But God didn't do this to abandon us later. Job, undergoing the severest of trials, argues in the same way:

> Your hands shaped me and made me.
> Will you now turn and destroy me?
> Remember that you molded me like clay.
> Will you now turn me to dust again? (Job 10:8-9)

The answer, of course, is a resounding "No!" Your life is precious in his sight. If you have life and breath, it is all because of God who has faithfully watched over your life from birth. How's that as an antidote for depression, discouragement, and feelings of rejection?

In his suffering, David not only had a problem with God and with himself. He also had a problem with others. David describes his enemies as strong, ravenous animals. He uses three terms: strong bulls, roaring lions, and vicious dogs.

> My enemies surround me like a herd of bulls;
> fierce bulls of Bashan have hemmed me in.
> Like lions they open their jaws against me,
> roaring and tearing into their prey.
> My enemies surround me like a pack of dogs;
> an evil gang closes in on me.
> (Psalm 22:12-13, 16, NLT)

Suffering can never be addressed apart from our relationships with others. As C. S. Lewis insightfully remarks: "When souls become wicked they will certainly use this possibility to hurt one another; and this, perhaps, accounts for four-fifths of the sufferings of men."[24] Abuse, whether it be sexual, physical, verbal, or emotional, can result in intense suffering in life that can only be relieved through forgiveness.

The profound and prolonged pain of losing our son was compounded by my personal struggle to forgive those ultimately responsible for his death. In those initial days and months, I struggled intensely with questions of justice and forgiveness. The wrong done leading to my son's death was not intentional. It was classified as accidental manslaughter, not murder. But this did not diminish my feelings of anger toward those responsible. My acute sense of justice that had proved to be one of the factors in my earlier depression once again manifested its pernicious head.

Those surrounded by insensitive "counselors" can also relate to the psalmist's words. Have you ever had someone say to you, "Hey, if the Lord loved you so much, why did he allow this into your life?" Some may not put the question so bluntly. But rather than sensitively listening to the indescribable pain and sorrow you may be experiencing at the moment, they insensitively jump ahead to the logic of what can be learned through the suffering. They resemble those who counseled Job in his distress: "But consider the joy of those corrected by God! Do not despise the discipline of the Almighty when you sin. For though he wounds, he also bandages. He strikes, but his hands also heal" (Job 5:17-19, NLT). Remember, this "counsel" was offered to a man who had just lost everything he owned, including his own health and family!

I personally believe, however, that there is more here than meets the eye in David's description of his enemies (Psalm 22:12-13, 16). David obviously isn't talking about literal bulls, lions, and dogs, though all three could be found in Palestine at this time. While David is most certainly describing his human enemies, he may also be describing the onslaught of demonic oppression. I believe we have here a picture of cosmic anarchy. In the Ancient Near East, animals were often a symbol of vicious demonic powers poised for attack. David's description of the lions opening their mouths against him is a Hebrew idiom associated with eating and swallowing.[25] The apostle Peter may have had these verses in mind when he writes: "Be alert and of sober mind. Your enemy the devil prowls around like a roaring lion looking for someone to devour" (1 Peter 5:8).

Maybe you feel surrounded by "bulls," "lions," and "dogs" right now. Maybe you are in a situation of abuse by someone else. Or maybe you are experiencing the battle fatigue that comes with being a child of God engaged in the spiritual warfare of the Christian life. Paul reminds us that our real battle is not against flesh and blood, but against the very powers of darkness themselves (Ephesians 6:10-12). This battle can quickly drain every ounce of emotional and physical strength we have if we fail to rely upon the Lord's resources available to us through prayer. As this is an aspect of suffering that is often ignored, I highlight it from several angles in the following chapters.

There is more in this Psalm . . . much more. We have only begun to sound its depths. We've explored the explicit, not the implicit. Up to this point, we have only seen suggestive hints of the full unveiling of God's help at daybreak which brings hope in our mourning. This will be the subject of chapter four.

In the ensuing days and weeks following Jonathan's death, my mind and emotions went from the question of *how* did this happen to the question of *why* did this happen. This was probably quite a normal process of working through the profound grief of losing a child. In the moment of tragedy, the immediate shock cries out for answers. The questions I asked, at least initially, were more of a practical than of a philosophical nature. I wanted to know the more concrete, tangible details of *how* before I was ready to deeply reflect on the more theoretical, intangible questions of *why*. Nevertheless, for the rational mind the *why* kinds of questions inevitably invade the aching soul. It is to those questions we turn in the following chapter.

CHAPTER 2

Why Does a Good God Allow Bad Things?

Whence evil—if there be a God?
—Epicurus

While it is evil that tortures human bodies,
it is the problem of evil that torments the human mind.
—Henri Blocher

The Old Testament judge, Gideon, asks: "But if the Lord is with us, *why* then has all this happened to us?"[26] I found this question particularly acute during the graveside service for my son. We had just come from the memorial service during which testimonies were shared and a biblical message of hope was delivered. The encouraging and sensitive words were like a calming balm for the weary soul, reminding me of the many biblical promises of life after death. This shot of biblical adrenaline filled me with hope, helping me look forward to a brighter future. But as family and friends gathered around the freshly dug grave and as the simple, wooden coffin was lowered into the vault, I was overwhelmingly confronted by the ever-persistent question of *why*. That profound and perplexing question reminded me of the abnormality of life as we know it. In the normal process of things, children bury their parents (as I had done) and not the other way around.

But life is not normal.

One writer has formulated the problem in these terms: "Sooner or later I must face the question in plain language.

What reason have we, except our own desperate wishes, to believe that God is, by any standard we can conceive, 'good?' Doesn't all the *prima facie* evidence suggest exactly the opposite?"[27] These are not the words of an atheist or skeptic. Nor are they written by the promoters of a smear campaign against Christianity. They are the words of C. S. Lewis, one of the greatest defenders of biblical faith during the twentieth century. He wrote those words while grieving the loss of his wife to cancer. As a believer, Lewis was dealing with the problem of evil. How can a good God allow bad things? Can we reconcile what the Bible says about God—that He is good, loving, just, and kind—with the harsh realities of pain and evil in the world all around us? These questions are the single greatest challenge to the Christian faith.

About the same time that my son died, three other young people in the church of which I was the lead pastor died in tragic and seemingly nonsensical accidents. One was a young Rwandan who had immigrated to the United States along with his family. Though he and his family had come to America to flee danger, danger found him. He was crossing a street with his bicycle when a careless driver hit him broadside and fled the scene of the accident. I'll never forget standing by his bedside in the Intensive Care Unit—touching his hand and praying with his grief-stricken mother—as he took his last few desperate breaths before passing through death's door. Several months later, a newly married young lady from our church was crossing a street in Seattle when another inattentive driver ran over her, killing her instantly. Then, only months later, one of the closest friends of our oldest daughter was killed in a tragic head-on collision while she was driving to her elementary school where she taught underprivileged children. She is buried only a few yards from my son.

Four young lives snuffed out in the space of fifteen months. *Why?*

THE COMPLEX CONUNDRUM

One of the first prayers I heard as a child was: "God is great, God is good. Let us thank him for our food." However true and full of childlike faith, the first part of that prayer highlights the conundrum posed by evil and suffering in the world. After all, if God is great would he not be *able* to prevent evil and suffering? And if God is good, would he not be *willing* to prevent evil and suffering? Or maybe God is not so great and good after all! Put in more personal terms, if God is all-loving and perfectly good, he must have *wanted* to protect my son. And if God is all-powerful and sovereign, he must have been *able* to protect my son. Yet my son died at the hands of inattentive hotel owners. Did God *plan* the death of my son by carbon monoxide poisoning? Or did he merely *permit* it to happen? Furthermore, whether or not it was part of God's planned or permissive will, he most certainly could have *prevented* it, could he not?

Why didn't he?

Such questions, when taken together, are part of what philosophers and theologians call the "theodicy problem." The word *theodicy* is fairly recent and carries with it an entire historical and philosophical context that I will mention later. Suffice it to say that the term derives from two Greek words, *theos* (God) and *dikē* (justice), which together convey the idea of God's justice—specifically God's justice in a chaotic world in which humanity experiences such horrendous and inexplicable suffering. Unless evil is, as author Philip Yancey puts it, "God's one great goof," then how are we to understand its origin and place in God's good creation?

Many claim that one cannot assert at the same time that there is an infinitely good God, that he is an all-powerful Creator, and that evil exists in the universe. For if God were all powerful, he *could* abolish all evil. And if God were all good, he *would* abolish all evil. Nevertheless, evil exists along with all of the suffering it entails. Stated in other terms, there seems to be an apparent inconsistency among four propositions:

I. God exists
II. God is all-powerful
III. God is all-loving and good
IV. Evil and suffering exist

I would suggest that these four statements can be boiled down to two for the majority of people in contemporary culture. Since (for most) evil undeniably exists as seen in innocent suffering, then the good, loving, and all-powerful God who many *want* to believe in must not exist.

That's the conundrum.[28]

DEFINING THE TERMS: EVIL, SIN, AND SUFFERING

It has been said that no theology is worth believing that cannot be preached in front of the gates of Auschwitz. We cannot adequately and honestly wrestle with the problem of evil without defining what we mean by God's sovereignty and goodness as well as evil's hideous nature. In other words, when we ask, *How can a good God allow bad things?*, we must ask at the same time, *Just what does bad mean?*

When it comes to evil, sin, and suffering, our thinking can be muddled. After the attacks of September 11, 2001, President George Bush wrote off a large segment of the world as the "axis of evil." Later, British Prime Minister Tony Blair proposed the rather idealistic goal of "ridding the world of evil." All of this begs the question of definition. So before going any further, it's important to define the terms from a biblical perspective. Just what are evil, sin, and suffering? And what is their interrelationship?

Evil is the rather abstract *opposite* of good as defined by God.[29] Evil, then, is not so much a thing but a lack of something. As many great theologians of the past have noted, evil is the absence or deprivation of good. Furthermore, evil expresses itself in two specific ways: *natural evil*, which most often does not *directly* involve the acts or will of mankind (volcanic eruptions, tornadoes, earthquakes, hurricanes, disease, etc.), and *moral evil*, which finds its origin in free moral agents (cruelty, crime, war, oppression, racism, genocide, sexual abuse, etc.).

The terms "evil" and "sin" must, however, be distinguished. In the Bible, the expression of moral evil by free moral agents is called sin, which stands in *opposition* to good as defined by God. The Bible often describes sin as "missing the mark" or "falling short" of something. In the Old Testament, the word most often translated *sin* also describes the elite left-handed marksmen from the tribe of Benjamin who could "sling a rock and hit a target within a hairsbreadth *without missing*" (Judges 20:16). In the New Testament, the Apostle Paul uses a similar term in Romans 3:23—"For all have sinned, and *fall short* of the glory of God." But what "mark" do we fall short of or miss? The answer is clear: "the glory of God." The glory of God is the magnificent display of the sum total of God's attributes. Another word used in the Bible to express the totality of God's attributes is the word *goodness*.[30] When we say God is good, we mean that in every way God's character and will represent the ideal. Psalm 18:30 says, "As for God, His way is perfect." People are good and things are good in so far as they measure up to the glory and goodness of God. To the degree that they don't, evil and sin are present.

Finally, suffering and death are the direct *outcome* of both evil and sin. For many in our postmodern world, the only real sin is suffering resulting from cruelty, and the only real evil is death. The symptoms of suffering and death, rather than the illness of evil and sin, become the "evil" to be overcome. For this reason the postmodern mind has great difficulty understanding the biblical narrative of Christ having conquered sin and evil, but not yet having abolished suffering and death (Hebrews 2:8; 1 Corinthians 15:25-28). Worse yet, any thought of a God who abolishes sin and evil *by suffering* is scandalous! Contrary to the postmodern perspective, however, the Bible views the problem of suffering and death as the consequence of evil and sin, not vice versa. While we see suffering as the central problem, God sees evil as the central problem.

While such definitions may be helpful for clarity's sake, they simply do not go far enough when addressing the problem of evil in relation to an all-powerful and all-good God. In many discussions that do attempt to address the problem, evil is spoken of in detached and abstract terms that limit our ability to conceptualize it in all of its hideousness. But if we are to truly and honestly wrestle with the conundrum posed by the biblical portrayal of God and evil, the latter must be tangibly incarnated in all its demonic horror. We must not speak in vague generalities that make it all too easy to sidestep the conundrum by attributing the ongoing presence of radical evil to the mysteries of God's providence. Furthermore, we must not trivialize evil, viewing it simply as "bad things." No, we must touch, see, smell, and feel evil in all its malefic hideousness if we are to rightfully address the conundrum.[31]

Two concrete examples will illustrate my point. One of the most gripping accounts of the Holocaust that I have read is by historian Philip Friedman. He provides this eyewitness account of a young Jewish girl living in the Warsaw ghetto during the Nazi occupation:

> Zosia was a little girl . . . the daughter of a physician. During an "action" one of the Germans became aware of her beautiful diamond-like eyes.
>
> "I could make two rings out of them," he said, "one for myself and one for my wife."

His colleague is holding the girl . . . One of the wittiest proposes to take the eyes out . . . The screaming penetrates our brains, pierces our hearts, the laughter hurts like the edge of a knife plunged into our body. The screaming and laughter are growing, mingling and soaring to heaven.

O God, whom will you hear first?

What happens next is that the fainting child is lying on the floor. Instead of eyes, two bloody wounds are staring. The mother, driven mad, is held by the women.

This time they left Zosia to her mother . . . At one of the next "actions," little Zosia was taken away. It was, of course, necessary to annihilate the blind child.[32]

For more than 6 million other Jews during the Holocaust, life became an evil nightmare void of meaning. I'm sure many of them thought long and hard about how God could "allow" such unimaginable, horrendous evil. How do we explain such radical evil? Furthermore, did God hear their cry for help?

Such questions have led many to doubt and eventually deny faith in a loving, all-powerful God. After all, if you believe, as I do, that our earthly existence has meaning and purpose and that humankind is far more than a mass of molecules resulting from cosmic chance, then the questions are unavoidable: Why such pain and suffering? What is its purpose? More specifically, how do we explain what happened to little Zosia or more generally the Nazis' brutality at Birkenau and Auschwitz?

Did God *plan* it? Merely *permit* it? In any case, why did He not *prevent* it?

Or consider another concrete example of evil recounted by one who is far more than an acquaintance.[33] Over fifty years have passed since that calamitous day. Claire was only nine at the time. She awoke that morning intent on spending time with her granddad, whose farm was just up the narrow country road from her home. Time with granddad was a much anticipated event. A game of checkers, a bowl of ice cream, a favorite television show—all of these and more made each visit a relished, unforgettable memory.

But on this day, a hideous event seared the mind and soul of this young girl in her feminine innocence. It, too, became an unforgettable, unshakable memory that would take root deep in her being and spread its ugly tentacles of self-doubt and codependency into her adult years. There is no greater sense of betrayal than when a trusted figure—a parent, grand-parent, or member of one's own family—suddenly breaks trust and victimizes a loved one. An atmosphere of childlike trust and innocent enjoyment was outwardly evident as Claire played a game of checkers with her granddad. Suddenly, the victimizer took advantage of his granddaughter's confident trust. Verbal innuendos prepared the way, leading to the profound trauma of sexual abuse. From that moment, life was never the same. A dark, deep secret not only cast a shadow over a young girl's life, but also initiated a complex process of self-incrimination and confused boundaries that could only be healed over time with God's enablement through trusted friends and counselors.

But why? Where was God at that tragic moment? Why did he allow evil to run its course? After all, does God not care for little children who are unable to protect themselves? Does Jesus not describe with utmost solemnity the harsh conse-quences for the one who causes "one of these little ones to stumble" (Matthew 18:6)? Why did he not step in and stop the victimizer and protect the victim? Beyond the question of why evil *persists* is the question of why God allowed it to *exist* in the first place. Such questions have led many to conclude that belief in an all-powerful and all-loving God is nothing but the residue of a childish fantasy.

THE ROCK OF ATHEISM?

While I have questioned my *understanding* of God—particularly the relationship between his sovereignty and the reality of evil and suffering—I've never doubted the *existence* of God. But given the experience of horrific evil and consequent suffering in the world, many conclude that the Christian God must not exist (Proposition I). Ironically, when Hitler was about to lose World War II, his mistress began wrestling with the problem of evil. Hearing the bombs fall on Berlin, Eva Braun wrote to a friend from Hitler's bunker: "It's enough to make one lose faith in God."[34]

Bart D. Ehrman, the author of *God's Problem: How the Bible Fails to Answer Our Most Important Question—Why We Suffer*, was a student with me at Moody Bible Institute in the early 1970s. In his testimony, he explains that he was raised a devout and committed Christian and made a personal profession of faith while attending a Youth-for-Christ club during his teen years. After high school, he began his undergraduate studies at Moody to train for the ministry. But during his Ph.D. studies at Princeton Theological Seminary, he began to question the historicity and reliability of the Scriptures. However, it was the problem of suffering—not problems with the Bible—that ultimately led to the watershed moment in his journey toward unbelief. He explains: "I realized that I could no longer reconcile the claims of faith with the facts of life. In particular, I could no longer explain how there can be a good and all-powerful God actively involved with this world, given the state of things. For many people who inhabit this planet, life is a cesspool of misery and suffering. I came to a point where I simply could not believe that there is a good and kindly disposed Ruler who is in charge of it."[35]

In my personal discussions with others concerning faith and the Bible, I have found that the most common question asked by believer and unbeliever alike is: "Why is there pain and suffering in the world?" While that question has been asked for centuries, it became particularly acute in Lisbon, Portugal, on All Saints Day, November 1, 1755. The unsuspecting population of some 250,000 residents awoke to an immaculately clear, sunny day. Many began their trek to worship in one of the many cathedrals spread throughout the city. Then at 9:40 a.m., all hell broke loose. On that calamitous day, one of the deadliest earthquakes in history reduced the opulent city to ruins. Seismologists today estimate the massive earthquake had a magnitude of 8.4 on the Richter scale, the equivalent of nearly 25,000 Hiroshima atomic bombs of which the devastating effects were felt over 1.2 million square miles, even reaching the coast of Brazil. This massive quake was followed at 10:10 a.m. by a terrifying tsunami driving 100 foot high waves that did far more damage than the earthquake itself. To make matters worse, for five days fires fanned by howling winds whipped through the city, asphyxiating any within 100 hundred yards of the blaze. The destructive effects of earthquake, wind, fire, and flood took their deadly toll, wiping out nearly one-third of Lisbon's inhabitants. Many believed it was the apocalyptic end of the world.

Confronted with such horror, many throughout the eighteenth century used the word *Lisbon* much like we use the word *Auschwitz* today. The undersea tectonic plates that precipitated the disaster produced not only massive physical destruction and death, but also philosophical shock waves that were just as violent. Ever since 1755, the history of European philosophy is best understood as the story of how people were attempting to come to grips with such horrendous evil in the world. Susan Neiman concludes in her recent book, *Evil in Modern Thought: An Alternative History of Philosophy*: "If one believes the world is ruled by a good and powerful father figure, it's natural to expect his order to be comprehensibly just . . . and whatever expectations remain are *unresolved residues of childish fantasy*. Thus the intellectual shock waves generated by Lisbon . . . are seen as the birth pangs of a sadder but wiser era that has learned to live on its own."[36] Little wonder that the German playwright Georg Büchner (1813-1837) described the problem of evil as "the rock of atheism."

My own Lisbon took place on November 28, 2004, with the death of my son. While not shaking the foundations of my belief in God's existence, this personal earthquake has forced me to grow in my understanding of his sovereignty and goodness. I've come to realize that to the degree I view God's sovereignty in terms of a divine playbook in which *every* detail of life—including both good and evil acts—has been decided beforehand, I will face the inevitable temptation to blame God for the Lisbons of my life. In doing so, I resemble insurance companies that describe natural disasters and tragedies as "acts of God." If it's bad, it's God's fault! To avoid this conclusion, some choose to turn a blind eye to evil and suffering all together.

THE THREE MONKEYS

See no evil, hear no evil, speak no evil. The well-known phrase, presumed to have Buddhist origins and often associated with three "wise" monkeys with hands covering either their eyes, ears, or mouth, is most frequently interpreted to refer to those who turn a blind eye to evil. Given the above conundrum of reconciling evil with the existence of an all-good and all-powerful God, some find a solution in the denial that sin or evil exist (Proposition IV).

A contemporary example of the denial of evil is Eckhart Tolle, author of the best-selling book, *A New Earth*. Eckhart packs thousands of years of teaching from Buddha, Jesus, Shakespeare, and even the Rolling Stones into what one of his publishers has called "a clean contemporary bottle." According to Tolle, "If evil has any reality . . . it has a relative, not an absolute, reality." He relates evil to denying "my intrinsic oneness" with all others and sin as simply forgetting that you are connected to the "Source."[37]

My father grew up in a home deeply committed to the teachings of Christian Science, which claims that sin, sickness, and death are merely an illusion. According to Mary Baker Eddy, the founder of this sect, "Evil has no reality. It is neither person, place nor thing, but is simply a belief, an illusion of the material sense."[38] And since evil has no reality, neither does sickness: "The sick are not healed merely by declaring there is no sickness, but by *knowing* there is none."[39] As a result of my grandparents' denial of sickness and refusal to request medical assistance, one of their sons who was seriously ill died at a young age. Confronted by the consequences of such an ill-founded belief, they later came to believe that not only does evil truly exist, but so also does the Son of God who has conquered evil.

Just as the tragic loss of my son never led me to question God's existence, neither did it lead me to doubt evil's existence. Nor was I tempted to redefine evil in more palatable, respectable terms. As I will demonstrate later, however, I have come to believe that many well-meaning Christians are in danger of doing just this. In a sincere desire to cling to an omni-controlling, deterministic conception of God's sovereignty, a subtle but inevitable tendency exists to redefine evil in light of the higher good of God's ultimate purposes, thus stripping evil of its evil character. But to deny, blur, ignore, redefine, reinterpret, or in any way minimize the most scandalous aspects of evil—whether it be natural or moral evil—is only to give it more opportunity to expand its pernicious tentacles. Thus the Scriptures call us to "hate what is evil; cling to what is good" (Romans 12:9).

The three "wise" monkeys are not so wise after all.

THINKING RIGHTLY ABOUT GOD

Yes, God is great, God is good, let us thank him for . . . *even the evil in the world that brings about so much human suffering?* The answer to that question depends largely upon how we define these two foundational pillars of God's character—his greatness and goodness.

Avid readers all have books that are part of a top ten list of favorites. In my younger years, one of the most important books (apart from the Bible) that fashioned my view of God was A. W. Tozer's *The Knowledge of the Holy.* His initial chapter is entitled "Why We Must Think Rightly About God," and his opening line has remained deeply imbedded in my mind and heart particularly in times of suffering and difficulty: *"What comes into our minds when we think about God is the most important thing about us."*[40]

Why is this?

The answer is straightforward. The way we *think* about God goes a long way in determining our *feelings* about God. For example, if we believe that an all-powerful and all-good God is somehow the *primary cause* of the evil that enters our lives, then our view of God's providential care will necessarily be shaped by this perspective. That is why, since my son's death, I have wrestled intensely with understanding just how God's all-powerful and all-loving character *interacts with* the reality of evil and suffering we all experience (Propositions II and III). Of course, as I mentioned earlier, if God is not *both* all-powerful and all-good, then he is not the God we would want to believe in anyway. But for the sake of clarity, I'll explore these two aspects separately.

GOD IS GREAT

Undeniably, the Bible teaches that God is great, i.e., *omnipotent* (Proposition II). The descriptive word itself comes from two Latin words—*omni,* "all," and *potens,* "powerful"—and means that *God is able to do all that he decides to do in confor-mity with his holy character and will.* Jesus himself said, "With man this is impossible, but with God all things are possible" (Matthew 19:26).

But herein lies the problem. If with God "all things are possible," then why does he not put a stop to such sense-less suffering in this world? Why does he not reach down to protect the Zosias and Claires of this world? Why did he not stoop down and shield my son from the deadly, toxic effects of carbon monoxide in his hotel room?

Why?

This problem is accentuated for those who claim that omnipotent means *omni-controlling.* A corollary of God's omnipotence is God's sovereignty, which is the exercise of God's power to rule over his creation. However, particularly since the time of Augustine in the fifth century, many have understood God's sovereignty in terms of a deterministic divine blueprint encompassing meticulous, exhaustive control over every detail of our human existence.[41] In other words, God does not merely *potentially* control all events, but he *actually* and *meticulously* controls all events. According to Augustine, the victim of evil "ought not to attribute [suffering] to the will of men, or of angels, or of any created spirit, but rather to His will who gives power to wills."[42] Calvin at times echoed a similar blueprint perspective. For example, he writes: "If someone falls into the hands of thieves or encounters a savage beast, if he falls into the ocean in a storm . . . or if a trav-eler in the desert finds whatever he needs to feed himself . . . Carnal reason will attribute all these good and bad events to chance. But those who have kept the teaching of Christ and who know that the hair on their head is numbered (Matthew 10:30), will look further, being convinced that all events are covered by God's secret plan."[43]

From this perspective, *all* that takes place happens because God decided it beforehand, down to the minutest details of our everyday lives, such as the grade a child makes on a particular exam or what I might eat for breakfast. Theologian Wayne Grudem reflects this viewpoint in his popular *Systematic Theology*: "The divine cause of *each event* works as an *invisible, behind-the-scenes, directing cause* and therefore could be called the 'primary cause' that plans and initiates *everything* that happens."[44]

Evidently, such a "behind-the-scenes, directing cause" is a type of all-encompassing divine blueprint minutely controlling everything that happens, *including evil*. Following the lead of Augustine, Calvin and many of the Reformers of the sixteenth and seventeenth centuries, an ever increasing number of contemporary evangelical theologians and philosophers conclude that the omnipotent God is the primary cause behind evil. Citing Ephesians 1:11 as a proof text that God "works all things according to the counsel of his will," two popular co-authors boldly state that this doesn't simply mean that "God manages to turn the evil aspects of our world to good for those who love him; it is rather that *he himself brings about* these evil aspects for his glory (see Ex 9:13-16; John 9:3) and his people's good (see Heb. 12:3-11; James 1:2-4)." They go on to explain further:

> This includes—*as incredible and as unacceptable as it may currently seem*—God's having even brought about the Nazis' brutality at Birkenau and Auschwitz as well as the terrible killings of Dennis Rader and even the sexual abuse of a young child: "The LORD has made everything for its own purpose, even the wicked for the day of evil" (Prov. 16:4, NASB).[45]

Unfortunately, similar statements can be found throughout the publications of popular authors in this "New Calvinistic" movement—statements that unequivocally impugn the character of God by attributing evil to God who "is light" and in whom "there is no darkness at all" (1 John 1:5).[46] That is why I have come to believe that a blueprint view of God's sovereignty inevitably leads to wrong thinking about God's relationship to evil and suffering. *We need to be far more zealous for the holiness of God than for a misconstrued concept of the sovereignty of God.*

Are we to believe that the Zozias and Claires of this world are to attribute their horrific suffering to God's will for them? In other words, is it (as Augustine contends) God's will that gives power to sex offenders and holocaust perpetrators who inflict unimaginable suffering upon others? Did God *will* the death of my son through unintentional homicide? Did God *will* the tragic circumstances surrounding the death of the three other young people in our church? Does God *will* every form of suffering that enters your life?

Such a perspective of God's greatness (all-powerful = deterministic control) along with a firm belief in his innate goodness inevitably lead to the conclusion that there must be a divine reason for everything that happens in life. This conviction is at the root of the many pious stock-and-trade answers that are sometimes offered under the guise of encouragement to those who are suffering, statements like: "God intended this to build your character," "Providence writes straight with crooked lines," or "Your suffering fits into God's mysterious plan in a way you just can't see right now." Admittedly, as to the latter point, God is *not* obligated to explain himself to you and me. Such biblical passages as Proverbs 25:2 ("It is the glory of God to conceal a matter") and Deuteronomy 29:29 ("The secret things belong to the Lord our God") make this clear. However, to say that God is not obligated to explain himself is not to immediately classify as *mystery* all apparent contradictions between our understanding of God's character on the one hand and the reality of evil and suffering on the other. *While the complex conundrums must be explored, outright contradictions must not be accepted.*

In my own process of grappling with these questions, I needed to further clarify just what I meant in that prayer I learned as a child: "God is great, God is good." Yes, God *is* great (all-powerful). But must God's omnipotence be equated with deterministic control, a type of exhaustive blueprint in which God is the primary cause of all that happens in the universe, including evil? Or does the Bible present a different perspective of God's sovereign omnipotence?

Though God is great (all-powerful), there are obviously certain things that even God *cannot* do. For example, most agree that God cannot do the illogical. Even an all-powerful God cannot violate the rules of logic that he himself established in the first place, such as creating colorless color, square circles, valleys without mountains, or married bachelors. Furthermore, God cannot do anything that is *not* in keeping with his holy character and will. For example, God cannot lie (Titus 1:2; Hebrews 6:18), God cannot cease to exist (2 Timothy 2:13), God cannot be tempted with evil or tempt others to sin (James 1:13), and God cannot transgress his innate goodness (Psalm 119:68). That is why I previously defined God's omnipotence to mean that God is able to do all that he decides to do *in conformity with his holy character and will*. As I will demonstrate in the following chapter, God—in conformity with his holy character and will—has chosen to entrust self-determinative freedom to those created as his image. Furthermore, this freedom, once entrusted, *cannot* be consistently revoked. Otherwise it is no longer genuine freedom.

As a child, I was enamored by the few puppet shows I witnessed. The little figurines on stage appeared so real, so alive, and their graceful movements and humorous interactions left me transfixed. Of course, what I *didn't* see were the invisible strings and hidden puppeteer meticulously controlling the entire scene. Though some may disagree, the metaphor of God as "puppet master" describes well the blueprint conception of divine sovereignty. From this perspective,

God exercises hands-on, exhaustive control over every detail of our existence, including both good and evil, "pulling the strings" (so to speak) of his marionettes on the stage of life. They *appear* to be acting on their own, but in reality their every move is directed by the puppeteer hidden from view. In other words, no matter how "free" we may consider ourselves to be, the omnipotent God is behind the scenes exercising absolute, unimpeded, and unabated control over every thought, action, word and circumstance of life. Absolutely nothing escapes God's preordained, predetermined script that serves as his blueprint. As composer and conductor of all that transpires from the beginning to the end and over everything between, God ordains and orchestrates life on planet Earth and throughout the universe down to the minutest details.

An alternative and more biblical metaphor of God's sovereignty is that of chess master. From this perspective, the beauty of the Creator's supreme sovereignty is not seen in "pulling the strings" in every detail of our lives, but rather in the profoundly and majestically wise way in which he is able to fulfill his ultimate purposes for humanity and the cosmos *all the while respecting the self-determining choices of both angelic and human beings*. We would consider a chess player to be insecure to the degree that he needed to meticulously control every move of his opponent in order to win the match. To the contrary, a chess master's confidence is derived from his ability to anticipate the possible and probable moves his opponent may make as well as his own responses to these moves. Indeed, there are certain non-negotiable aspects of God's redemptive plan that are determined beforehand and are irrevocable and unchangeable. The divine Chess Master, however, takes into account not only the certainties of his redemptive plan, but also the incalculable number of probabilities and possibilities that are inherent to the dignity of self-determining human beings created as the image of God. Just as a world-class chess master wins to the degree that he is able to foresee and then outmaneuver the moves made by his opponent, our all-wise God is able to foresee and outmaneuver every decision and action by free moral agents so as to inevitably and most assuredly accomplish his eternal purposes.

Does such a perspective of God's greatness diminish God's sovereign power? Not at all! It rather exalts his sovereignty and matchless wisdom.[47] The accomplishment of God's sovereign purposes is no longer *entirely* dependent on determinative decrees that meticulously mandate every detail of human existence. It is rather dynamically but most assuredly accomplished through morally free agents who have the choice to willingly submit to the good intentions of their loving Creator. Yet in making this choice, God has not only made suffering possible, but he has also made it meaningful. Because of freedom, I can choose to trust God to work in such a way that evil and the consequent suffering it entails result in good in my life and in the lives of others (Romans 8:28).

GOD IS GOOD

God is great (Proposition II). But God is also good (Proposition III). That's the rub—the delicate dance between God is great and God is good. When it comes to the conundrum of understanding the relationship of an all-powerful and all-good God to evil and suffering in the world, the last thing anyone wants to forfeit is the goodness of God. Fortunately, the Bible affirms the truth of God's goodness time and time again: "You are good and what you do is good" (Psalm 119:68).[48]

Could it be that the biblical writers, like Job, all the while confronted by horrific evil, never questioned God's existence because they had also experienced so much of God's goodness? After all, if (in the minds of some) evil and suffering provide evidence *against* God's existence, shouldn't the presence of good in the human experience count as evidence *for* his existence? As A.W. Tozer writes: "The whole outlook of mankind might be changed if we could all believe that we dwell under a friendly sky and that the God of heaven, though exalted in power and majesty, is eager to be friends with us."[49]

Yet there are times when we may not *feel* that way! At such times we must question what it means to affirm that God is good. In speaking with the rich young ruler, Jesus said, "No one is good—except God alone" (Luke 18:19). In other words, the only way to even begin to understand the concept of *good* is to define it in relation to God.

Just what does the Bible mean when it speaks of God's goodness? I previously stated that when we say God is good we mean that in every way God's character and will represents the ideal. As such, God is the final standard of good, and all that he is and does is worthy of approval. However, it is precisely here that the problem begins for anyone who honestly grapples with the reality of evil and suffering in light of God's goodness. That God could intervene to protect the Zozias and Claires of this world but does not lead many to question his goodness.

This problem is particularly acute for those who hold to (or assume) a deterministic blueprint view of God's sovereignty. For in this case, God not only does not *prevent* innocent suffering, but also intentionally *plans* such suffering. The question is unavoidable: If God is all-powerful in the sense of exhaustive, meticulous control over every detail of life (both good and evil) and if God is all-good in the sense that all he is and does is worthy of approval, then how do we account for the continuation of such pervasive evil and suffering without impugning the character of God?

Faced with this conundrum, there is the subtle tendency to redefine the meaning of God's goodness rather than deny it all together. In other words:

> Whatever happens is caused by God
> Whatever is caused by God is good
> Whatever happens is good.

In this case, the concept of *goodness* is so transformed that it no longer has any meaning. Concerning this tendency the prophet Isaiah sternly warns: "Woe to those who call evil good and good evil, who put darkness for light and light for darkness" (Isaiah 5:20). It might be argued that we, as humans, cannot truly understand *good* and *evil* from God's perspective. But as N. T. Wright forcefully reminds us: ". . .there must be *some* substantial continuity between what we mean by good and evil and what God means; otherwise we are in moral darkness indeed."[50]

To avoid impugning the character of God, some suggest that God's sovereign will is like a beautiful tapestry with a well-planned pattern. Looked at from the underside, we see a hodgepodge of many threads of varying lengths, some filled with knots and tangles and going off in different directions. But looked at from the topside, it's an intricately woven work of art that colorfully displays the magnificent work of the Creator. While we tend to focus on the knots and tangles on the underside, someday we'll see the tapestry from God's perspective in all of its splendid design. From start to finish, the master Weaver doesn't merely *allow* certain threads, but he carefully and intentionally *chooses* them. Eventually we'll see that every intended twist and knot had its proper place in the overall design of aesthetic beauty.

One of the verses often referred to in support of this perspective is John 9:1-3. The disciples ask Jesus, "Rabbi, who sinned, this man or his parents, that he was born blind?" Apparently the disciples believed, as did the Jewish audience, that God must somehow be behind this man's suffering. However, Jesus replies, "Neither this man nor his parents sinned, but this happened so that the works of God might be displayed in him." A casual reading of this passage would seem to indicate that God *planned* for this man to suffer a lifetime of blindness in order that God would be glorified in healing him. But is this what the verse actually says?

In response, it is significant that Jesus explicitly tells us what ultimately brings God glory—it is the *healing* of the blind man, not his *suffering*. Furthermore, the verse should not be understood to mean that God was in some mysterious way behind this man's suffering in the first place. Unfortunately, many translations add a phrase such as "But this happened. . ." (NIV) or "but he was born blind" (NET)—neither of which are found in the original text. Such phrases are added because some type of reason for the suffering is implied in the disciples' question. However, the Greek phrase of verse 3 is best translated simply as "*But let* the works of God be manifested in him."[51] In this case, Jesus was not *answering* the disciple's question as much as *negating* their question. In effect, Jesus says, "You ask *why* this man was born blind? Wrong question! The real question is *what now*? The only thing that matters is seeing the work of God revealed *now* in opposition to evil!" It is this that brings glory to God. What is needed is not answers to the question *why,* but action in response to the question *what now.* As Blocher reminds us, "Evil is not there to be understood, but to be *fought*."[52]

That this is the preferred understanding of this verse is seen in the immediate context. Jesus goes on to speak of his miracle as a work of the "light" that stands in opposition to the works of "darkness" (vv. 4-5). And this is no isolated case. Throughout the gospels, Jesus stands vehemently opposed to such evil and suffering, *never* behind it. Is this to say that good cannot come out of evil? Of course not. Throughout the Scriptures, there are many cases where evil is turned for good. But this is quite different from saying that God brought about the evil in the first place. Does not the Apostle Paul vehemently condemn those who slanderously claim "Let us do evil that good may result?" (Romans 3:8). Evil is God's enemy.

So the question remains on the table: Apart from *denying* God's innate goodness or *redefining* evil in light of the tapestry of a higher good, how do we reconcile the truth that in every way God's character and will represent the ideal with the reality of such pervasive evil and suffering in the world?

According to the creation account of Genesis 1, all that God created was good, an affirmation repeated seven times (the number of perfection) in chapter one alone. One of the good things that the all-good God created was morally free creatures (whether people or angels), able to choose between good and the opposite of good, that is, evil. In fact, such a choice on God's part actually highlights the beauty of his sovereignty! As A. W. Tozer so succinctly states: "Man's will is free, because God is sovereign. A God less than sovereign could not bestow moral freedom upon His creatures. *He would be afraid to do so.*"[53]

God could have created androids, preprogrammed to always make the right choice in conformity with God's moral will. Yet what would be lacking is love. Where there is no possibility of choice, there is no possibility of authentic love. Coerced, controlled love is not love at all. Furthermore, in order to create a world where genuine love is possible, God excluded another possibility: the guarantee of a world where his will is always done. Is that not why Jesus taught his disciples to pray, "Thy will be done on earth as it is in heaven" (Matthew 6:10)? In creating moral agents with the possibility of choice, God also made evil possible.

The expression of genuine love demands libertarian choice. As C. S. Lewis asks, "Why, then, did God give them free will?" He then answers: "Because free will, though it makes evil possible, is also the only thing that makes possible any love or goodness or joy worth having. A world of automata—of creatures that worked like machines—would hardly be worth creating."[54]

Potential evil that results in actual evil carries with it the natural consequences of evil. In the same way that an all-powerful God *cannot* do the illogical or consistently intervene in the natural laws that he himself established, so also an all-good God *will not* consistently step in to alleviate the natural consequences of evil and sin in the world. In a game of chess, one player can occasionally make arbitrary concessions to his opponent by allowing him to take back a move made inadvertently or by depriving himself of a castle. But if he did this consistently, there would be no game at all. Similarly, if God were to intervene to miraculously counteract the fixed laws of nature and the inevitable and painful consequences of wrong "moves" on our part, then we would find that we have excluded life itself.[55]

There is something else an all-good God will not do. An all-good God will not *consistently* alter the laws of nature every time someone faces potential harm. Nor should he. Just as God causes his sun to shine on the evil and the good and sends rain on the righteous and unrighteous (Matthew 5:4), so also both the evil and the good get sick or hurt. My hammer serves me well to drive a nail into the wall. But when I miss the nail and hammer my hand, I suffer. Could God miraculously intervene to transform my hammer into a type of super soft gel and spare me the pain? In principle, he could, just as Jesus *did* intervene to rebuke a violent storm on the Sea of Galilee (Luke 8:23-25), just as he *did* intervene to protect three of his servants from a fiery furnace (Daniel 3:1-26), and just as he *could have* miraculously intervened to rid the polluted air of the toxic carbon monoxide that killed my son. While a world in which all people alike suffer the same natural dangers poses problems, a world in which certain people are *consistently* exempt from those same dangers would cause even more problems.

In January 1852, a search party discovered the lifeless body of English missionary Allen Gardiner. Having encountered fierce weather, he and his fellow missionaries shipwrecked on Tierra del Fuego, an island shared by Chile and Argentina in the southernmost portion of South America. Gardiner and his companions were isolated and physically broken. Human error and lack of provisions led to disease, starvation, and finally death. Nevertheless, despite his suffering, Gardiner recorded Psalm 34:10 in his diary: "The young lions do lack, and suffer hunger: but they that seek the Lord will not want any good thing." Later, facing imminent death, he managed to feebly write one final entry into his journal: "I am overwhelmed with a sense of the goodness of God."[56]

As for Gardiner, the natural dangers and consequent suffering we do experience should not lead us to doubt God's goodness or believe that he stands behind each instance of suffering as the primary cause. For example, a world that consistently operates according to divine intervention is not compatible with a world inhabited by morally free agents who relate to one another in meaningful ways. As I will demonstrate in chapter three, God chose to create a world with significantly free people who make moral choices between good and evil. If God were to consistently intervene to inhibit such choices as well as their consequences, he would revoke our significant freedom resulting in an inferior world.[57]

Furthermore, is it not true that no matter how much God in his goodness reduced suffering in our fallen world, we would still think he did too little? Suppose we evaluated all suffering on a scale of one to ten, with ten describing the worst suffering imaginable and one representing the unpleasant yet tolerable. Let's say that "losing your home in a tornado" received a level ten rating while your friend's "mild sunburn" received a level one rating. If God eliminated level ten, would not level nine become the worst? And what if God reduced all suffering to a level three? Would not level three now seem unbearable? Any evaluation of God's goodness based strictly on his elimination of evil and suffering will, in the end, leave us unsatisfied.[58]

In light of God's inherent goodness, there is a final thing God will not do. He will not intervene to bring absolute justice to a world marked by the proliferation of evil and suffering until the appropriate time. God patiently delays absolute justice, not to make life miserable, but to make life possible. Sin carries with it not only physical and emotional consequences, but also spiritual and eternal consequences. If we are to continue to live with the opportunity to experience God's remedy for both, justice must wait (2 Peter 3:9; 1 Timothy 2:4).

Yes, what comes into our minds when we think about God is the most important thing about us. God *is* great and God *is* good. God never was, is not now, and never will be the source of evil as its primary cause. God stands *over* evil as its sovereign and *against* evil as its archenemy, but never *behind* evil as its primary source. God opposes evil, restrains evil and channels evil. God works for good in the midst of evil and even on occasion will use evil committed by free moral agents in order to judge evil. In this way, God turns evil against evil and will ultimately destroy evil. But he himself is *never* the source or primary cause of evil.

Only in rejecting the notion that God stands behind evil can I confidently trust him to accompany me through evil in the present and ultimately abolish evil in the future. It is this profound confidence in God's greatness and goodness that brings deep assurance to my heart in times of suffering and loss. We do indeed live under friendly skies. The God of heaven, though exalted in power and majesty, is eager to be friends with us!

Nevertheless, a storm cloud has gathered in those friendly skies—a storm cloud of evil that has brought inestimable suffering to humanity as the image of God as well as to all creation. So Epicurus' question remains to be answered: "Whence evil—if there be a God?"

CHAPTER 3

An Enemy Has Done This!

There are some people . . . who . . . assert that God is,
in himself, the cause and author of sin . . . If I should attempt
to refute them, it would be like inventing a long argument
to prove that God is not the Devil.
—John Milton, *De Doctrina Christiana*

Through the open window I hear the rhythmic music of joyful believers. The harmony of their voices and the movement of their bodies remind me that I'm in Africa. The vibrant sound of praise continues for hours, reverberating throughout the surrounding neighborhoods. The joy in the believers' faces and the hope of which they sing seem to push back the otherwise overwhelming stench of urine and garbage in the streets.

Three years after the death of our son in the Land of the Morning Calm, I visited the East African country of Rwanda, *Le Pays des Milles Collines* (The Country of a Thousand Hills). Still reeling from my own grief, I was confronted by the horror of mass genocide that had rivaled—and in some cases surpassed—that of the Nazi death camps.

For decades following World War II, animosity between the Hutu and Tutsi tribes cast a dark shadow over this land of hills, lakes, and laughing children. By 1994, this dark shadow became a storm cloud of gratuitous evil delivering a torrent of unimaginable suffering and death. The horror of the apocalyptic massacre is beyond description. Women and children were often the direct target of the sadistic killers. Women were beaten and ultimately murdered, often in the sight of their families. Some were systematically raped and sexually mutilated as a weapon of genocide, often intentionally by known HIV-infected males. Children often looked on helplessly before being hacked to death with machetes. Others were forced to participate in the massacre by killing their friends or neighbors. Though many ran to churches for refuge, these places of worship became mass graves. The devastating frenzy of violence, bloodshed, and merciless killing left the streets littered with rotting corpses that were eventually devoured by roaming dogs. Entire families were annihilated simply because they belonged to a particular tribe. Even today, bodies are still being uncovered where they had been ruthlessly buried in mass graves. Erected on many of these sites are small memorials declaring, "Never Again!" Others have simply passed into oblivion and will never be found. Those who survived continue to carry the deep physical and emotional scars of a tragedy the world must never forget.

The memory of my visit to the National Genocide Memorial in Kigali, Rwanda, in 2007, is deeply imbedded in my soul. I was accompanied by a Rwandan colleague from the church I pastored at the time, who himself had lost some thirty members of his extended family in the senseless, atrocious massacre. The remains of one family member were only recently found. While I had lost a son due to accidental manslaughter, my colleague had lost an entire family due to barbarous, cold-blooded murder. In one hundred days, nearly one million people throughout the country were viciously murdered—one by one, day after day, hour after hour, minute after minute; ten thousand people a day, four hundred people each hour, seven people each minute. Motivated by revenge and hatred in response to years of racial discrimination promulgated by colonial powers, the killers called their victims, "cockroaches." And what do you do with a cockroach? You stomp it, crush it, and extinguish its life. In the meantime, the world withdrew and watched as a million people were mercilessly murdered. Lieutenant General Roméo Dallaire, in charge of the United Nations peacekeeping troops at the time and whose authority had been usurped due to political maneuvering, "watched as the devil took control of paradise on earth and fed on the blood of the people."[59]

Confronted with such examples of horrific evil and needless suffering, many conclude that God does not exist. How could he? For if he were all powerful, he could intervene and put an end to such evil. And if he were all good, he would intervene to protect the innocent. But in Rwanda he did not . . . and throughout the world often does not even now. Rather paradoxically, Dallaire came to a different conclusion. In his own words: "I know there is a God because in Rwanda I shook hands with the devil. I have seen him, I have smelled him and I have touched him. I know the devil exists, and therefore I know there is a God."[60]

THE GROANING OF CREATION

"Whence such evil—if there be a God?" In response to that question the Apostle Paul, in a passage that N. T. Wright describes as "the deepest New Testament answer to the 'problem of evil,'"[61] points us in the right direction:

> Yet what we suffer now is nothing compared to the glory he will reveal to us later . . . Against its will, all creation was subjected to God's curse. But with eager hope, the creation looks forward to the day when it will join God's children in glorious freedom from death and decay. For we know that all creation has been groaning as in the pains of childbirth right up to the present time. And we believers also groan, even though we have the Holy Spirit within us as a

foretaste of future glory, for we long for our bodies to be released from sin and suffering. (Romans 8:18-23)

The groaning of creation is a type of parable reflecting its underlying illness. It's as if the moral evil of mankind inevitably results in the land mourning and even vomiting out its inhabitants.[62]

Present suffering. Frustration. Longing. Groaning. Decay. And *death*.

Little wonder that the writer of Ecclesiastes exclaims: "So I loathed life because what happens on earth seems awful to me" (Ecclesiastes 2:17, NET). What seems so awful to the sage is what the Apostle Paul describes as a world profoundly marked by the catastrophic consequences of evil.

Fortunately, that's not the end of the story! All is *not* lost! The end of the story will be "glory" for those who believe in *His* story (Romans 8:18). But that's getting ahead of ourselves. We must first better understand "from whence such evil?" For that, we must reflect deeply on the end, the beginning, and everything between.

HUMANITY AS THE *IMAGO DEI*

Genesis, the book of beginnings, brings us face-to-face with God's original intentions for humanity.[63] Genesis 1 beautifully describes in poetic form the historical realities of humanity's beginning. This dramatic account cannot be read without the distinct impression that humankind stands as the apex of the created order. All that precedes the grand finale of God's creation of humankind, though receiving the divine affirmation as "good," is clearly distinguished from humanity who alone exists as the very image of God. The inspired wording is unmistakable:

Then God said, "Let us make mankind in our image, in our likeness, and let them rule over the fish of the sea and the birds in the sky, over the livestock and all the wild animals, and over all the creatures that move along the ground." So God created mankind in his own image, in the image of God he created them; male and female he created them. (Genesis 1:26–27)

The setting is idyllic. Man as the image of God stands in perfect harmony with his Creator, with fellow man (Eve), and with all of creation. No need is unmet. No want is unsatisfied. No happiness could be greater.

How could humanity wander from all of this?

To answer that question, we need to understand the significance of what it means to be created in the image of God. In many ways, this concept is foundational for understanding not only the groaning of creation in the present, but also the unfolding biblical drama of redemption with its promise of hope and restoration. If the revelation of who we are as the image of God were absent from the Bible, we would exist as nothing more than a dominant animal. Of course, this is not the case. As the image of God, we were created a little "lower than the angels" and not, as some would have us believe, a little higher than the animals (Psalm 8). The noble description of mankind as the *imago Dei* defines our dignity, telling us who we are. But it also clarifies our destiny, reminding us of who we are to become. So if we get this wrong, we get many things wrong as it pertains to the origin of evil and suffering in the world. For where there is no dignity, there is no morality. As F. R. Barry has noted, "God created man in his own image. All the rest of the Bible is a commentary on that phrase."[64]

ROMANCE AT THE HEART OF THE UNIVERSE

Genesis 1:26 reads, "Then God said, 'Let *us* make mankind in *our* image.'" Hidden away in the unexplained "us" and "our" of this verse is the veiled allusion to the most intimate of loving relationships between Father, Son, and Holy Spirit. God is a social being, and as such has enjoyed eternal fellowship within himself. God is one essence, yet exists as three persons. Likewise, humanity as image exists—not singularly—but as two (man and woman) and then in relation to the many. At the end of Genesis 1, God saw all that he had made and it was "very good" (Genesis 1:31). However, while man exists *apart* from woman, God's pronouncement is telling: "It is *not* good" (Genesis 2:18). The image is not complete until the creation of Eve. As the French philosopher Gabriel Marcel has stated, "To exist is to coexist."

But there is more. Not only does humanity as image speak of solidarity of relationship, but also of intimacy and transparency of *loving* relationship. Pastor and theologian Augustus Strong (1836-1921) writes, "Love is an impossible exercise to a solitary being."[65] Adam and Eve were both naked and they "felt no shame" (Genesis 2:25). This is not merely a description of their literal, physical state, but also of something far more profound. Even as they were physically naked, sharing their bodies with each other, so also they were psychologically and spiritually transparent, sharing their souls with each other without fear of exploitation. In this way, the relational loving intimacy of Father, Son, and Holy Spirit was reflected in the creation of humanity as the image of God.

The relational oneness of the great Three-in-One is the template expressing God's most cherished intentions for all of humanity—*relational love*. Centuries later, John, the "apostle of love," pens these words concerning the very essence of God: "God is love" (1 John 4:16). Love is not simply a quality that God possesses, but that which he is by his very nature, just as "God is light" (1 John 1:5) and "God is spirit" (John 4:24).

Does it then not make sense that this relational God of love yearns for the intimacy of loving relationship *with* and *among* those created as his image?

Yes, romance is at the heart of the universe. From the very beginning, God intended mankind to experience the ecstasy of loving community (John 17:20-26). God desires a relational universe, not a robotic universe. Our Creator values an intimate, loving relationship *with* mankind rather than meticulous, coercive control *over* mankind. Furthermore, a loving relationship between the Creator and humanity and the relationships within humanity itself are what most glorifies God (John 17:24).

Irenaeus of Lyon, the second century Greek theologian and missionary to Gaul (today's France), once said: "The glory of God is a human being fully alive."[66] But for humans to be fully alive, there must be love. And for there to be love, there must be choice. As certain as a square cannot exist without four sides and as certain as a valley cannot exist apart from two hills, so love by its very nature cannot exist apart from choice. It cannot be determined, programmed, predestined, decreed, or coerced. Furthermore, for there to be choice, there must be the freedom to choose. And the freedom to choose, though having such potential for good, also carries with it enormous potential for evil, which in turn brings suffering.

DESTINED TO RULE

God created mankind not only for loving relationships, but also with the delegated authority to rule over the earth. That this is true is clearly seen from the structure of Genesis 1:26, which is best translated, "Let us make mankind *as* our image . . . *in order that they* might rule."[67] This function of dominion over the earth is further described in verse 28 as "subduing" ("bring into bondage") and "ruling" (to tread down, subdue). Humanity itself is the image of God; the commission to rule is the function of the image, that to which mankind is called and capable of *because of who he is*. This is God's *Magna Carta* for all human progress. Mankind's divinely given mandate is to populate, cultivate, and preserve the earth that God has placed under his care. Yes, God fashioned mankind out of the dust to reign!

The idea of humankind as God's official representative on earth is revolutionary in light of many of the ancient religions surrounding Israel, which taught that mankind is helplessly and irreversibly caught up in fatalistic, rhythmic cycles of fertility. No such pessimistic fatalism or deterministic control can be seen in the author's words. Rather as the royal human race, we are God's ennobled servants entrusted with the mandate to bring untold blessing to this earthly realm.[68]

The implications of this mandate are breathtaking! To entrust such a mandate to mankind implies a sort of "divine abdication."[69] Throughout Scripture, God chooses to work through mediators. In doing so, he "abdicates" his rule to those who represent the apex of his creation. As God's vice-regents, we have been entrusted with divinely delegated "say-so," enabling us to carry out the mandate to rule over the earth. Such a mandate necessitates that those commissioned make a self-determinative choice to fulfill their privileged role as God's vice-regents of the earth (Psalm 8). While such delegation of "say-so" does not entail the *certainty* of evil in the human race, it inevitably entails the *possibility* of evil.

THE BREATH OF LIFE

We fulfill our role as the image of God, not only to the degree that we *rule* over creation, but also to the degree that we *resemble* our Creator. That is why in Genesis 1 mankind is further described as the "likeness" of God.

In what ways, then, do we as humans resemble God? Most likely the answer is to be found in that God imparted the "breath of life" to Adam's body of dust (Genesis 2:7). Having the breath of life sets us as humans apart as unique among all living beings. Though even the animals are termed "living beings" (2:19), *only* human beings are described as the image of God infused with the breath of God. This "breath" does more than animate the first man, Adam, and his descendants; it defines our essential personhood. While there is no passage of Scripture that unequivocally defines the elements of personhood, the Bible does reveal certain personality features shared by both God and humans and which seem to describe how we as humans resemble God. Larry Crabb, in his insightful book *Understanding People*, summarizes these similarities under four foundational concepts:[70]

Evaluative thinking. As personal beings, both God and humans can rationally evaluate what is happening. God's thoughts are as profound as they are vast (Psalm 90:5; 139:17). Furthermore, God reasons and invites those created as his image to reason with him: "Come now, let us reason together, says the Lord: though your sins are like scarlet, they shall be as white as snow" (Isaiah 1:18, RSV). We can do this because we have the innate capacity to consider and draw conclusions: "When I consider your heavens, the work of your fingers, the moon and the stars, which you have set in place, what is mankind that you are mindful of them, human beings that you care for them?" (Psalm 8:3-4).

Emotional experiencing. As we have already seen in Chapter 1, God is not without emotion. God's heart was "deeply troubled" as he witnessed the evil of the human race in the days of Noah (Genesis 6:6). As the perfect image of the Father, our Lord is described as a "man of sorrows" (Isaiah 53:3) who experienced deep sadness when Lazarus died (John 11:33-36), felt anger when the temple became a market place (John 2:14-17), and is pleased when we do his will (Hebrews 13:21). Similarly, when confronted by suffering, we often *feel* as Job did: "The churning inside me never stops; days of suffering confront me" (Job 30:27).

Deep longing. As Jesus, the perfect image of God, looks out over wayward Jerusalem, he laments, "Jerusalem, Jerusalem, you who kill the prophets and stone those sent to you, how often I have longed to gather your children together . . ." (Matthew 23:37). Such longings express profound desire that is much deeper than mere emotion. As those who are the likeness-image of God, we also experience deep, inner longings. The psalmist declares, "All my longings lie open before you, Lord; my sighing is not hidden from you" (Psalm 38:9). In the New Testament, Paul speaks of a similar longing so profound that it expresses itself in groans, "Meanwhile we groan, longing to be clothed instead with our heavenly dwelling" (2 Corinthians 5:2). Both God and human beings have the capacity to long deeply.

Active choosing. Both God and humans can intentionally pursue a chosen direction. According to Ephesians 1:9-11, God intentionally pursues his plan to bring "all things in heaven and earth under Christ." As those who resemble our Creator, we also can choose whether or not to do his will: "Anyone who chooses to do the will of God will find out whether my teaching comes from God or whether I speak on my own" (John 7:17). Along with the moral capacity of choice, however, comes the possibility of whether or not to continue in a loving relationship with the Creator. *We cannot be moral creatures without being significantly free creatures.*

In his book, *The Screwtape Letters,* C. S. Lewis depicts a demon who whines about the unique way in which God created humans in his image:

> We must never forget what is the most repellent and inexplicable trait in our Enemy; He *really* loves the hair-less bipeds He has created. . . . He really *does* want to fill the universe with a lot of loathsome little replicas of Himself—creatures whose life, on its miniature scale, will be qualitatively like His own, not because He has

absorbed them but because their wills freely conform to His. We want cattle who can finally become food; He wants servants who can finally become sons.[71]

So what went wrong?

THE IMAGE DEFACED

In the early 1900s, the London *Times* asked a number of writers for essays on the topic, "What's Wrong With the World?" British writer and philosopher G. K. Chesterton's reply was the shortest and most concise:

> Dear Sirs:
> I am.
> Sincerely yours,
> G. K. Chesterton[72]

The writer of Ecclesiastes seems to agree: "God made men and women true and upright; we're the ones who've made a mess of things" (Ecclesiastes 7:29, MSG). Apparently, the problem was not the fruit on the tree, but the pair on the ground!

Just how did we make such a mess of things? Ultimately, where does all this evil and suffering find its source? Part of the answer is found in the tragic drama recorded in Genesis 3:6-8. There we read:

> When the woman saw that the fruit of the tree was good for food and pleasing to the eye, and also desirable for gaining wisdom, she took some and ate it. She also gave some to her husband, who was with her, and he ate it. Then the eyes of both of them were opened, and they realized they were naked; so they sewed fig leaves together and made coverings for themselves. (Genesis 3:6-8)

It is not surprising that these early chapters of Genesis remind us three times of humanity's identity as the image of God (Genesis 1:26–27; 5:3; 9:6). This is the high ground from which humanity fell. Then the downward trend of sin and death quickly came to the forefront. Sin entered mankind's experience as a malignant, deadly abnormality, compromising humanity's divinely endowed role as God's image.

Nothing in the creation narrative would lead us to believe that God had somehow predetermined Adam and Eve's sinful choice. God says to Eve: "What is this that *you* have done?" and not "What did *I* cause you to do?" (Genesis 3:13). Indeed, the Fall of man was not the "push" of God. God created mankind with the *capacity* to sin, but not with the *necessity* to sin. In fact, throughout the narrative of the Fall, God stands in opposition to sin, not in collusion with sin. While God is the author of the *fact* of human freedom, He is not responsible for the *acts* of human freedom.[73] God endowed humanity with significant freedom, but God is not responsible for the misuse of that freedom. Therefore, the mystery of evil is about God's creation and not about God's character.

The tragic results of self-assertive sin profoundly marred humanity's privileged role as God's image, tarnishing the three expressions of who we are as the image of God: *relationship*, *rule*, and *resemblance*. First, sin dealt a death blow to our *relational* capacity. With the intrusion of sin came alienation, both between man and God and between man and fellow man. Explicit trust and transparency—illustrated by man's nakedness—vanished, leaving insecurity and fear. Humanity was now fractured at its core. The transparency and intimacy characteristic of mankind as the image of God have now degenerated into shame, alienation, and blame. Prior to sin's intrusion, mankind enjoyed the bliss of relational harmony. Now the blame game begins: "*The woman you put here with me*—she gave me some of the fruit of the tree, and I ate it" (Genesis 3:12). And the blame game brings suffering. While human speech was given to enhance man's relational potential, it is now wielded as an instrument of divisiveness. Divisive words between Adam and Eve later became a bold act of murder in their son, Cain (Genesis 4:1-8). Such discord and resultant suffering is the expression of death; and for Adam, Eve, Cain, and Abel, as well as all of humanity, death was now a certainty (Genesis 3:3).

Secondly, sin struck at our innate *resemblance* to our Creator. Humanity's essence and role as the "likeness image" of God was severely compromised, bringing devastating consequences in each of the four foundational elements of our personhood as described above—darkening our mental capacity (Romans 1:21), disorienting our emotions (Proverbs 14:17), misdirecting our deepest longings toward that which can never satisfy (Jeremiah 2:13), all resulting in willful disobedience to God (Ephesians 2:2). Self-sufficiency, alienation, and fear are also expressions of mankind having become a sinner at heart. Adam and Eve realized they were naked. Suddenly the God-given garments of innocence, holiness, and perfect love were stripped away like one's clothes at the end of the day.

In Genesis 3, we find the first obituary recorded in the Bible. The repeated refrain is not surprising: "and he died." That the world is one giant cemetery stands as a memorial to sin's devastating consequences. Little wonder that the biblical doctrine of original sin is the only one attested to by the daily news. Quite frankly, it all seems so unfair . . . such evil, pain, and suffering. But as Peter Kreeft reminds us: "Original sin is unfair, just as a baby inheriting a heroin addiction is unfair."[74]

Finally, sin struck at our mandate to *rule*. Though mankind was created to have dominion as God's vice-regent over all the earth, a creature—the very embodiment of Satan—exerted dominion over man and thus disrupted creation order. Consequently, humanity became estranged from the very creation over which he had been given dominion. Ravaged by the insecurity of sin, mankind demonstrated an unwilling-ness to fill the earth and subdue it (Genesis 1:26–27; 9:1–3). Having been raised out of the dust to reign, instead to the dust mankind will return; not to reign, but to die. That very dust is now cursed on account of humanity's disobedience: "Thorns and thistles" and "painful toil" became part and parcel of mankind's struggle to fulfill his role as God's image over an alienated world (Genesis 3:17). God had blessed humanity with the divine mandate to procreate and fill the earth. Paradoxically, mankind filled the earth by promul-gating violence. The result was and is death. Sin has tilted the cosmos. Evil was now crouching at humanity's door (Genesis 4:7); and from that day forward, all of creation has been groaning as in the pains of childbirth (Romans 8:22). Though we ever remain the image of God, we nevertheless must now contend with both physical and spiritual disease, deformity, suffering, and ultimate death.

The tragedy of it all is highlighted by scholar and author Nancy Pearcey when she writes:

> Our value and dignity are rooted in the fact that we are created in the image of God, with the high calling of being His representatives on earth. In fact, it is only because humans have such a high value that sin is so tragic. If we were worthless to begin with, then the Fall would be a trivial event. When a cheap trinket is broken, we toss it aside with a shrug. But when a priceless masterpiece is defaced, we are horrified. It is because humans are the masterpiece of God's creation that the destructiveness of sin produces such horror and sorrow.[75]

Humanity's endowment with such an incredible potential for good and personal satisfaction necessarily entails an incredible potential for evil and personal suffering. Because of satanically inspired sin, collective mankind as God's likeness image was marred, his representative role on earth was perverted, and he became alienated in his relationship with God and fellow man. Ever since, the titanic effects of sin have reverberated throughout the entire human race. A priceless masterpiece has been defaced. Defaced, but not destroyed. Effaced, but not erased. Obscured, but not obliterated.

Nevertheless, the question remains, "Whence such evil—if there be a God?"

NOW THE SERPENT

Genesis 3 begins with three words, the significance of which have altered the course of human history: *"now the serpent"* (Genesis 3:1).

> Now the serpent was more crafty than any of the wild animals the Lord God had made. He said to the woman, "Did God really say, 'You must not eat from any tree in the garden'?" The woman said to the serpent, "We may eat fruit from the trees in the garden, but God did say, 'You must not eat fruit from the tree that is in the middle of the garden, and you must not touch it, or you will die.'" "You will not certainly die," the serpent said to the woman. "For God knows that when you eat from it your eyes will be opened, and you will be like God, knowing good and evil." (Genesis 3:1-5)

The Scriptures leave an impenetrable veil over the origin of evil in the universe. The appearance of the serpent is left unexplained. We must await further revelation before drawing conclusions as to the primeval angelic rebellion that certainly predates the Fall of man. Though few details are given, several passages indicate that certain angels fell from their original condition as members of God's heavenly council or angelic army.[76] Beyond this, we know next to nothing about the initial choice of some angels to sin. What we do know is that Satan—*by his free choice*—was the first cause of evil in the universe, and you can't back up any further than that. While the book of Genesis does not explain the origin of angelic evil, it clearly states where evil does *not* have its source. Evil was not inherent to God or to mankind. What is explicit is that Satan as a free agent attacks the very apex of God's creation. His entire strategy is a perversion of humanity as the image of God leading to inestimable suffering in the world.

We need a paradigm shift when it comes to how we view our present world so ravaged by evil and suffering. Since the time of Augustine in the fourth century, many theologians and philosophers have attempted to explain evil and suffering as a human phenomenon without taking sufficiently into account supernatural evil. It's almost as if the opening phrase of Genesis 3, "Now the serpent. . ." was absent from the text. This negligence, combined with a blueprint view of God's sovereignty emphasizing meticulous, exhaustive control over the details of life, has inevitably led to the quest for a *divine* reason for the evil and suffering that enters our lives. The Bible, however, points us in a different direction.

We are in need of a paradigm shift.

AN ENEMY HAS DONE THIS!

Since the Fall, all human suffering can ultimately be traced to these three causes: Satan, sin, and sinners . . . and in that order. The Bible never minimizes the influence of supernatural evil all around us. In fact, we cannot understand the message of the Bible apart from recognizing the theme of spiritual warfare that is found from Genesis to Revelation. As J. R. R. Tolkien wrote, "It does not do to leave a live dragon out of your calculations, if you live near him."[77]

After Satan's sudden and pernicious intrusion into human experience and God's promise to eventually crush the head of the serpent (Genesis 3:15), Satan recedes into the background.

We see no further direct mention of him in the successive chapters of Genesis. We might conclude the serpent and his horde of fallen angels have gone into hiding. But he is there, performing his insidious work. In fact, there are only four chapters in the Bible that are absent of spiritual warfare— Genesis 1 and 2 and Revelation 21 and 22. Everything in between is marked by conflict between God and Satan. Little wonder that the God of the Bible is consistently compared to a warrior.[78]

Particularly since the rise of modern critical approaches to the Scriptures, there are some who dismiss outright the multitude of biblical passages that unabashedly affirm the existence of angelic and demonic powers. In short, they have "exorcised" such passages from the Bible. Walter Wink states:

> We moderns cannot bring ourselves by any feat of will or imagination to believe in the real existence of these mythological entities that traditionally have been lumped under the general category 'principalities and powers.' . . . It is as impossible for most of us to believe in the real existence of demonic or angelic powers as it is to believe in dragons, or elves, or a flat world.[79]

However, such an approach falls prey to Satan's greatest weapon, which is to convince the world that he doesn't exist. There is no doubt that the biblical writers considered Satan and his minions to be personal, cosmic beings that are directly or indirectly involved in every aspect of natural and moral evil in the world.

When it comes to the topic of supernatural evil, no one has more concisely stated the potential of error than C. S. Lewis: "There are two equal and opposite errors into which our race can fall about devils. One is to disbelieve in their existence. The other is to believe, and to feel an excessive and unhealthy interest in them. They themselves are equally pleased by both errors and hail a materialist or a magician with the same delight."[80]

"Materialist" or "magician": neither of these approaches does justice to the clear, unequivocal language of the Old and New Testament. As for the Bible's teaching on Satan and his demons, we only have three options: dismiss what the Bible says as irrelevant for our day and culture, reinterpret the biblical teaching so that it is more palatable to our scientific mentality, or accept it as a true picture of reality. We must not be materialists or magicians when it comes to the influence of supernatural evil on humanity. Unfortunately, far too many believers in the Western world view evil almost entirely from a naturalistic mindset and too quickly gloss over the words, "Now the serpent. . ." (Genesis 3:1). As a result, the explanations proposed for understanding the pervasive evil and suffering in the world today often do not take seriously enough the pernicious influence of the cosmic powers so frequently mentioned in the Scriptures.

In Milton's *Paradise Lost*, the chief of staff of the hellish forces is called "pan-*demon*-ium." The name is fitting and describes well the fact that all forms of evil are ultimately incited by Satan and his demonic minions who seek to sow pandemonium throughout the world with the goal of destroying humanity as the *imago Dei*. As Paul reminds us: "Our struggle is not against flesh and blood, but against the rulers, against the authorities, against the powers of this dark world and against the spiritual forces of evil in the heavenly realms" (Ephesians 6:12). From the perspective of Scripture, the tragic events on earth are a mere reflection of turmoil in the heavenlies (Isaiah 24:21). Not only has humanity fallen, the entire cosmos is tilted. Does this not explain why Satan can offer to Jesus the power and glory of the kingdoms of the world? Satan's proposition is justified: the kingdoms of this earth *are* under his temporary control and influence. Likewise John writes: "We know that we are children of God and that the whole world is under the control of the evil one" (1 John 5:19-20).[81]

The "world" of which John speaks is the same as that of which Jesus speaks in the parable of the weeds and the wheat (Matthew 13:24-20; 36-43), an account that gives us perceptive insight into the ultimate source of evil in human experience:

> Here is another story Jesus told: "The Kingdom of Heaven is like a farmer who planted good seed in his field. But that night as the workers slept, his enemy came and planted weeds among the wheat, then slipped away. When the crop began to grow and produce grain, the weeds also grew. The farmer's workers went to him and said, 'Sir, the field where you planted that good seed is full of weeds! Where did they come from?' 'An enemy has done this!' the farmer exclaimed. 'Should we pull out the weeds?' they asked. 'No,' he replied, 'you'll uproot the wheat if you do. Let both grow together until the harvest. Then I will tell the harvesters to sort out the weeds, tie them into bundles, and burn them, and to put the wheat in the barn.'" (Matthew 13:24-30, NLT)

What is explicitly clear in this parable of the wheat and the weeds is that the mystery of evil is *not* to be found in some unfathomable blueprint decreed by God and by which evil becomes God's ordained means of accomplishing good. Rather, the entire context of this parable is one of spiritual conflict between the kingdom of God and the kingdom of Satan. Jesus had previously said the kingdom was under violent attack (cf. Matthew 11:2), and on many occasions he engaged the enemy through healing the sick, delivering the oppressed, and even calming the chaos of fallen creation (Matthew 8:26). This onslaught of evil is sourced in both human and demonic forces (Matthew 11:12; 12:28; Mark 3:27). In this parable, evil is not viewed as a mere discolored thread that ultimately lends stunning beauty to the great tapestry of God's plan of the ages. It is rather a subversive countermovement to the kingdom of God. Furthermore, this conflict is not limited to the past or the future. *It is now.*

As to the details, Jesus' explanation is straightforward:

> Then, leaving the crowds outside, Jesus went into the house. His disciples said, "Please explain to us the story of the weeds in the field." Jesus replied, "The Son of Man is the farmer who plants the good seed. The field is the world, and the good seed represents the people of the Kingdom. The weeds are the people who belong to the evil one. The enemy who planted the weeds among the wheat is the devil. The harvest is the end of the world, and the harvesters are the angels. Just as the weeds are sorted out and burned in the fire, so it will be at the end of the world. The Son of Man will send his angels, and they will remove from his Kingdom everything that causes sin and all who do evil. And the angels will throw them into the fiery furnace, where there will be weeping and gnashing of teeth. Then the righteous will shine like the sun in their Father's Kingdom. Anyone with ears to hear should listen and understand!" (Matthew 13:36-43, NLT)

In contrast to the understanding of some, the "field" in this parable is *not* the church, but the world. The "farmer" is the Messiah, the Son of Man, who plants *only* the good seed, referring to the sons of the kingdom. And the "weeds" are the "sons of the evil one," emissaries of Satan (cf. John 8:44; 1 John 3:10), who have been planted throughout a cursed world and carry out his bidding by means of a counter-sowing. The action of "rooting up" speaks of destruction by the judgment of God (cf. Matthew 15:13; Jude 12). Jesus had already said the kingdom was under violent attack (Matthew 11:12), and throughout his ministry, he forcefully confronted demonic opposition. *God's kingdom is certain to advance; but no doubt about it, there will be opposition!*[82]

The disciples may have been silently asking the same question posed by the farmer's workers: "Sir, the field where you planted the good seed is full of weeds! Where did they come from?" In other words, "God, are you the source of this evil? Are you to blame?" Such questions reflect the moral outrage that is to be expected when confronted with evil and all of its horrendous consequences. Nowhere does Jesus rebuke his disciples for this question of protest. Nowhere does he say, "You should not ask such questions!" He simply answers their question (and ours), unequivocally attributing evil, not to the inscrutable plan of God, but to the work of the devil: *"An enemy has done this!"* (v. 25). It is not the *envoy* of the owner who introduced evil, but rather the *enemy* of the owner. The owner of the field is in no way depicted as cooperating with the enemy, but as opposing the enemy! The landowner is not to blame. To the contrary, he plants good seed, not bad seed.

Is not Jesus' statement insightful with respect to the various theodicies that attempt to solve the question of how a good God can allow bad things? In line with the recompense theology of Job's counselors, are the weeds of life merely the cause-and-effect relationship of sin to sorrow? Or are the weeds intentionally sown as part of God's meticulous, mysterious plan designed to bring about a higher good? Or are they simply inexplicable as part of the mysterious providence of God who must have a good reason for everything? Like the weaving of a beautiful tapestry of which we only see the underside at present, will the weeds one day be seen in their proper light as threads carefully and intentionally chosen by the Weaver? In response to all of these questions and many more like them, the parable shouts out a resounding, "No!"

For "God is light and in him is no darkness at all" (1 John 1:5). Furthermore, "God is love" (1 John 4:8), and as such he is *not* responsible for the weeds of evil and all its consequent suffering. Who then is responsible? The enemy! The weeds of the Rwandan genocide, of Germany's Holocaust, of ravaging world wars, of child abuse, of human trafficking, of world pandemics, and of every evil imaginable are ultimately sown by the seed of the serpent who has been striking at the heel of the seed of the woman since the Fall of humanity (Genesis 3:15). Only when this is understood can we embrace a biblical worldview in which evil and suffering are not about God's mysterious plan, nor do they present an unsolvable intellectual problem.

Some have mistakenly interpreted this parable to mean that, since good and evil are inextricably linked together making it difficult to distinguish between the two, it's best to leave well enough alone; otherwise, we might do more harm than good. However, such a hasty, superficial reading of the text totally misses the point and leads to disastrous consequences. Such a perspective would lead to an attitude of moral indifference with regard to the evils of this world: child abuse, domestic violence, terrorism, genocide, and all horrors of living in a sin-sick world. Furthermore, such a passive indifference never characterized the life of Jesus, himself the perfect "image" of God, who throughout his ministry opposed evil and the suffering it caused. Never once did Jesus look at one caught in the clutches of evil and suffering and conclude that such affliction was somehow part of God's good plan for that individual. And neither should we!

Notice that in this parable, the farmer is unable to take steps to remedy the situation. Why? His inability doesn't stem from ignorance or from impotence. To the contrary, the farmer understands and controls (in his way) the situation. His inability stems from the fact that rooting up the weeds also would require rooting up the wheat. The time of judgment must wait. The disciples mistakenly wanted Jesus to come into the field of this world with a machete and slash away at evil and uproot it definitively. But if God were to do this today, who could stand? As D. A. Carson appropriately asks, "Do you really want nothing but totally effective, instantaneous justice? Then go to hell."[83]

———⧉———

God's purpose in the present age is not judgment, but salvation. The question is no longer, "What is the *source* of evil and suffering?" but rather "What is the *solution* to evil and suffering?" Today, the cross is God's way of dealing with evil. Jesus did not come into the world to condemn the world, but that the world through him might be saved (John 3:17). God is not willing that any should perish but that all should come to repentance (2 Peter 3:9). His purpose today is not rooting out the evil, but restraining it by planting the good. After all, there is deep truth in the charitable saying of Augustine, "Those who are weeds today, may be wheat tomorrow." It is only at the final judgment that all will be made right and the field of this world will experience freedom from the power of the evil one (Daniel 7:14; Revelation 11:15). Then "the righteous will shine like the sun in their Father's Kingdom" (Daniel 12:3). Ultimately, the Kingdom of God will prevail over the powers of darkness (Matthew 16:18). "Whoever has ears, let them hear" (Matthew 13:43).

There is indeed hope in our present mourning!

CHAPTER 4

Hope in the Mourning

The other gods were strong, but Thou wast weak.
They rode, but Thou didst stumble to a throne.
But to our wounds only God's wounds can speak,
And not a god has wounds but Thou alone.
—Edward Shillito, "Jesus of the Scars"

They will look on me, the one they have pierced,
and they will mourn for him as one mourns for
an only child, and grieve bitterly for him
as one grieves for a firstborn son.
—Zechariah 12:10

A few months after Jonathan's death, my wife, Mary Alice, had a dream. Or was it a vision? Jonathan appeared to her and said, "Don't move my room!" We didn't. We left it exactly as it was for years following his death. We laundered his clothes that I brought back from South Korea and neatly placed them in his closet. We rearranged the straw mat he used for sleeping exactly as he had left it before his departure. On the small desk that Jonathan had rarely used (always preferring to sit Korean style on the floor to do his studies), we placed front and center a bamboo plant that he had given to his sister. Around this plant we laid out several of his Korean grammar books and papers that proudly displayed the degree to which he had already begun to master that difficult language. Elsewhere were pictures and mementos of his younger years, such as his cowboy hat and a walking stick he had meticulously carved while as a young boy in southern France. Though Jonathan's belongings and mementos were there, Jonathan was not.

Absence. Emptiness. Stillness. Sadness. And we grieve bitterly, for he was our firstborn son.

Is there any hope in the mourning?

GLIMMERS OF HOPE

To answer that question, we must take a closer look at the ultimate answer to evil; for in doing so, we also discover the ultimate answer to suffering. The unfolding drama following the fall of mankind in Genesis 3 reveals in no uncertain terms the tragic consequences of evil. Mankind was created as the image of God with all the divinely endowed privileges this entailed—loving *relationship* with God and fellow man, authoritative *rule* over God's creation, and the innate *resemblance* of his Maker derived from the "breath of life." Yet through one act of disobedience, humanity's essence and role as the *imago Dei* was profoundly marred, giving birth to a world marked by suffering and death (Romans 5:19).

The tragedy of humanity's progressive defacement as the image of God is highlighted by one Hebrew word—*toledoth*—used repeatedly throughout the early chapters of Genesis. While the term is sometimes translated "generations" or "descendants," it is best understood as "this is what became of . . ." The expression is fitting, for it serves as a header for each major section of the book that details the horrendous devolution of mankind as he journeyed away from his Creator.[84] Nevertheless, while each section is marked by the progressive defacing of God's masterpiece, we happily find in each tokens of grace, rays of hope, and glimmers of the gospel inspiring confidence in God's final solution to the problem of evil and suffering.

The first and foundational glimmer of hope is found in the immediate context of humanity's sinful rebellion. In Genesis 3:15, God initiates his redemptive program with a promise as he speaks to the serpent:

> And I will put enmity between you and the woman, and between your offspring and hers; he will crush your head, and you will strike his heel.

This verse is like a crossword puzzle you can't solve until someone gives you a keyword: Christ. Known as the *proto-evangelium* (first gospel), this promise reminds us of the certain fulfillment of God's ultimate victory over evil and all the suffering it brings. It describes the missional God of the Bible, motivated by a supreme and sacrificial love for all humanity, breaking through in time-space history to deliver mankind from the clutches of satanically inspired evil.

Far beyond any antagonism between snakes and human beings, the intent of the passage is to direct our attention to the serpent and his "seed" on one hand and the woman and her "seed" on the other. In both cases, the seed is both individual and collective in nature. The seed of the serpent refers to those who belong to the evil one and ultimately to Satan himself (John 8:44; 1 John 3:8). On the other hand, the seed of the woman speaks of the people of the promise and ultimately of Christ himself (Revelation 12:1-5; Galatians 3:16, 19). The crushing of the serpent's head points to the ultimate and definitive victory over evil (Hebrews 2:14-15; Romans 16:20; 1 John 3:8). The striking of the heel of the woman's seed speaks of the fact that even the Victor would not come away unscathed in the process.

Should I, as his follower, expect anything less?

As we have already seen, Jesus also refers to these same "seeds" in the parable of the Weeds and the Wheat. The Son of Man sows the good seed, which speaks of the sons of the kingdom. On the other hand, the enemy (Satan) sows weeds, which speak of those who belong to the evil one (Matthew 13:24-30; 36-43). Jesus leaves no doubt as to who is responsible for sowing the seeds of evil. Likewise in Genesis 3:15, the ultimate source of evil is unmistakably identified. God's rhetorical question to Eve (and Adam) places the responsibility for evil squarely on the shoulders of humanity—"What is this *you* have done?" (v. 13). However, God's declaration of a curse upon the serpent takes us beyond the human phenomenon of sin to the cosmic problem of supernatural evil—"Because *you* (the serpent) have done this. . ." (v. 14). In stark contrast to the ongoing dignity of humanity *despite* the Fall (Psalm 8; Hebrews 2:6-8), the curse obliged the serpent from that day forward to "eat dust," an expression indicating debasement, humiliation, and ultimate defeat (Psalm 44:25; 72:9; Isaiah 25:12).

That ultimate defeat, however, must await the right time (Galatians 4:4). In preparation for that propitious moment, God's relentless love intervened by means of three other glimpses of the gospel that are inclusive in scope. In the confusion and scattering of the nations at Babel, God chooses a seed in Abraham that will ultimately bring blessing to the peoples of the earth (Genesis 12:1-3; Galatians 3:6-18). Centuries later, God's tokens of grace became more precise in his covenant made with David, providing the means by which the universal blessing promised to Abraham would come to the nations (2 Samuel 7:1-17). Finally, God's promises to Abraham and David find their ultimate fulfillment in the New Covenant sealed by Christ's victory on the cross over sin, Satan, and ultimately over all suffering in the world (Matthew 26:28).[85] Furthermore, it is this victory acquired by the Crucified Conqueror that grants us the promise of hope in our mourning that is so graphically described in Psalm 22.

HELP IN OUR MOURNING

SEE CHRIST IN HIS SUFFERINGS

Psalm 22 is a messianic song of lament that ultimately points us toward the Son of David, the Morning Star. He alone can help us as we journey from the dark night of suffering into the daybreak of hope. But to fully embrace his help, we must first see our suffering through the lens of Christ in *his* sufferings.

In this psalm of lament, David has thus far urged us to do three things in times of suffering:

- Passionately cry to God for help in time of need (vv. 2, 11, 19);
- Recall God's faithful character (vv. 3-5);
- Remember God's unfailing acceptance and love (vv. 9-10).

David does just that—recalling God's character and love, he pours out his heart in unrelenting prayer: "Every day I call to you . . ." (v. 2), "Do not stay far from me . . ." (v. 11), and "Snatch me from the lion's jaws . . ." (v. 21).

Did God hear and answer David's passionate cry for God's presence and deliverance? Does he hear and answer our cry? While not reflected in certain translations, the psalmist triumphantly exclaims in verse 21, *"You have answered me!"* (v. 21). Yet David's confident declaration begs the question, "How?" *How* did God respond to David's anguished prayer as he endured such affliction? *How* does he respond to our cries for help in times of suffering? A casual reading of the psalm leaves a puzzling veil over the answers to those questions.

My wife and I spoke with our son only hours before his death. He called us while on his ninety minute journey by train from the university in Asan, South Korea, to Seoul. We spoke of future plans and possibilities. Jonathan shared with us that he had discovered his "third home" in the Land of the

Morning Calm. Then we prayed. I prayed for God's hand of protection and direction in my son's life. That was the last time we spoke.

Did God hear my prayer? Did God answer my prayer?

Many believe that, given the amount of unjust suffering in this world, God (*if* God exists) simply doesn't hear our cries for help and probably never has. Elie Wiesel, author of the Pulitzer Prize-winning book, *Night*, was imprisoned at the age of fifteen in the Nazi labor camp Monowitz-Buna, a sub-camp of Auschwitz. He describes in his own words the account of a *pipel*, a young boy whose father had been shipped to Auschwitz after having been discovered concealing a cache of arms. The *pipel* had a "delicate and beautiful face" that Wiesel describes as the face "of a sad little angel." When the young boy refused to cooperate with his interrogators, the SS sentenced him to death along with two other prisoners who had collaborated with the boy's father.

> One day, as we returned from work, we saw three gallows, three black ravens, erected in the *Appelplatz*. Roll call. The SS surrounding us, machine guns aimed at us: the usual ritual. Three prisoners in chains—and among them, the little *pipel*, the sad-eyed angel. The SS seemed more preoccupied, more worried, than usual. To hang a child in front of thousands of onlookers was not a small matter. The head of the camp read the verdict.
>
> All eyes were on the child. He was pale, almost calm, but he was biting his lips as he stood in the shadow of the gallows. This time the *Lagerkapo* refused to act as executioner. Three SS took his place. The three condemned prisoners together stepped onto the chairs. In unison, the nooses were placed around their necks. "Long live liberty!" shouted the two men. But

the boy was silent. "Where is merciful God, where is He?" someone behind me was asking.

At the signal, the three chairs were tipped over. Total silence in the camp. On the horizon, the sun was setting. . . Then came the march past the victims. The two men were no longer alive. Their tongues were hanging out, swollen and bluish. But the third rope was still moving: the child, too light, was still breathing. . . And so he remained for more than half an hour, lingering between life and death, writhing before our eyes. And we were forced to look at him at close range. He was still alive when I passed him. His tongue was still red, his eyes not yet extinguished. Behind me, I heard the same man asking: "For God's sake, where is God?" And from within me, I heard a voice answer: "Where He is [sic]? This is where—hanging there from this gallows. . ."[86]

For Wiesel, the horrors of the death camp proved the absence of God. He and his fellow Jews most certainly and sincerely cried out to God as did the psalmist: "My God, my God, why have you forsaken me? Why are you so far from saving me, so far from my cries of anguish?" (Ps. 22:1). But their experience of unimaginable suffering led many to believe that they were forsaken, forgotten, and without hope.

Paradoxically, Wiesel's question contains its own answer. To his own question, "Where is He?" he responds: *This is where—hanging there from this gallows.*" That is precisely the message of David's hope-filled lament of Psalm 22! At the moment when God seems most absent, he is most present—suffering *with* us and *for* us on the gallows of the cross.

GOD ON THE GALLOWS
The origin and solution to evil are found in two stories. The first story focuses on two trees in a garden, a temptation, and

the Fall of mankind who tries to be like God. The second story also focuses on a tree (Calvary) near a garden of suffering, another temptation, and another man (the "second Adam") who *is* God, who resisted temptation, and who died and rose from the dead.[87]

As David pens Psalm 22, he is experiencing extreme opposition and intense suffering that literally brings him to death's door. But the agonizing language of lament goes far beyond what David himself could have experienced. Nothing in this psalm leads us to believe that he is describing his own personal experience of execution. The language rather describes what becomes historically true only in the "seed" of the woman, the Son of David. To our knowledge only the Messiah experienced the pain of dislocated bones (v. 14), the physical collapse of his bodily structure (v. 14), extreme thirst and loss of vigor (v. 15), the piercing of his hands and feet (v. 16), and the plundering of his possessions in anticipation of his imminent death (v. 18). Using figurative and hyperbolic language, the Spirit of God speaks through the pen of David to give us this raw, graphic account of the Son of David's excruciating suffering on the cross. In so doing, his words are like an X-ray that penetrates into our Lord's thoughts, inner life, and emotions during his crucifixion. Here we see the anguish of Christ's passion; we see his soul laid bare. C. H. Spurgeon writes: "It is the photograph of our Lord's saddest hours, the record of his dying words . . . the memorial of His expiring joys. David and his afflictions may be here in a modified sense, but, as the star is concealed by the light of the sun, he who sees Jesus will probably neither see nor care to see David." Little wonder that Spurgeon entitles this psalm the "psalm of the cross."[88]

Without a doubt, the graphic portrait of Psalm 22 is of God on the gallows; so much so that the psalm has been called the "Fifth Gospel" account of the crucifixion. The irony of it all is that the Jewish and Roman leaders responsible for Jesus' death had no idea they were fulfilling the words of this psalm written nearly one thousand years earlier. Yet by fulfilling these words, they demonstrated that Jesus was indeed the Messiah, the very fact they denied!

OUR SUFFERING GOD

Dietrich Bonhoeffer once wrote: "Only the suffering God can help."[89] In the first book of the Bible, it is predicted that Jesus would suffer by the bruising of his heel (Genesis 3:15); the last book of the Bible describes Jesus as the one "slain from the creation of the world" (Revelation 13:8). From Genesis to Revelation, the sufferings of Christ are a predominant but *scandalous* theme. The descriptive word is appropriate, "scandal" referring to an offense that creates public outrage—an outrage brought about by suffering. That's precisely why so many through the centuries have failed to grasp the connection between Christ's suffering and evil— it's a case of mistaken identity (John 1:10-11; 1 Corinthians 2:8). As prophesied by Isaiah, the majority of Jesus' contemporaries totally misunderstood that Jesus *must* suffer and die (Isaiah 53:4).[90] They were expecting the Messiah to "bare his holy arm in the sight of all the nations. . ." (Isaiah 52:10). The stirring picture is of God rolling up his sleeve, baring his mighty biceps, and taking up his weapon in order to crush his enemy. But the arm that Jesus' contemporaries saw was not the muscled, mighty arm of a weightlifter; instead, it was the suffering arm of a humble servant. Very unimpressive! Even Jesus' inner circle of disciples didn't understand. Peter received one of Jesus' strongest rebukes when he protested against the need for Christ to suffer (Matthew 16:23-25). For the majority of the religious elite, Jesus didn't fit the bill of what humanity was looking for in a messiah. Could this one truly be the "strong arm of the Lord"? Could this one truly be God's final solution to evil and suffering in the world?

Fallen humanity expected a mighty warrior; God came to us as a helpless baby. We wanted someone to rid us of sorrow; God chose to identify with us in sorrow. He did this first by taking on a human Jewish body of flesh and bones, cartilage and nerve cells, blood and sinew, "sharing in our humanity" (Hebrews 2:14). He suffered the normal trials and heartaches, the fatigue and disappointments of life on planet earth. He experienced hunger pains as an infant, bruises from falling as a young boy at play, the pangs of thirst after a long journey, and the deep emotions of loss following the death of his friend, Lazarus. Though being the Son of God who created the mathematics table, as the Son of Man, he had to learn the mathematics table.

In addition to his intimate identification with you and me in our humanity, he also experienced indescribable suffering at the hands of evil men. They joked about his birth and called him an illegitimate son. His brothers misunderstood him and didn't believe him. Others called him a drunkard and a glutton and said he was possessed by the devil. As he began his ministry, he encountered the assault of hell itself in a face-to-face encounter with Satan (Matthew 4:1-11). And as he ended his ministry, he experienced the deepest agony of the soul known to mankind in the Garden of Gethsemane where he became "sorrowful and troubled" as he endured profound spiritual, mental, and emotional distress (Matthew 26:37). As the prophet Isaiah describes him: "He was despised and rejected—a man of sorrows, acquainted with deepest grief. We turned our backs on him and looked the other way" (Isaiah 53:3, NLT).

Should it really surprise us that many today still "look the other way"? Any concept of a suffering God as the solution to a suffering world is foolishness to human reasoning (1 Corinthians 1:23). After the publication of his book *The God Delusion*, outspoken atheist and Oxford professor Richard Dawkins spoke of the grandeur of what yet may be discovered by the science of the future. Dawkins concluded: "I don't see . . . Jesus coming down and dying on the Cross as worthy of that grandeur . . . [that] strike[s] me as parochial. If there is a God, it's going to be a whole lot bigger and a whole lot more incomprehensible than anything that any theologian of any religion has ever proposed."[91]

Unfortunately, it is not merely agnostics and atheists who resist the idea of a suffering God. Over the centuries, theologians have formulated what is known as the doctrine of God's *impassibility*, a doctrine closely connected to a blueprint view of God's sovereign omnipotence. Beginning with the assumption that God cannot be affected by anything external to himself, the term conveys the idea that God is "without passions" or emotions. Even the well-known Westminster Confession goes so far as to state that God is "infinite in being and perfection, a most pure spirit, invisible, without body, parts, or *passions*; immutable, immense."[92]

However, the God of the Bible is not like the stoic Buddha removed from the fray of human ills and stripped of all emotion. A multitude of biblical passages demonstrates that our Three-in-One relational God experiences a broad range of emotions. For example, when God saw the evil of mankind, "His heart was deeply troubled" (Genesis 6:6). The prophet Isaiah describes God's profound emotions regarding the distress of his people, "In all their distress he too was distressed" (Isaiah 63:9). In relation to the Spirit of God, we are told not to grieve the Holy Spirit (Ephesians 4:30) who intercedes for us with "wordless groans" (Romans 8:26). Finally, Jesus Christ—the pure reflection of what God is like—was a man of sorrows who shed tears (Luke 19:41), grieved loss (John 11:35), experienced sadness and sorrow (Matthew 26:37), and felt distress (Luke 12:50). Far from being "without passion," the God of the Bible is frequently described as being a God of *compassion*, a term derived from two Latin words *cum* ("with") and *pati* ("to suffer").

The Hellenistic philosophy of stoicism that permeated the Greek world at the time of Christ argued that God, by his very nature, was beyond all feeling. On the other hand, the Epicureans of the day believed the gods lived in the perfect bliss of happiness, totally detached from the suffering in this world. As for many of the Jewish leaders, their view of God (not at all represented by the Old Testament) was that his holiness kept him from sympathizing with humankind. But it was into this world—the world of the Stoics, Epicureans, and Jews—that Christ as the very image of God came and suffered![93]

Contrary to Richard Dawkins, what God has done is truly a "whole lot bigger and a whole lot more incomprehensible" than anything we humans could have imagined. The God of the universe does not withdraw from our suffering, but draws close to us in our suffering. He took the high road, which is the wise road of humility, sacrifice, and suffering in order to vanquish the self-seeking arrogance of our sin. God's wisdom is so often upside down in comparison to man's wisdom.

The writer to the Hebrew believers describes the encouragement this truth brings to us in our suffering:

> For we do not have a high priest who is unable to sympathize with our weaknesses, but we have one who has been tempted in every way, just as we are—yet was without sin. Let us then approach the throne of grace with confidence, so that we may receive mercy and find grace to help us in our time of need. (Hebrews 4:15-16)

To be our helper in time of need, Jesus *had* to suffer in his earthly body. Jesus' scars are a badge of honor that renders him capable of compassionately identifying with us in our suffering. Only through the suffering of an obedient life, enduring temptation, and the agony of the cross could Jesus be our deliverer, our "Pioneer." As such, Jesus is a trailblazer, one who breaks new ground for those who follow him. He's the file leader, the path finder, the captain of a company of suffering followers!

I'll never forget entering the mortuary in Seoul, South Korea, where Jonathan's body was embalmed. The smell of incense pervaded the dark, eerie room. The flicker of lit candles cast a dancing shadow over the numerous statues of Buddha where adherents mourned their loved ones. There sat the detached Buddha—arms folded, eyes closed, legs crossed, a half-smile plastered on his iconic lips, a stoic look on his austere face—seemingly immune to the silent agony of those in the throes of grief. I could almost hear the Buddha's hopeless words: "Birth is suffering; decay is suffering; illness is suffering; death is suffering. Presence of objects we hate is suffering; separation from objects we love is suffering; not to obtain what we desire is suffering."[94] What then shall we do in our suffering of loss? The Buddha replies: "Let therefore no man love anything; loss of the beloved is evil. Those who love nothing and hate nothing have no fetters."[95] The depressing atmosphere of hopelessness only served to heighten my own emotional distress and left me at a breaking point.

At that moment, in my own heart and mind, I turned away and fixed my gaze on the disfigured, lonely figure on the cross—arms outstretched, eyes open, feet pierced, lips parched, a compassionate look of infinite love on his face— assuring me of his intimate, tangible presence in suffering. I was reminded of Jesus' suffering presence with my son even as those toxic fumes enveloped his body. I remembered, too, that it is the truth that God is present in my suffering—not that he in some way planned my suffering—that brings comfort. And I took comfort in Jesus' hope filled words that give assurance of his suffering presence now, with us—Jonathan's parents and siblings—who continue to endure the pangs of an empty place around the table of our hearts.

CRIME AND COMPASSION

My wounds are healed by my Lord's wounds (Isaiah 53:5). And his wounds are preeminently those of the cross. For on that bloody tree the compassion of the cross conquered the crime of the crucifixion. "God's love comes to us soaked in divine blood," writes Randy Alcorn. "One look at Jesus—at his incarnation and the redemption he provided us—should silence the argument that God has withdrawn to some far corner of the universe where he keeps his hands clean and maintains his distance from human suffering."[96]

Jesus was in critical condition even before the crucifixion began. After Jesus' trial in which he was found guilty of blasphemy for claiming to be God, Pilate ordered him to be flogged (John 19:1). This brutal beating left Jesus on the verge of death. He was tied to a post and beaten at least 39 times—probably more—with a whip woven together with jagged bones and lead. The blows cut deep into the underlying tissues, producing a spurting of arterial bleeding. According to the third-century historian, Eusebius, "The sufferer's veins were laid bare, and the very muscles and tendons and bowels of the victim were open to exposure."[97] That is why the prophet Isaiah says that ". . . there were many who were appalled at him—his appearance (probably referring to his face) was so disfigured beyond that of any human being and his form (probably referring to his body in general) marred beyond human likeness—" (Isaiah 52:14). Those who observed the Messiah's trial, torture, and crucifixion were "appalled;" that is, they were amazed, shocked, and horrified at the brutality with which Jesus Christ was treated.

Upon arrival at Skull Hill, Jesus was nailed to the cross. "They have pierced my hands and feet," writes the psalmist (Psalm 22:16). Crucifixion was a particularly gruesome and painful means of death and appropriately described as *excruciating*, which literally means "a pain like the pain of crucifixion."

Beyond the unimaginable pain of the cross was the shame of the cross. Today, the symbol of the cross is worn by many, believers and unbelievers alike. Ornate, delicate, attractive, often coated in gold or silver, the crosses worn today reveal how little we grasp the awful shame and profound horror of this form of capital punishment. Who today would wear around their neck a piece of jewelry in the shape of a gas chamber or an electric chair? Among the three official methods of capital punishment in the Roman world—crucifixion, decapitation, and burning alive—crucifixion was considered the most shameful and brutal. In the honor-shame culture of the Roman world, crucifixion was the *summum supplicium* ("ultimate punishment"), reserved for political rebels and slaves. As Cicero once wrote: "Even the word, cross, must remain far not only from the lips of the citizens of Rome, but also from their thoughts, their eyes, their ears."[98]

This shame was intensified by the mocking ridicule of the crowds: "They divide my garments among themselves and throw dice for my clothing," writes the psalmist (Psalm 22:18). You can almost hear the Roman soldiers as they bargain for the coveted clothes of this controversial figure named Jesus: "Here, Antonius, you take the head shawl; and Felix, you the sandals. Julius, do you want the tunic? It's too valuable to tear. Let's throw dice for it!" All the while they were arguing over who gets what, the God-man Jesus Christ was offering his eternal blood to free mankind from the clutches of Satan, sin, and death.

But we must make a distinction. We must see the difference between Jesus' human suffering and his saving suffering, between the crime of the crucifixion and the compassion of the cross. Human intermediaries like Judas, the Jewish leaders, and the Roman rulers—all of these could inflict suffering on Jesus. But only God could take the most heinous crime of humanity and turn it into a tale of compassion. As one has said, "Christ was God's Lamb—not Pilate's. God provided the redeeming blood—not Caiaphas."[99]

From the standpoint of the compassion of the cross, God the Father led his own Son to Calvary. Was this against Jesus' will? If so, it would have been as much of a crime as that committed by the Jewish and Roman leaders! But it was *not* against Jesus' will. The cross was not "divine child abuse." Jesus' words leave no doubt: "The reason my Father loves me is that I lay down my life—only to take it up again. No one takes it from me, but I lay it down of my own accord. I have authority to lay it down and authority to take it up again. This command I received from my Father" (John 10:17). His suffering was the quintessential expression of God's goodness. Yes, the greatest crime of humanity became the outpouring of God's compassion at the cross. Jesus didn't just take notes on our suffering. He didn't merely observe our sorrow from afar. He plunges headlong into our pain and sorrow and takes it all upon himself.

Many do not believe in the existence of God because of the existence of evil. But God has definitively responded to this objection not in mere words, but in deeds and tears. God's scandalous love is the ultimate answer to the perplexing question of evil, suffering, and injustice in the world. We want deliverance from the symptoms, called suffering; God has provided healing of the illness, called sin and evil. The irony of it all is that he suffered and died precisely because he was carrying *our* sin and *our* sorrow. While God does not fully explain our suffering, he does compassionately share in our suffering. And by sharing in our suffering, he demonstrates that he is sovereign over suffering. For only by sharing in our suffering could the sovereign God turn the crime of the crucifixion into the compassion of the cross. In taking evil upon himself, he has conquered evil for others.

THE CRUCIFIED CONQUEROR

The cross is a "T" formed by two cruel, rough beams of wood on Calvary's hill.[100] Jesus' hands were nailed against the crossbeam which he falteringly carried through the streets of Jerusalem on the way to Skull Hill. His feet were nailed to the upright stake upon which his body was laid before being raised in front of a mocking crowd. This cruel tree in the shape of a "T" highlights the three realities that converge at Calvary: the crime of the crucifixion, the compassion of the cross, and the incomprehensible sovereign wisdom of God. In the infinite wisdom of divine sovereignty, Jesus Christ stretched out his arms on the cross and brought together the crime of the crucifixion and the compassion of the cross in order to once-for-all conquer Satan, sin, and the suffering of this world.

While the cross does not explain the ultimate origin of evil, it does put on display the profound perversity of evil carried out by free moral agents (human and angelic) against the very embodiment of undefiled love. Everything in history before the cross and after the cross is brought into perspective by the cross, including all the evil and suffering in this world. As N. T. Wright reminds us, ". . . the story the gospels are trying to tell us is the story of how the death of Jesus is the point at which evil in all its forms has come rushing together."[101]

One form of evil that put Jesus on the cross was human in origin. In Peter's message to the crowds at Pentecost, he unequivocally places the responsibility for the crucifixion at the feet of evil men: ". . . you, with the help of wicked men, put him to death by nailing him to the cross" (Acts 2:23). No room is left for any suspicion of God's complicity in the evil of the cross. As I have previously argued, the "wicked" human beings responsible for Christ's crucifixion were (as "image bearers") self-determining moral agents acting out of their own free will. Nevertheless, they had acquired *by their own choices* a "wicked" character that manifested itself in the most heinous crime of history.

Author Henri Nouwen tells the story of a family he knew in Paraguay. The father, a doctor, spoke out against the military regime in that country and its human rights abuses. In response, the local police arrested the doctor's teenage son and tortured him to death. Enraged citizens wanted to turn the boy's funeral into a huge protest march, but the doctor chose another means of protest. At the funeral, the father displayed his son's body as he had found it in the jail—naked, scarred from electric shocks, cigarette burns, and beatings. The people of the town filed past the corpse, which lay not in a coffin but on the blood-soaked mattress from the prison. It was the strongest protest imaginable, for it put injustice on grotesque display.[102]

Isn't that what God did at Calvary? The cross that held Jesus' body, naked and scarred, exposed all the violence and injustice of this world. At once, the cross revealed what kind of world we have and what kind of God we have; a world of gross unfairness and suffering, but a God of sacrificial, scandalous love who "handed over" his Son for us all (Acts 2:23; Romans 4:25). The cross is the quintessential expression of three emotionally laden words uttered by the Three-in-One relational God: "I love you."

However, another form of evil—and the ultimate source of evil—was supernatural in origin. This is already hinted at in Psalm 22. Help at daybreak comes when we are delivered from the "strong bulls" (v. 12), vicious "dogs" (v.16), and "roaring lions" (v. 13) that seek to devour us (cf. 1 Peter 5:8). In predicting his death, Jesus told his disciples that "now the prince of this world will be driven out" (John 12:31). The gospel writers remind us that Satan entered into Judas just before he betrayed Jesus (John 13:2, 27). When the chief priests and temple guard came to arrest Jesus in the garden of Gethsemane, he told them, "But this is your hour—when darkness reigns" (Luke 22:53). Some years later, looking back on the significance of Christ's cross-work, Paul tells us the "rulers of this age" crucified the "Lord of glory" (1 Corinthians 2:7-8). While contextually this refers primarily to the human rulers responsible for the crucifixion, the frequent connection in Scripture between heavenly powers and human authorities would lead us to suspect demonic involvement behind the scenes (Isaiah 24:21; Daniel 10). That this is true is confirmed by John's unequivocal words: "The reason the Son of God appeared was to destroy the devil's work" (1 John 3:8). On the cross, the Crucified Conqueror dealt a death blow to the perversity and persistence of evil by breaking the power of the devil (Hebrews 2:14-15).

If Satan is the ultimate source of evil, death is the "secret goal" of evil.[103] By breaking the power of Satan at the cross, Jesus Christ dealt definitively with both the source and goal of evil. God did this at the cross by disarming "the powers and authorities" and making a "public spectacle of them, triumphing over them by the cross" (Colossians 2:15). It is Jesus' victory over the supernatural powers of evil—the theme known as *Christus Victor*—that brings into perspective all the other aspects of Christ's redemptive work on the cross.

It is on Calvary's hill that the "impenetrable mystery of evil meets the paradoxical mystery of the cross."[104] By an unprecedented maneuver of his inscrutable wisdom, God entraps the crafty serpent in his own entangled web. On the "T" of Calvary, the evil of evil was vanquished by the undefiled goodness of God according to his "deliberate plan and foreknowledge" (Acts 2:23). The psalmist reminds us: "The Lord is known for his justice; the wicked are trapped by their own deeds" (Psalm 9:16). Evil sought to take advantage of undefiled goodness by "striking the heel" of the Messiah, putting him to death. The Lord responds like a champion, causing his opponent's own momentum to work against him, which crushes his head, entrapping him in his own evil. In this way, God, in his inscrutable wisdom, uses evil against evil and overturns the strategies of his adversary. In orchestrating the crime of the crucifixion, Satan defeated himself!

Whether human or angelic in origin, the cross reveals God's definitive response to the persistence of evil. David's final affirmative shout—"He has done it!" (Psalm 22:31)—is the Son of David's final, victorious last word from the cross: "It is finished!" (John 19:30). The "it is finished" of Calvary is God's answer to every injustice of this life. It is God's word of assurance that evil and all the suffering that accompanies it has been once-for-all defeated at Calvary. At the foot of the cross we find the answer to a suffering universe. There, and there alone, we find the infinite wisdom of God that combines into one great act of redemption the crime of the crucifixion and the compassion of the cross. There God turned evil back on itself by the greatest display of supreme love the universe has ever witnessed. The most vehement, abominable expression of evil—the crucifixion of the incarnation of love—is the very thing that definitively conquered evil. This truth consoles us in our pain and comforts us in our suffering as we await the Crucified Conqueror who will one day right all wrongs and wipe away all tears from the eyes of those who believe.

In the days and weeks following Jonathan's death, I found myself repeating the words of Mary and Martha to Jesus upon receiving word of their brother's death: "Lord, *if you had been here* my brother would not have died!" (John 11:21, 32). In my own dark night of the soul I cried, "Where *were* you, God? Where *are* you, God? Did you not hear our prayer for protection over my son?" But at one particular moment, I heard afresh the consoling words of my heavenly Father speaking into my pain: "Where was I? The same place I was when *my* Son died." God's watchful care is not from a distance; it's up close, ultimately demonstrated in God sending his only Son—"a man of suffering and familiar with pain" (Isaiah 53:3)—to be our companion in grief. There is no suffering, loss, tragedy, or pain with which he is not familiar. God *was* there and *is* where he has always been since that infamous Good Friday when Jesus Christ experienced the brute force of satanic evil. At that moment, when God seemed most absent, he was most present. As Cornelius Plantinga, Jr., writes: "We do not refer each other to the cross of Christ to explain evil. It is not as if in pondering Calvary we will at last understand throat cancer. We rather lift our eyes to the cross, whence comes our help, in order to see that God shares our lot and can therefore be trusted."[105]

Over the years since my son's death, I've come to realize that my deepest consolation in distress is found, not in a meticulously omni-controlling God, but in a suffering God. No passive appeal to God's sovereignty (God is in control) can bring lasting solace to the Zosias and Claires of this world who have been slaughtered and molested at the hands of free (but fallen) moral agents. Only the image of a suffering God can calm the deepest recesses of the human heart where only groans express the otherwise inexpressible sorrow.

LOOK TO THE PROMISE OF THE RESURRECTION

Yes, only a suffering God can help. But not a God who *only* suffers. Apart from the resurrection of the Son of David, his suffering of death would be of little help. If the cross of Christ defeated evil, the resurrection of Christ defeated death, for death is the hidden objective of all evil. Death is separation, and separations need bridges. If God's Son *never* suffered and died, his provision for us earthlings would be like a bridge broken on the near end. He could not identify with us in our suffering. But if God's Son *only* suffered and died, his provision would be like a bridge broken on the far end. He could not deliver us from our suffering. Thankfully, the resurrection of Jesus Christ—the one mediator between God and man (1 Timothy 2:5)—is the guarantee that the bridge to authentic life is not broken on either end.

In the days following Jonathan's death, my wife began to ask God to raise him from the dead. I hesitantly prayed that prayer once or twice myself. I wanted to hear Jesus say, "My child, get up" (Luke 8:54). After all, did not some godly women mentioned in the Bible receive their loved ones back from the dead (Hebrews 11:35)? If God can, by his all-powerful pronouncement of "Let there be . . . ," overcome primeval chaos, he most certainly could also, by that same life-giving declaration, bring my son back to life. Yet I struggled inwardly. If God did not answer my previous prayer for Jonathan's physical protection, how could I trust him now for his physical resurrection? Or should we have even prayed for such a stupendous miracle in the first place?

The answer to those questions gradually came to me as I meditated on Psalm 22 and its best commentary as recorded in Hebrews 2:5-18. As we have seen, the psalmist does not explicitly describe *how* God answered his prayer. He simply but confidently affirms, "You have answered me!" (v. 21), and then goes on to confidently declare in verse 24, "For he has not despised or scorned the suffering of the afflicted one; he has not hidden his face from him but has listened to his cry for help." We must depend on later revelation to connect the dots that span the thousand years between the experience of the psalmist David and the experience of the Son of David.

While we do not know the precise way in which God answered David's prayer historically, we do have indications of how it was answered prophetically. Looking back on the Son of David's sufferings, the writer to the Hebrew Christians pens these words: "During the days of Jesus' life on earth, he offered up prayers and petitions with loud cries and tears to the one who could save him from death, and *he was heard* because of his reverent submission" (Hebrews 5:7-8). Could it be the psalmist points us to the fact that the ultimate answer to his prayers as well as those of his counterpart, the Messiah, would be in the form of resurrection in the future rather than rescue in the present? For in spite of his prayer, "My Father, if it is possible, may this cup be taken from me . . ." (Matthew 26:39), the Son of David was not delivered *from* evil, but he was delivered *through* evil—or better, by *overcoming* evil (cf. Matthew 27:40-43). God answered the Son of David's prayer in a different way and at a different time than requested. Jesus prayed to be delivered on Good Friday, but he was delivered on Easter Sunday. He prayed to be preserved from death, but he was resurrected from death. Just as the Son of David's submission to death definitively conquered the penalty and power of evil, so also his resurrection from death is the guarantee that those who believe will one day be delivered from the very presence of evil. Jesus' historical, bodily resurrection is proof positive that "He has done it" (Psalm 22:32).

That Christ's resurrection and future world dominion are in view is confirmed by the citation of David's words in Hebrews 2. Having joined the multitude of the afflicted and become one with us in our suffering, the risen Son of David now calls us his brothers and sisters: "I will declare your name to my brothers and sisters; in the assembly I will sing your praises" (Psalm 22:22; cf. Hebrews 2:10-12). While it is the psalmist David who pens these words, it is the Son of David who speaks these words to those of us who are his spiritual siblings in suffering ("brothers and sisters," Hebrews 2:11-12). Furthermore, according to the psalmist's words, all of this takes place in the context of the future reign of the resurrected Messiah when ". . . all the ends of the earth will remember and turn to the Lord, and all families of the nations will bow down before him" (Psalm 22:27). Yes, a better day is coming! We don't see it now and we don't feel it now, but someday everything that opposes the righteous, just rule of Christ will be brought into submission to him. That includes death, disease, pain, grief, suffering, loss, and all relational disharmony. It includes everything that at times makes our present life so painful and distasteful. For in that day, "The earth will be filled with the knowledge of the glory of the Lord as the waters cover the sea" (Habakkuk 2:14).

With this in mind, should we not also expect that in our suffering God may answer our prayer in a different way and at a different time than requested? Remember, the key idea of Psalm 22 is this: *In times of suffering, God hears and answers our cries for help according to his own perfect plan.* Consider Abraham. To this pilgrim of faith, God gave the promise that through his descendant all the nations of the earth would be blessed. But then, in a paradoxical turn of events, God asks him to sacrifice the very fulfillment of that promise. It just doesn't make sense! Sometimes God seems to contradict God . . . but only for the moment. God's answer to the seeming paradox may not be seen until the resurrection. That's precisely what Abraham concluded. For even if Isaac had been slain, "Abraham reasoned that God could even raise the dead" (Hebrews 11:19). That is also, it seems, what the psalmist David and the Son of David believed based on Psalm 22. The *ultimate* fulfillment of God's promises in our lives is deferred until the resurrection: "Now we see only a reflection as in a mirror; then we shall see face to face (1 Corinthians 13:12).

Remember the superscription of Psalm 22, "Help at Daybreak"? Here's the answer to the "spoiler." The historical, bodily resurrection of Jesus Christ is the promise of resurrection to life for all who believe. Because of his resurrection at daybreak that first Easter morning, there is hope in our mourning. So our prayer for our son's resurrection was valid. After all, true healing—of which resurrection is the epitome—is never returning to what we once were, but rather becoming all we were meant to be. Jonathan now experiences true healing, as do all Christ followers who have died. His body now buried in Troutdale, Oregon, awaits a "better resurrection"[106] which I will describe in greater detail in Chapter 10.

When we lived in Belgium, I visited on several occasions the well-known site of Waterloo. June 18, 1815, was a momentous day for the people of Europe, and the Battle of Waterloo would decide their fate. Sir Arthur Wellesley, Duke of Wellington, was commander of the English Army along with the allied forces of Prussia, Russia, and Austria. As a united front, they marched out to put an end to Napoleon Bonaparte's ambitious plan to conquer all of Europe. The fate of history lay in the balance. The historic battle ended at nine o'clock that night. In excited anticipation of news of the outcome, the English townspeople waited with bated breath. News from the battlefront was flashed homeward across the English Channel by signal lamps at a cathedral's bell tower—much like Morse code in more recent times. However, as if on cue, a dense fog settled in, obscuring the view of the cathedral. The only discernible words were "Wellington . . . defeated." All of England was thrown into a panic as the disturbing news of defeat began to spread. Then, as quickly as it had arrived, the fog began to lift revealing the rest of the message: "Wellington . . . defeated . . . the enemy." Despair became delight as the message spread like wildfire!

Similarly, darkness descended as Christ hung on Skull Hill. Even his disciples believed his final words "It is finished" meant nothing more than "Jesus . . . defeated." Nailed to a cross, declared dead by experienced soldiers, buried in a rock tomb—what else were they to believe? But three days later everything changed. Their despondency and perplexity were transformed into a shout of victory: "Jesus . . . defeated . . . death!" What a difference! The disciples now understood what both the psalmist David and the Son of David meant by the victory cry: "He has done it!"

ENJOY GOD FOREVER AND ENCOURAGE OTHERS TO DO THE SAME

Thus far in Psalm 22, the inspired poet has given five words of counsel, offering us hope in our mourning:

- Passionately cry to God for help in time of need (vv. 2, 11, 19);
- Recall God's faithful character (vv. 3-5);
- Remember God's unfailing acceptance and love (vv. 9-10);
- Identify with Christ in his sufferings (vv. 1-18);
- Look to the promise of the resurrection (vv. 21-22).

The psalmist now leaves us with a final word of "help at daybreak," enabling us to walk—albeit with a limp—through the suffering of this life. It is this: *Enjoy God forever and encourage others to do the same* (vv. 22-31).

The melancholy tone of David's lament in Psalm 22 begins in verse one with an agonizing cry of despair and then descends downward for twenty-one verses. Suddenly in verse twenty-two, the melody is lifted an octave higher as the mood of the psalmist spirals upward, culminating in a triumphant declaration of victory: "He has done it!" Assured of God's definitive intervention, the psalmist now describes God as both the source and object of his praise: "*From you* comes the theme of *my* praise. . ." (v. 25). That is the essence of biblical lament—*praise when God's presence seems hidden.* The image of a suffering Savior assures us of God's presence in our suffering. The truth of a resurrected Savior assures us of ultimate deliverance from suffering. And both call us to a life of praise in the midst of suffering.

In our process of grieving and healing as parents, we have discovered that praise both expresses and brings delight. While grief tends to insulate and isolate, praise decentralizes the soul, moving the worshiper in pain toward the true and only source of enduring happiness—God himself. Again, Lewis states it eloquently when he writes: ". . . we must suppose ourselves to be in perfect love with God—drunk with, drowned in, dissolved by, that delight which, far from remaining pent up within ourselves as incommunicable . . . flows out from us incessantly again in effortless and perfect expression, our joy no more separable from the praise in which it liberates and utters itself than the brightness a mirror receives is separable from the brightness it sheds."[107]

Such profound delight in God is not only the experience of the psalmist, but also his encouragement to others, including you and me. The poet expresses his *joie de vivre* even in the midst of horrendous pain and suffering as he offers a final toast to the company of the afflicted: "May your hearts live forever!" (v. 26). I can almost hear the festive sound of glasses clinking in joyous celebration of life—authentic life—forever! And the wellspring of such festive joy is found, not in the absence of difficulty, but in the presence of God.

This psalm has also taught me that "to glorify God and enjoy him forever" is not merely an individual affair. It is best experienced in community. But not just any community; it is the community of the "seed." The psalmist reminds us: "Posterity (i.e., seed) will serve him; future generations will be told about the Lord" (v. 30; cf. Isaiah 53:10). Is this not the same seed of the woman (i.e., the people of the promise) spoken of in Genesis 3:15? And is this not the good seed (i.e., the sons of the Kingdom) of which Jesus speaks in Matthew 13:36-43? It is in this assembly that David both weeps and worships (v. 22). And it is to this company of the afflicted that he expresses both his pain and praise (v. 25). As Peterman and Schmutzer have written, "Lament is a standing invitation to worship in pain, among the pained, not in spite of pain."[108]

In the days, weeks, and months following the death of my son, I worshiped "in pain." I cried when I prayed, and I cried when I preached. Sometimes—and often at the most unexpected moments—I cried before congregants and congregation. Gradually, the tears of grief became tears of healing as I expressed my pain and praise "in the assembly." For in our tears, we see his tears; and because of his tears, our tears will someday be wiped away.

—⊶⊷—

The fact that Jesus died my death must determine how I live my life. If our Savior's human and saving sufferings lead us to trust him, his exemplary sufferings call us to follow him. In the same way that the Pioneer of our faith was "made perfect" through suffering, so also are we his followers—which is the theme of Part 2 of this book. The Apostle Peter reminds us: "For God called you to do good, even if it means suffering, just as Christ suffered for you. He is your example, and you must follow in his steps" (1 Peter 2:21, NLT). It's no coincidence that the man who penned these words was himself unjustly treated under Nero's reign. Considering himself unworthy to be crucified in the same position as his Lord, he requested to be crucified upside down. In so doing, he encourages us to follow in the path of Jesus of the scars:

> If we have never sought, we seek Thee now;
> Thine eyes burn through the dark, our only stars;
> We must have sight of thorn-pricks on Thy brow,
> We must have Thee, O Jesus of the Scars.
> —Edward Shillito, from "Jesus of the Scars[109]

Interlude –
Jacob at the Jabbok

CHAPTER 5

Blessing from Brokenness

*I've come to believe that only broken people
truly worship. Unbroken people—happy folks who enjoy
their blessings more than the Blesser—say thanks to God
the way a shopper thanks a clerk.*
—Larry Crabb

*The Lord cannot fully bless a man until
He has first conquered him.*
—A. W. Tozer

We often don't realize that Jesus is all we need until Jesus is all we have. I cannot honestly say that I've been in that position. Or if I have, I haven't stayed there very long. For days, weeks, months, even years after the death of our son, I *felt* at times as if I had been stripped down naked and that Jesus was all I had. Yet even in such desperate times, I found my soul could all too easily slip back into a complacent status quo spirituality that relishes the gifts more than the Giver and the blessings more than the Blesser.

During such times, the biblical account of Jacob began to take on fresh meaning in my own pilgrimage toward a different kind of happiness—a happiness the Bible sometimes calls God's "blessing." Jacob's circuitous, tortuous journey underscores time and again just how much God wants to bless his people. Maybe that's why the narrator of Genesis, the Book of Beginnings, devotes an entire twenty-five chapters to tracing the blessing God wants to pour out, not only into this man's life, but also through him toward the nations of the world. Furthermore, Jacob was desperate for the blessing of God on his life. So much so that—as the prophet Hosea tells us—he wept and begged for God's favor (Hosea 12:4).

But it is here that Jacob's trouble begins—and ours as well. Solomon reminds us: "It is the *blessing* of the Lord that makes rich, and he adds no sorrow to it" (Proverbs 10:22). Furthermore, the weeping prophet Jeremiah adds: "For he does not willingly bring affliction or grief to anyone" (Lamentations 3:33). Our God, who is always at work to maximize good and minimize evil, does not willingly add unnecessary sorrow. Like Jacob, however, we so often do! We want to experience God's blessing, *but on our terms.* Not only do we frequently mistake what God's blessing entails, but we also have our own misconstrued ideas of how to attain it.

Jacob's life is a graphic illustration of both tragic errors. He needed to acknowledge his arrogant ego and deceitful ways and exchange both for a personal, life-transforming encounter with the Giver of every good gift. However, the blessing of such an encounter must begin with brokenness. That is precisely what happens. As the story begins, Jacob walks with a strut; as the story ends, he walks with a limp. Throughout we discover that the crooked contours of his life only serve to highlight the matchless beauty of the grace of God who calls himself the God of Jacob.

The crucial turning point in Jacob's experience is graphically recounted in Genesis 32:22-31.

> But during the night he got up and took his two wives, his two maidservants, and his eleven children and crossed the ford of the Jabbok. He got them safely across the brook along with all his possessions.
>
> But Jacob stayed behind by himself, and a man wrestled with him until daybreak. When the man saw

that he couldn't get the best of Jacob as they wrestled, he deliberately threw Jacob's hip out of joint.

The man said, "Let me go; it's daybreak."

Jacob said, "I'm not letting you go 'til you bless me."

The man said, "What's your name?"

He answered, "Jacob."

The man said, "But no longer. Your name is no longer Jacob. From now on it's Israel (God-Wrestler); you've wrestled with God and you've come through."

Jacob asked, "And what's your name?"

The man said, "Why do you want to know my name?" And then, right then and there, he blessed him.

Jacob named the place "Peniel" (God's Face) because, he said, "I saw God face to face and lived to tell the story!"

The sun came up as he left Peniel, limping because of his hip. (This is why Israelites to this day don't eat the hip muscle; because Jacob's hip was thrown out of joint.)[110]

In reading this brief account of only ten verses, all kinds of questions come to mind: Who is this mysterious "man"? Why is he fighting Jacob in the first place? Why was he not able to defeat the patriarch from the outset? Why does he cripple Jacob's thigh? What is the significance of Jacob's change of name? Finally, what is the significance of Jacob's limp following this event?

In attempting to answer these questions, commentators through the centuries have offered some rather ingenious interpretations of this narrative.[111] Personally, I see in this account how God can take me as I am and—*through broken-ness*—fashion me into what he wants me to be.

At the Jabbok, Jacob met his match at midnight and was never to be the same again. Here we find vintage Jacob, the one who still struggles in his own strength to experience the blessing already promised. His only obstacle to experiencing it was himself. What transpired that momentous night near the brook, Jabbok, revealed who Jacob was and who he was to become. It was only through a limp that Jacob would learn to lean on the One who alone could satisfy the deepest desires of his heart. When the sun goes down, his name is Jacob; but when the sun comes up, his name is Israel.[112]

THE HEEL CATCHER

To understand what this wrestling match signified for Jacob—as well as for you and me—we need to back up and remind ourselves of the patriarch's pilgrimage of faith up to this point. Jacob is one of the many unlikely heroes so remarkably and nobly mentioned in God's "Hall of Faith" as detailed in Hebrews 11. Nevertheless, Jacob's struggle with the "man" in this account epitomizes an intense struggle with God and others that began even before birth.

Exceptional difficulty often precedes exceptional events in life. Jacob's father, Isaac, had already wrestled with God for twenty years, pleading in prayer for the blessing of an heir. Finally, God responded and his wife, Rebekah, became pregnant with twins (Genesis 25:21). But this was no normal pregnancy. The twins tumbled and kicked within her like a herd of stubborn goats! The description in the Hebrew text implies a violent struggle that must have left Rebecca in physical and emotional turmoil, so much so that Rebekah despairs of life: "If it's going to be this way, why go on living?" she says to herself. So she prays that well-known prayer, "Lord, why is this happening to me?" In response, the Lord explains: "You're going to have twins! More than that, the kicking in your womb is prophetic. The twins in your womb are two nations that are butting heads. One will overpower the other and the older will serve the younger." The struggle for supremacy had already begun.

At the moment of birth, the two infants arrive in a near dead heat. Esau comes out first, but only by minutes. Because he's red all over and covered with thick hair like a fur coat, he's named Esau (red), a term that later describes his descendants, the Edomites. Jacob emerges next, grasping his brother's heel. The name Jacob is a play on the Hebrew word for "heel." The French word *talonner* brings out the original idea: "to follow closely behind" in the sense of protecting. Jacob was to be a rearguard. For Jacob's parents, it was a rather affectionate name and carried no negative connotation at the moment of birth. As we will see, however, his name began to take on another meaning, that of "heel catcher," "trickster," or "supplanter."

What took place in the womb was already an indication of what would happen out of the womb. Jacob became as crooked as the pejorative meaning of his name implied. Grasping the heel of his brother in the womb was a preview of his grasping character in life, which is placed on full display as he cunningly steals the birthright from his brother, Esau (Genesis 25:29-34). As a skillful wrestler attempts to overthrow his opponent by grasping his heel, Jacob's name describes his relations with others and with God. The prophet Hosea reminds us: "Even in the womb, Jacob struggled with his brother; when he became a man, he even fought with God" (Hosea 12:3, NLT).

These two brothers are far from identical twins. Esau is wild, woolly, and adventurous, preferring the chase and the kill. He's an outdoorsman, a man's man, a hunter, a nomad. In contrast, Jacob is more sedentary and quiet tempered, preferring domestic life around family. He's a young man tied to his mother's apron strings. As the story unravels, however,

Jacob is seen to be the superior hunter who catches Esau in his own trap!

One day, while Jacob is cooking some stew, Esau arrives from the field, famished after a long day's hunt. Upon arriving, he sees and smells the lentil stew that Jacob is preparing. Ironically, the stew is literally termed "red stuff," the perfect trap for his older brother, Esau (red). Falling for the ploy, impulsive Esau cries out: "I'm starved! Give me some of that red stew." Actually, the term is used twice: "Red stuff, red stuff, feed me!" The rabbis used the term "feed me" to describe cramming food down the throat of an animal. At that critical moment, "The cunning hunter fell into a better hunter's trap, becoming prey to his own appetite."[113]

It is here that Jacob's true colors begin to show. "Make me a trade," he says, "My stew for your birthright." Esau takes the bait without hesitation. "I'm famished!" he replies. "What good is a birthright if I die here on the spot!" To seal the deal, Jacob agrees to the trade only if Esau is willing to swear that once exchanged, there's no turning back. The oath is taken, the stew is given, and the birthright becomes Jacob's.

The birthright Esau forfeited included the privilege of being the chief of the tribe and spiritual leader of the family. It also entitled the bearer to a double portion of the father's land and possessions. Most importantly, it carried with it the promise of personal, national, and universal blessing, including the possession of Canaan and intimate covenant fellowship with God.[114] The New Testament commentary clearly places the responsibility for the ordeal on Esau's shoulders: "Make sure that no one is immoral or godless like Esau, who traded his birthright as the firstborn son for a single meal. You know that afterward, when he wanted his father's blessing, he was rejected. It was too late for repentance, even though he begged with bitter tears" (Hebrews 12:16-17, NLT).

As in the fall of humanity, spiritual blessing is traded for temporary satisfaction. Jacob and Esau knew what they wanted, and what they both wanted wasn't God. The "red man" wanted the "red stew." The "heel catcher" wanted the blessing, but on his own terms and in his own way. While Esau is motivated by lesser desires, Jacob is willing to use fleshly means to obtain better desires. Somehow the Giver of all good gifts, whether it be stew or birthright, was lost in the mix.

The saga of Jacob's wrestling match with his brother doesn't end there. The greatest struggle between the two occurs later when Jacob, following the counsel of his eaves-dropping mother, participates in a ruse to deceive his father, Isaac, and become the recipient of the much coveted patriar-chal blessing (Genesis 27). While Jacob obtained the birth-right by manipulation, he received the blessing by outright deceit. In his quest for a blessing, Jacob acted in a manner that deserved a curse. When Esau learned he had lost the blessing, he cried out: "Isn't he rightly named Jacob? . . . He took my birthright, and now he's taken my blessing!" (Genesis 27:36). Little wonder that when Jeremiah the prophet describes the heart as being deceitful above all things he literally says, "The heart is a Jacob" (Jeremiah 17:9). Though Jacob tried to grasp everything—from heels to birthright to blessing—he failed to grasp the significance of grace.

But all that was about to change.

THE HOUND OF HEAVEN

Jacob and Esau grew up in a God-fearing home. Though far from perfect, even quite dysfunctional at times, their family was nevertheless a context of faith inseparably linked to the promises of God. Jacob and Esau were about fifteen years old at the death of Abraham (cf. Genesis 25:7). I'm sure they had sat on their grandfather's lap as young children, listening attentively to stories of God's faithfulness in choosing the patriarch and in promising to bring blessing through him to all nations. They learned of his call out of a pagan land and of God's promise to bring untold blessing to him and through him to all the nations of the earth (Genesis 12:1-3). Would Abraham not have told Jacob and Esau of the miraculous birth of their father, Isaac, and of God's gracious provision of a sacrifice on Mount Moriah? In spite of such a rich spiritual heritage, the faith of Jacob's grandfather (Abraham) and father (Isaac) was not yet his own. When Isaac, much later in life, asked Jacob how he had found the wild game so quickly, Jacob simply replied, "The Lord *your* God gave me success" (Genesis 27:20).

This, too, was about to change.

Aware of Esau's determination to get revenge by killing his brother, Rebekah tells Jacob: "Get out of here. Run for your life . . . *go east* . . . far away, all the way to Haran where my brother Laban lives." Frequently in this Book of Beginnings to go *east* is to move away from the presence of the Lord. Adam and Eve not only hid from God, they also went *east* (Genesis 3:24). Later, Cain went *east* "out from the Lord's presence" (Genesis 4:16-17). Following the Ararat departure, the people migrated *eastward* in hopes of making a name for themselves (Genesis 11:2). Lot chose the whole Jordan Valley to the *east* (Genesis 13:11). Figuratively, to *go east* is to add sorrow upon sorrow to the Lord's rich blessing in our lives. Jacob is no exception to this. Now *persona non grata* in his homeland, he heads east. For over twenty years, the heel-catcher will live in the *east* . . . running from his brother, from his inheritance, from God.

In fleeing his home, Jacob may have wondered if the blessing of the birthright was his after all. Would he truly inherit the full benefits of the promises given to his grandfather and to his father? Ironically, Jacob is running away from the very blessing God had promised, just as we often do.

But God met him anyway. And he didn't wait for Jacob to take the initiative.

Of course, that's just like God, the "Hound of Heaven." The expression comes from a poem written by Francis Thompson, a nineteenth century British poet. Thompson was the son of a physician and studied medicine himself before discovering his gifts as a writer and poet. Though a Christ-follower, Thompson struggled with homelessness, poverty, and even an addiction to opium. For a period of time, he lived on the streets of London and Manchester, selling matches and newspapers to support himself until an anonymous prostitute gave him temporary lodging. Though he died of tuberculosis in 1907 at the age of 47, the profound depth of his writings earned him the favor of such literary giants as G. K. Chesterton and J. R. R. Tolkien. In Thompson's renown 182-line poem, "The Hound of Heaven," he describes the unfailing mercy and compassion of God that relentlessly pursues him as it did Jacob:

> I fled Him down the nights and down the days;
> I fled Him down the arches of the years;
> I fled Him down the labyrinthine ways
> Of my own mind; and in the mist of tears
> I hid from Him . . .
> From those strong Feet that followed after, followed after.
> But with unhurrying chase and unperturbed pace,
> Deliberate speed, majestic instancy,
> They beat—and a Voice beat,
> More instant than the feet:
> "All things betray thee who betrayest me."[115]

In his study of Thompson's life and poetry, J. F. X. O'Conor writes:

> As the hound follows the hare, never ceasing in its running, ever drawing nearer in the chase, with unhurrying and unperturbed pace, so does God follow the fleeing soul by His Divine grace. And though in sin or

in human love, away from God it seeks to hide itself, Divine grace follows after, unwearyingly follows ever after, till the soul feels its pressure forcing it to turn to Him alone in that never-ending pursuit.[116]

No words better describe God's unrelenting love for Jacob, the fugitive now running from the birthright and blessing already received but not yet experienced. Hosea, the prophet sums it up when he writes: "He found him at Bethel and talked with him there—the Lord God Almighty, the Lord is his name!" (Hosea 12:4).

As night approaches, the fugitive, Jacob, beds down in the desert where he takes a stone, lays it under his head, goes to sleep, and begins to dream (Genesis 28:10-22). In his dream, he receives a vision of God standing on top of an angel-filled stairway to heaven: "There, a ladder! And look, angels! And oh my, the Lord himself!" he exclaims. Through a series of word-plays, everything in this account points upward to heaven, toward the vision of the Lord himself. Following the vision, Jacob takes his stone pillow and sets it upright as a pillar, a sort of model of the stairway that he had seen.

The place where the encounter unfolds was relatively insig-nificant. It was just a "place" near a town called Luz. Yes, an *ordinary* place. In fact, the narrator repeats the term six times to get across the point (Genesis 28:11, 16, 19). But for Jacob, this inconspicuous, out-of-the-way place became "Bethel," the very house of God; the stone for his head became an altar; and the fugitive deceiver became a disciple. At Bethel, heaven and earth touched!

Is it not just like God to work in the ordinary places and circumstances of life? With God, ordinary places of trials and suffering can become extraordinary places of spiritual encounter and transformation. Gradually, the veil is lifted from our eyes, and we exclaim as Jacob: "Surely the LORD is in this place, and I was not aware of it" (Genesis 28:16).

In New Testament terms, this was Jacob's "conversion." For the first time in Jacob's rebellious journey, he caught a glimpse of the heavenly realities behind the earthly promises. He was beginning to realize the birthright and blessing consisted of far more than family privileges and a piece of real estate. For Jacob, this stairway was the offer of a personal, intimate encounter with God, the Giver of every good gift. But it was not limited to Jacob. The vision was the promise that this same blessing of personal encounter would be offered to the entire world. Over 1,700 years later, Jesus himself would refer to this event to describe what his first followers experienced by placing their faith in the Messiah. In speaking to Nathanael and his fellow disciples, Jesus says: "I tell you the truth, you will all see heaven open and the angels of God going up and down on the Son of Man, the one who is the stairway between heaven and earth" (John 1:51, NLT).

Here, in this ordinary place, God gives Jacob three extraordinary promises, all based upon Jacob's possession of the birthright: the promise of property, the promise of protection, and most importantly, the promise of the Lord's presence (Genesis 28:13-16). In spite of such extraordinary promises, Jacob tries to cut a deal with God. He had walked the aisle and even signed a pledge card, promising to tithe from what God would give . . . *if*:

> *If* God will indeed be with me and protect me on this journey, and *if* he will provide me with food and clothing, and *if* I return safely to my father's home, then the Lord will certainly be my God. And this memorial pillar I have set up will become a place for worshiping God, and I will present to God a tenth of everything he gives me" (Genesis 28:20-22, NLT).

God's promises to Jacob were unconditional: "*I am* with you and will watch over you wherever you go, and *I will* bring you back to this land. *I will* not leave you until I have done what I have promised you" (Genesis 28:15). There was no "*if* you . . . *then* I." In contrast, Jacob's promises to God were conditional: "*If* . . . *if* . . . *if* . . . then . . ." (Genesis 28:21). While God had tested Abraham, Jacob here tests God. He bargains with God more than submits to God. Rather than recalling God's loyal love in the past, he conditions his worship upon God's faithfulness in the future. Because he wasn't really at the end of himself, he hadn't *truly* begun with God. Just like the prodigal, he wanted his inheritance more than the One who provided it. While his stone pillow had become a pillar, his pillar would only become an altar *if* God came through! His mother, Rebekah, had also struggled with the same dependency upon circumstances to give life meaning: "*If* Jacob takes a wife from among the women of this land . . . my life will not be worth living" (Genesis 27:46). Only when Jacob realized that God was all he had, would he discover that God was all he needed.

That would only come at the cost of a limp!

Jacob left Bethel with a new gait in his step, finally arriving in the land of the east where he would spend the next twenty years (Genesis 29–31). He was blessed, but not yet broken. Though blessed materially, Jacob suffered relationally. Just as Jacob had deceived, so he was now deceived over a period of twenty years. Promises given, were broken. Wages set, were changed. Demands made, were modified. Jacob went from the status of a son to that of a slave. He wanted blessing, but what he got was treachery. As Alexander Whyte describes it: ". . . he is taken down to Padan-aram, where he is cheated out of his wages, and cheated out of his wife, and cheated, and cheated, and cheated again, ten times cheated, and that too by his own mother's brother, till cheating came out of Jacob's nostrils, and stank in his eyes, and became hateful as hell to Jacob's heart."[117] Jacob was forced to drink his own medicine. And it was very bitter.

What we call God's discipline is simply the expression of God's love as experienced by a fool. God's discipline is the form love takes when we run from it, just as darkness is the form light takes when we turn from it and run into our own shadow. We ourselves cast the shadow of God's discipline and ultimate judgment. God shines ever faithfully with love, as the sun with light. He does not change—we do.[118] Sometimes love has to leave people alone so they will learn from suffering what they refuse to learn from blessing (cf. Romans 2:4). In all of Jacob's adversity, the Hound of Heaven was constantly nipping at the heels of the "heel catcher," reminding him: "All things betray thee who betrayest me."

Jacob had sown the wind; he now reaps the whirlwind. No wonder he flees Laban and begins his journey back to the land of promise. Jacob faces another crisis, however, as he approaches the land of Canaan. Though the relational problems with his father-in-law, Laban, are now behind him, before him lies the ominous threat of his brother, Esau. No doubt, Esau's murderous threats are still ringing in Jacob's ears. When Jacob left his home, Rebekah promised him: "When your brother's anger cools down, I'll send for you." Rebekah thought her favorite son would only be gone for a few days (Genesis 27:44). But twenty years passed and, as far as we are told, Jacob never heard from his mother again. He could only conclude that his brother was as hot-headed as ever. Jacob needs reassurance. The question uppermost in his mind is, "Will God continue to bless me as he has up to this point?"

A FOXHOLE PRAYER

To provide that assurance, God grants Jacob insight into the out-of-sight with a second encounter with angels, who are sent as ministering servants in his moment of trial (Genesis 32:1-2; cf. Hebrews 1:14; 2 Kings 6:17). The encounter reminds Jacob that the company of angels accompanying him from heaven is far greater than the armies of Esau approaching on the horizon. So, Jacob names the place "Mahanaim," meaning "two camps."

Immediately following the vision, Jacob receives confirmation of Esau's approaching army of four hundred men. Convinced they are not coming with gifts and ready to hand out hugs, Jacob panics. Quickly forgetting the angelic revelation he had just received, Jacob immediately reverts to his normal, scheming ways. Jacob's motto seems to be "God helps those who help themselves." The subtle play on words in the passage highlights the degree to which he missed the point. Having encountered heavenly messengers intended to reassure him in a time of crisis, Jacob now sends human messengers to appease his brother. And having seen two "camps"—one heavenly and his own—he now divides his own into two, substituting his "camp" for God's (Genesis 32:7-8). He reasons that if Esau attacks the first camp, the remaining camp has a chance to survive. In this way, he can cut his losses if his manipulative expression of respect is not well received. When faced with difficulty on the horizon, Jacob prays only *after* he plans—as we so often do. It will soon become clear that Jacob's reconciliation with Esau was the result of his prayer and not of his scheming.

Jacob needed to replace fear of his circumstances with faith in God's promises. Instead, calculating Jacob reverts to his default mode of attempting to manipulatively control his circumstances by sending a bribe and parading his wealth (Genesis 32:13-18). He failed to grasp an important principle: Fear God, and you will fear nothing; do not fear God, and you will fear everything (cf. Luke 12:4; John 4:18). Jacob chose the latter.

Jacob's prayer is a typical foxhole prayer (Genesis 32:9-12). Jacob wanted the blessing of physical protection, a blessing now threatened by the impending encounter with his brother, Esau. Jacob had not yet come to the point where he wanted an encounter with the living God more than he wanted the blessing of safety, or any other blessing for that matter. Yes, he speaks of God's loyal love to his forefathers, confesses his own unworthiness, and relies upon God's promises of a continuing line of descendants. Nevertheless, Jacob's prayer still reflects the conditional *if* of his Bethel encounter. Rescue from his brother was still more important than intimate relationship with God. Furthermore, it seems Jacob had already forgotten the privileged implications of the birthright and blessing from which he had been running for the past twenty years. He instructs his servants to address Esau and his approaching army as those who are superior: "my master Esau," "your servant Jacob," and "my lord" (Genesis 32:4, 5, 18). These statements clearly demonstrate just what Jacob was willing to sacrifice. Jacob prays for protection from his brother; what he yet needed, however, was protection from himself . . . and from God!

GOD'S GYMNASIUM

In the shadows of the night, Jacob gets up, takes his two wives, maidservants, and eleven children and sends them over the Jabbok, a winding river located midway between the Sea of Galilee in the north and the Dead Sea in the south. The place name Jabbok speaks of a wrestling, crooked, twisting river. What better image to describe Jacob's life up to this point. Indeed, the trickster Jacob was just as crooked as the river he is about to cross! Before Jacob can cross the Jabbok and enter into God's blessing, he must fight.

Having sent his family members and possessions to the other side of the Jabbok, Jacob is alone. It's time for Jacob to grapple *in solitude* not only with who he is and who God is, but also with what God's blessing truly consists of and how to attain it. After all, Jacob's real problem was not Esau, but God. His intimacy of relationship with God (or lack of it) invariably determined his view of himself and his relationship with people. Like Jacob, we sometimes need to be sealed off and isolated. God often makes wise use of suffering to slow us down, to help us put on the brakes in our fast-paced lives so we can consider who we are, what we are doing, where we are going, and who God is. It might be an unexpected illness, a midnight phone call, a financial crisis, or the loss of a loved one that awakens us to our urgent need of soul care, and most importantly of God's care.

Yes, Jacob is alone. Or at least he thinks he is! Suddenly out of nowhere, a "man" abruptly initiates a no-holds-barred wrestling match with Jacob. To describe the all-out struggle, the author chooses a term that derives from a word meaning "dust." Jacob got dusty in this wrestling match! Within minutes, there was a takedown, an escape, a reversal, and a near fall. There was no referee to call illegal holds or technical violations. The long, indecisive bout continues on throughout the night. Round one, two, three. Alexander Whyte describes it well when he writes: "Whether in the body, Jacob to the day of his death could never tell; or whether out of the body, Jacob could never tell; but such a night of terror and of battle no other man every spent."[119]

In the shadows of the night, Jacob could not immediately identify this "man." Given Jacob's obsessive fear of his brother, he may have initially concluded the aggressive antagonist was Esau himself or maybe one of his special agents who had stealthily sneaked around to the other side of the winding ford to lay in wait until the opportune moment. He most certainly didn't think it was God or someone sent from God, for he had just asked God to rescue him, not to fight with him! In any case, believing his adversary to be like any of the others he had encountered in his life, Jacob thought he could cunningly outwit him.

It would not be until round three that Jacob discovers he is fighting a heavenly heavyweight. Did Jacob remember his grandfather, Abraham, telling him stories of having been visited by angels who took the form of men? Or of his distant relative, Lot, who had received a similar angelic visit? The ancient rabbis suggested that the angel was Jacob's guardian angel. Really? Had Jacob become so crooked that even his protective angel attacked him? No, it's clear from other Old Testament passages that this unidentified "man" was not just any angel, but *the* Angel of the Lord (cf. Exodus 3:1-6; Numbers 22:31). The prophet Hosea confirms this understanding with his inspired commentary: "He struggled with the angel and overcame him; he wept and begged for his favor . . . the Lord God Almighty, the Lord is his name!" (Hosea 12:3-4).

Jacob did not choose the struggle, the God-Man did! Here, as at Bethel, the Hound of Heaven takes the initiative. Up to this point, Jacob had expended a great deal of energy wrestling with others, trying to get what he wanted. It was always Jacob, the "heel catcher," who chose his opponents as well as his strategy. I'm certain Jacob tried every move in the book—cradle, crotch lift, duck-under, and even an aggressive gut wrench. Each move speaks of Jacob's varied attempts based on heredity and trickery to experience God's blessing. That's what made this midnight match with the God-Man so relentless, lasting until daybreak.

Jacob finds himself in God's gymnasium, not his own. The term comes from an ancient Greek term meaning to be "stripped naked." For the first time, Jacob had to truly fight. He could no longer depend upon his shrewd strategies and cunning deceit to obtain what he wanted. No, he had to be stripped naked and taken to the mat so he could see himself for who he really was before God. In this wrestling match, Jacob could only win by losing.

Our toughest battles in life are not with ourselves, with others, with adverse circumstances, or even with our archenemy, Satan himself . . . *but with God.* As so often happens with us, Jacob finds himself fighting against the very One who can help him overcome his secondary opponents. Indeed, when God is no longer our ultimate refuge, he becomes our ultimate threat. Some directly blame God for the suffering in their lives, believing that if he *controls* all things he necessarily *causes* all things—including their suffering. Others indirectly blame God, reasoning that if he did not plan the suffering, he most certainly should have prevented it. *Why didn't he?* So we wrestle on through our night of misery, stubbornly resisting the ever persistent, but deeply compassionate bark of the Hound of Heaven.

Given Jacob's track record, one might have expected he would be the one to take advantage of the other. But no, Jacob is crippled by his assailant and at his point of greatest strength. The narrator drops a hint as to some of the dynamics of this night-long duel between Jacob and the God-Man: "When the man saw that he could not overpower him . . ." (Genesis 32:25). Could not overpower him? The Angel of the Lord, God himself, could not get the best of this trickster?

God's love always pursues and persuades, but never coerces. God never relates to us *homo sapiens* as automates. He never abuses the limits of our free choice to love, intrinsic to our identity as those created as the image of God. Just as there are natural laws that God will not ignore, so there are also spiritual laws. The evangelist Mark reminds us, "He could not do any miracles there, except lay his hands on a few sick people and heal them" (Mark 6:5). Why? Did this mean that Jesus' power was insufficient? No, for the text goes on to say: "He was amazed at their lack of faith." The problem was not insufficient power on the part of Jesus, but insufficient faith on the part of the people. In their striving, the God-Man can only bring Jacob so far.

When the God-Man saw he couldn't get the best of Jacob, he simply "touched him," dislocating his hip (v. 25). If God's finger could dislocate the heel catcher's hip, think of what his strong arm could have done! But the God-Man chose to touch Jacob rather than crush Jacob. Satan crushes, God touches. Satan wants to destroy us, sifting us like wheat (Luke 22:31). God wants to touch us, purifying us like gold (Job 23:10). Even as years later the seraphim's purging touch of Isaiah's lips brought forgiveness (Isaiah 6:7), so here the angel's loving, compassionate touch of Jacob's hip brought brokenness.

God's discipline in our lives, though intentional, is more often than not gentle. The entire wrestling match may have resembled the Japanese art of self-defense termed *aikido*, which uses an opponent's own momentum to work against him. As is often the case in our experience, it may be that Jacob harmed himself in his aggressive wrestling match with God. Though God does not coerce, he does intentionally, wisely, and lovingly work through the harsh circumstances of our lives to bring us to the end of ourselves and to the beginning of an intimate encounter with himself.

Jacob must have felt this strategic move on the part of the angel was unfair. But God has a way of afflicting the comfortable as well as comforting the afflicted. When he does, we cry out: *Not fair!* We feel that God has done us wrong, that we don't deserve such difficulty, or that God isn't playing by the rules. But in Jacob's case, God *did* play by the rules. For more than twenty years, he allowed Jacob to exercise his self-determinative freedom to go east in his flight from the land of promise. Though Jacob ran from the land of promise, he could never escape God's hand of promise. And that divine hand now deliberately but lovingly touched Jacob at his point of greatest strength. God needs to throw us off balance at times and take us to the mat. That's what suffering does. It "plants the flag of truth within the fortress of a rebel soul."[120]

Jacob was broken and recreated at the same time. Jacob's physical disability became a testimony to his spiritual victory. God chose him, God loved him, but God needed to break him. The God-Man's deliberate touch apparently resulted in musculoskeletal damage as well as neurological injury to the sciatic nerve all the way to the heel of the "heel catcher." But more importantly, in touching Jacob's strongest sinew, it shriveled, along with the wrestler's persistent self-confidence. Until now, the only wrestling hold Jacob knew was to steal a man blind. But now, God broke Jacob's physical strength in order to bless him with true spiritual and moral strength. Jacob's resulting limp would teach him to lean on God rather than himself. The "heel catcher" had finally come to the point of wanting God's blessing more than his own selfish desires.

In the morning twilight, Jacob could not see. But he was able to hear his heart, a heart that had now begun to be weaned away from the good in order to know and experience the best. The divine touch allowed Jacob to move from fighting his foe to tenaciously embracing his foe. Whatever the cost, he wanted God's blessing. Jacob, the schemer, finally comes to realize that the blessing of God must be obtained on God's terms, not his. Up to this point, Jacob, in his scrappy persistence, had wrestled with God because he thought he had a chance of winning. Now he begins to understand what it really means to win with God.

At that moment, the God-Man said: "Let me go; it's daybreak." It seems that God is testing the authenticity of Jacob's desire. Sometimes God hides his face so we might all the more earnestly seek his face (cf. Isaiah 8:17). Centuries later, Jesus' disciples were conversing with the resurrected Messiah on the road to Emmaus. Their hearts burned within them as they listened to Jesus expound the Scriptures that spoke of both his agony and glory. As they approached the edge of the village, Jesus acted as if he were going on without them until his followers insisted: "Stay and have supper with us!" (Luke 24:13-32). That is the cry of authentic desire, a longing for the person and presence of the Giver more than the gifts that he provides.

So Jacob cries out: "I'm not letting you go until you bless me!" Jacob can no longer fight, but he can hold on, clinging in desperation to the One who alone can truly bless. God wants us to be desperate. And nothing makes us desperate like suffering, of which Jacob had experienced his share. He is now on the verge of brokenness. His request is no longer conditioned on God providing a pleasant life, like his bargaining at Bethel: . . . *if* . . . *if* . . . *if*. It is now a passionate cry for God himself. Jacob began the night as a wrestler, trying to get the upper hand. He welcomes the dawn as a worshipper, desperately clinging to God.

Only broken people truly worship. Twenty years earlier, Jacob's earthly father inquired as to his true identity. On that occasion, Jacob lied, saying, "I am Esau." In doing so, he stole the blessing. Now his heavenly Father poses the same question and Jacob speaks the truth, uttering his name with all its damning significance: "My name is Jacob. *No, my name is heel catcher, deceiver, schemer, grabber, usurper, shyster, con artist!*" At that very moment, Jacob was stripped down naked. Heslop writes, "His strength was broken; his will was broken; his thigh was broken; he was helpless, and he helpless fell into the arms of Christ."[121]

While Jacob received his earthly father's blessing wrongfully, he obtained his heavenly Father's blessing rightfully. He would never understand the true meaning of this divine encounter until he understood and fully embraced the horrid significance his name had come to signify. Jacob's defeat was his victory. He began the night as a wrestler, trying to get the upper hand; he welcomes the dawn as a worshipper, desperately clinging to God. Jacob entered the wrestling match as the "heel catcher," the deceiver; he was about to exit as Israel, the one who wrestles with God and for whom God fights.

THE GOD WRESTLER

It is not unusual to fight the wrong battles in life. We often wrestle with ourselves, with others, or even with the Devil, forgetting that we can only resist the "demon" in ourselves and others by first submitting to God (James 4:7). Jacob's confession of his name was the sure sign of his submission to God.

Upon Jacob's confession of all that his dreadful name had come to signify, the God-Man says: "Your name will no longer be Jacob, but Israel, because you have struggled with God and with humans and have overcome" (Genesis 32:28; cf. Hosea 12:4). While the account says he "overcame" with God, he only overcame by losing. Jacob had finally come to the point of seeing his spiritual illness and confessing his personal need. There is both a blessing and a defeat. The former is dependent on the latter in the sense that the blessing came through the defeat. The old Jacob had to be defeated so that the new Israel might be blessed. Jacob could not win with men until he had "lost" with God, for "the secret of victory is losing the right battle."[122] After all, this was the only victory that really mattered. As for Jacob, so for all of us—there is a battle we can't afford to win.

At that critical moment, the God-Man attributes to Jacob a new name, Israel, meaning "God fights" or "God-wrestler."[123] A new name speaks of a new character. Personal encounter with God always brings transformation of character. The name is both a motto and a reminder that God wrestles on behalf of those who genuinely wrestle with him. The name would forever evoke the memory of this midnight match, reminding God's people for ages to come that God fights for them. God wrestles to bring us to a place of brokenness and surrender to his will.

Having received a new name, Israel now asks the name of the God-Man: "What is your name?" (Genesis 32:29). In

Ancient Near Eastern culture, the greater always named the lesser, for to attribute a name is to exercise authority. Even as Adam named the animals, exhibiting his rightful authority over them, so the God-Man manifests his supremacy in naming his opponent. But the opposite is unthinkable. We can never manipulate or control God, his governing of the universe, or his fatherly care of our lives. So the man said, "Why do you want to know my name?" In other words, "Think about it, and you will know the answer."

Right then and there, the God-Man blessed Jacob.

Jacob's prayer for deliverance was now answered. Having been delivered from himself, he met God. Consequently, he was ready to meet his brother, Esau. So Jacob names that place Peniel, saying, "It is because I saw God face to face, and yet my life was spared" (Genesis 32:30). Up to this point, Jacob had experienced three significant encounters with God: the "house of God," the "angels of God," and the "face of God." At Bethel, Jacob saw God in a dream; at Peniel, he saw God face to face. It was the face of God that radically changed Jacob, the "heel catcher," into Israel, the "God wrestler." This was the essence of the blessing that Jacob received! All the blessings guaranteed at Bethel—property, prosperity, and protection—were still intact. Now, however, Jacob had come to experience the most vital and foundational blessing—*personal encounter with God's person and presence.* Jacob finally saw God as he really was, not as he wanted him to be. In that encounter, Jacob's prayer for deliverance was answered. Having encountered God face to face, he could now look his brother directly in the eye.

Jacob could have named the setting of his midnight match "Place of Fear" or "Place of Suffering" or something similar. We often look back on our times of wrestling with God and focus on the pain rather than on what the pain produces, or we fix our attention on the suffering rather than on the profound satisfaction of encountering God in new and fresh ways. As suffering wrestlers with God, both Jacob and Job finally arrive at the same spiritual destination: "I had only heard about you before, but now I have seen you with my own eyes" (Job 42:5, NLT).

As the sun set, Jacob was fearful and apprehensive. As the sun rose, he was broken and blessed. Having confronted and confessed his own crookedness, he was now ready to cross the crooked Jabbok and enter the Land of Promise. He does so having received what he wanted and what he didn't want. He wanted God's blessing. But with the blessing came a limp, which characterized Jacob's gait for the rest of his life. Jacob entered this midnight match physically whole, but spiritually lame. He now crosses the Jabbok physically lame, but spiritually whole.

I can only imagine the surprise on the face of Jacob's family members. Seeing the crippled patriarch cross the stream, they are puzzled by his stride. One of his sons asks, "Is he limping?" Another one replies, "Maybe he tripped in the dark and injured his leg!" As Jacob approaches, they realize this was no simple stumble in the shadows of the night. His hair is disheveled, his clothes are dirty and torn, and his leg is bruised.

His family members crowd around him and ask, "Dad, what happened? Who accosted you?" "Gather around family," Jacob replies. "You will never believe what I'm about to tell you!"

But they did! That is why to this day many Israelites don't eat the hip muscle—because the God-Man touched the tendon of Jacob's hip.

Having won with God, Jacob was now ready to win with men. So he limps and leaps into the arms of his estranged brother. In fact, the loving touch he received from the God-Man kept him limping and leaning for the rest of his life (Exodus 47:31). The epitaph of this unlikely hero is recorded for us in Hebrews 11:21: "By faith Jacob, when he was dying, blessed each of Joseph's sons, and worshiped as he leaned on the top of his staff."

——— ⚬⚬⚬ ———

As Jacob journeyed from Bethel to Peniel, so must we. However, we can never experience the blessedness of Peniel until we pass by the brokenness of the Jabbok. We only see God as we see him in his Son and follow in the steps of Jesus of the scars.

In a beautiful poem called "The Thorn," Martha Snell Nicholson writes:

> I learned He never gives a thorn
> without this added grace,
> He takes the thorn to pin aside the veil
> which hides His face.[124]

In his long, arduous struggle with God, Jacob experienced the painful thorn prick of his own crooked, manipulative decisions as he went east, away from the presence of the Lord. Nevertheless, the Hound of Heaven persevered in relentless pursuit, little by little stripping away the hardness of heart to bring about a profound transformation of character. God's severe mercy made wise use of the "thorns" of Jacob's waywardness to pin aside his human self-confidence, allowing him to encounter God as never before. At that point, Jacob saw and desired the Blesser more than the blessings and the Giver more than the gifts. He finally let go of his own contrived dreams in order to embrace the One who could make far better and unimaginable dreams come true (Ephesians 3:20).

Divine blessing begins with human brokenness. For us who are, like Jacob, so frequently obstinate of heart, God has to rip the "Jacob" out of us, stripping away every plausible source of false happiness to bring us into authentic happiness.

Timothy Keller states it well: "But to grow into a true 'free lover' of God, who has the depth of joy unknown to the mercenary, conditional religious observer—we must ordinarily go through a stripping. We must feel that to obey God will bring us no benefits at all. It is at *that* point that seeking, praying to, and obeying God begin to change us."[125]

We can only be successful with God to the degree that we are crippled in our own self-sufficiency. Just as water always flows to the lowest level, so God's greatest blessings flow down on the humble of heart. To become victors, we must be vanquished. This is the paradoxical nature of the pilgrimage of faith, of which Jacob's birth order was a consistent reminder. But that's just like God, constantly reversing the expected order of things.

Centuries later, the fully incarnate God-Man, Jesus Christ, defined in unmistakable terms the upside-down order of God's economy:

Whoever wants to save his life will lose it. (Mark 8:35) The last shall be first, and the first shall be last. (Matthew 20:16)

Whoever wants to become great among you must be your servant. (Matthew 20:26)

Whoever wants to be first must be your slave. (Matthew 20:27)

Yes, in the kingdom of God, the way up is down and the way to save your life is to lose it.

Jesus not only spoke of these paradoxes that characterize the journey of faith; he also lived it. The God-Man, Jesus, demonstrated in his life and death the humble brokenness that he lovingly brought to the rebellious patriarch. As Jacob crossed the crooked Jabbok, Jesus crossed the filthy Kidron. The brook

Kidron, today called the *Wady Sitti Miriam*, lies between the eastern walls of Jerusalem and the Mount of Olives. In the Old Testament era, it was the graveyard of the poor and despised as well as the junkyard for disposing of unwanted idols during times of revival.[126] As such, this foul river and valley became a symbol of deep sorrow, distress, and death.

The evangelist John reminds us: "When he had finished praying, Jesus left with his disciples and crossed the Kidron Valley. On the other side there was a garden, and he and his disciples went into it" (John 18:1). It was only after crossing the Kidron—that symbol of human shame and sorrow—that Jesus entered the garden of Gethsemane and prayed: "My Father, if it is possible, may this cup be taken from me. Yet not as I will, but as you will" (Matthew 26:39). But that "cup" was not taken from him. The same God-Man who was willing to patiently wrestle with Jacob was later willing to sacrificially die for Jacob—as well as for you and me.

Part 2 –
Growing Through Suffering

CHAPTER 6

A Martyr's Advice on Suffering

The man who has not suffered—
what does he know anyway?
—Rabbi Abraham Heschel

Consider it pure joy, my brothers and sisters,
whenever you face trials of many kinds.
—James the Just (James 1:2)

T he limp Jacob received at daybreak kept him limping and leaning into God's blessing until the sunset of his life. The greatest blessings of God come to those who are deeply broken before God. We must not merely see ourselves in Jacob, we must see "the Jacob" in ourselves. For that to take place, our loving, sovereign God makes wise use of the raw realities of life in a fallen world to bring us through brokenness into the deepest joy imaginable—a joy that springs from personal encounter with the Giver of every good gift. At that moment, we realize that Jesus is all we really need.

Since the death of my son, I have found encouragement in the life and teaching of another biblical character. James, the author of the New Testament epistle that goes by his name, encountered the Hound of Heaven after years of spiritual flight in the opposite direction. Though James lived with Jesus for nearly thirty years as his half-brother, he remained a staunch unbeliever well into his adult years. Speaking of the unbelief of Jesus' own family members, the evangelist John reminds us: "For even his own brothers did not believe in

him" (John 7:5). But like Jacob, James had a Peniel experience of personal encounter with the resurrected God-Man,
Jesus Christ, which changed his life forever (1 Corinthians
15:7). Because of his righteous life, he became known as
James the Just. Because of his consistent habit of kneeling
in intercession on behalf of other believers, some called him
"The Man with Camel Knees." But it is the virtue of humility
that particularly characterized James' life. In his letter to
persecuted but sometimes proud believers, he reminds us that
humility is necessary to embrace God's grace. "God opposes
the proud, but gives grace to the humble" (James 4:7, NLT).

While we can never merit God's grace, pride is the one
thing that can keep us from God's grace. James not only taught
this truth repeated so frequently in Scripture, he also lived it.
Although he grew up as a sibling of the Messiah and later
became a respected leader in the emerging Jerusalem church,
he nevertheless refers to himself in this letter simply as "a slave
of God and of the Lord Jesus Christ" (James 1:1, NLT). For
the Greeks, the term "slave" was abhorrent and revolting. And
in the Roman Empire, animals had more rights than slaves.
Though James had the choice of several other nobler words
for a slave in his native language, all of which can be translated "servant," he chose the term that speaks of one who has
no rights of his own and whose whole life is swallowed up in
serving his master.

Because James was broken before God, he was bold
before men. One of the earliest historians of the early church,
Hegesippus, describes in detail the circumstances surrounding
James' martyrdom.[127] During the Feast of Passover, AD 63,
the religious leaders of Jerusalem urged James to exert his
influence by restraining the crowds from believing in Jesus as
the Messiah. Upon his refusal to do so, they led him to the
pinnacle of the temple in Jerusalem that overlooked the same
Kidron Valley that Jesus crossed on his way to execution (John
18:1). Here they attempted to persuade him to renounce

Jesus as the Son of God. Rather than deny Christ, James the Just boldly preached Christ to the crowds below: "Jesus is the promised Messiah! He is sitting at the right hand of God, and shall come again in the clouds of heaven, to judge the living and the dead!" As the onlookers lifted their voices in praise to God, the religious leaders lifted their hands to lay hold of James and throw him off the temple roof into the valley below, a drop of about one hundred feet. Miraculously, the impact did not kill James. Camel Knees immediately began praying for his persecutors: "Lord, forgive them for they do not know what they are doing." While his persecutors were stoning him to death, another man ran up with a large staff and struck James in the head bringing instant death.

James lived what he preached. That's what makes his advice so powerful and pertinent to any who suffer. As for the original readers of this short letter, their countrymen persecuted them, the rich and powerful oppressed them, various physical afflictions weakened them, and through it all the temptation to renounce their faith in the Messiah enticed them. But it is to these believers that James writes this most remarkable statement: "Consider it pure joy, my brothers and sisters, whenever you face trials of many kinds" (James 1:2).

Pure joy? How can that be? Is James saying that affliction, trials, suffering, and temptations can be turned from foe to friend? In answering those questions, James tells us several facts about trials. These, in turn, give us insight into the rich blessing awaiting those who endure adversity.

FACT #1: TRIALS ARE INEVITABLE

James writes: "Consider it pure joy, my brothers, *whenever* you face trials of many kinds" (James 1:2). Trials in our earthly pilgrimage are unavoidable and to be expected. As the universal "leveler," they touch poor and rich alike (James 1:8-11). Suffering is not an elective in life; it's a required course for all who live on planet earth this side of eternity. This is especially true for those who claim to follow in the steps of Jesus, the one "familiar with suffering" (Isaiah 53:3). How could it be otherwise?

We can grow *through* trials, but we never grow *out* of trials. Some have the misconception that great difficulties are for the young Christian, while great delights are for the mature. Both the Bible and Christian history tell us otherwise. Evagrius Ponticus, an early Christian theologian of the fourth century, writes: "The further the soul advances, the greater are the adversaries against which it must contend." Throughout his letter to afflicted believers, James presents the Christian life as perilous and full of obstacles that must be overcome. Many of the greatest biblical heroes faced some of their severest trials later in their journey of faith. This certainly proved true for Jesus' band of disciples of whom the vast majority suffered martyrdom by being burned, crucified, stoned, or beheaded.

Such a perspective does not sit well with many of us. Surrounded daily by multiple creature comforts, we begin to adopt an attitude of avoiding pain at any cost to the point of feeling traumatized by the slightest inconvenience. Dr. Paul Brand, an orthopedic surgeon who spent the first part of his medical career in India in the treatment of leprosy patients, writes: "In the United States . . . I encountered a society that seeks to avoid pain at all costs. Patients lived at a greater comfort level than any I had previously treated, but they seemed far less equipped to handle suffering and far more traumatized by it."[128] Our cultural experience in turn begins to affect our view of suffering. In some ways, it is easier to stand up against adversity than against prosperity. Ease has ruined far more people than trouble ever did.

Many of the early Christians saw pain and adversity as an opportunity to follow in the footsteps of the suffering Pioneer of their faith, Jesus Christ. For them, the goal of life was not to escape suffering, but to endure suffering for the glory of

God. They thought more in terms of the "right to suffer" rather than the "right to happiness." Believing otherwise only sets us up for bitterness. We must remember that some of Jesus' harshest words were in response to Peter's resistance to suffering: "Get behind me, Satan. For you are not setting your mind on the things of God, but on the things of man" (Mark 8:33).

FACT #2: MANY TRIALS ARE UNPREDICTABLE

One well-known cartoon image of Charlie Brown pictures him pondering his plight in life. He thinks, "For one brief moment I was happy. But just when I thought I was winning in the game of life, there was a flag thrown on the play and life dealt me a blow." James seems to be referring to the same unpredictability of adversity when he writes: "Whenever you *face* trials of many kinds" (James 1:2). The *New King James Version* conveys better the meaning of the text: "When you *fall* into various trials." We find the same term in the story of the Good Samaritan who cared for the man who *fell* into the hands of robbers (Luke 10:30, NET). He didn't plan it, nor did he expect it. It just happened, like Jacob encountering the "man" out of nowhere. Elsewhere, Jesus speaks of eighteen people who died when a tower unexpectedly fell on them (Luke 13:5). They weren't anticipating it, nor were their family members who consequently grieved their loss. Likewise, our trials are rarely predictable. We "fall" into them . . . an unwelcome doctor's report, the bitter news of the sudden death of a family member, or the stress of a job loss.

James speaks of this fragility of life and unpredictability of circumstances later in his letter: "Look here, you who say, 'Today or tomorrow we are going to a certain town and will stay there a year. We will do business there and make a profit.' How do you know what your life will be like tomorrow? Your life is like the morning fog—it's here a little while, then it's gone" (James 4:13-14, NLT). James does not discount the importance of planning for the future. He does, however, warn us against *presumptuous* planning that does not consider the unpredictability of life. Unless we fully embrace the fragility and unpredictability of life and unreservedly entrust ourselves to the Father's care, we will inevitably and selfishly plan for our future with the goal of avoiding difficulty at all costs.

FACT #3: TRIALS ARE VARIABLE

In this short but remarkable phrase, James conveys a third fact about trials in life—they are diverse. James writes: "Whenever you face trials of *many kinds*" (James 1:2). James carefully chooses a term—"many kinds" —that in the Old Testament described Joseph's multicolored robe (Genesis 37:3) and later the variegated color of flowers or woven carpets. Our trials in life range from minor inconveniences to major crises, from the dirty diaper type to the death and depression type. Each trial carries with it varying levels of emotional, spiritual, and physical impact. It is easier to say, "My head is aching," than to say, "My heart is aching."

Trials also vary as to their source. We experience some trials because of our sin. A stingy person suffers need (Proverbs 11:24), an idle person experiences hunger (Proverbs 19:15), and those who keep bad company experience harm (Proverbs 13:20). Other trials come from empathetic identification with the suffering of others, such as those who "mourn with those who mourn" (Romans 12:15) or who, like Paul, share in the trials and anguish of others (2 Corinthians 2:4). Still other trials are experienced by those who suffer for their testimony of faith in Christ (Hebrews 10:33).

Adversity also varies in both duration and intensity, the latter being determined by multiple factors that influence our expectations and how we experience our circumstances. As I write this chapter, I'm traveling in the West African country of Senegal. Our driver probably lives on a monthly salary of about 112,000 CFA (approximately $200 American dollars) a month. The pastoral colleague with whom I'm traveling receives the meager equivalent of $250 a month. Many in this country live on far less. As we drive past village after village of seemingly content peasant farmers and small business owners, St. Francis of Assisi's statement rings true: "Blessed is he who expects nothing, for he shall enjoy everything." Yes, the gauge by which we determine the intensity of adversity is frequently determined by our context and previous experience.

Trials are also diverse in the suffering they produce, whether just or unjust. Jesus, when questioned about some Jews butchered by Pilate as they were sacrificing in the Temple in Jerusalem, confronts both the just and unjust aspects of suffering:

> Now there were some present at that time who told Jesus about the Galileans whose blood Pilate had mixed with their sacrifices. Jesus answered, "Do you think those Galileans were worse sinners than all the other people from Galilee?" Jesus asked. "Is that why they suffered? Not at all! And you will perish, too, unless you repent of your sins and turn to God. And what about the eighteen people who died when the tower in Siloam fell on them? Were they the worst sinners in Jerusalem? No, and I tell you again that unless you repent, you will perish, too. (Luke 13:2-5)

The question in both situations is the same: Did God give these people what they deserved? In other words, was their suffering just or unjust? The answer Jesus provides is insightful. All suffering is "just" in the sense that we belong to the fabric of fallen humanity. As such, we deserve the ultimate and just penalty of sin, which is death. Thus Jesus changes the import of their question in order to remind them and us: "Unless you repent, you will perish, too." At the same time, some suffering is unjust. Thus the pertinence of Jesus' question: "Were they the worst sinners in Jerusalem?" The expected answer is "no." Author Ron Dunn writes, "With these words Jesus lifts the burden of guilt from every hurting heart. He makes it explicitly clear that those slaughtered by evil rulers like Pilate or those killed in a freak accident such as happened at Siloam are not objects of divine retribution."[129] Tragedies are commonplace and to be expected in a world out of sync with the will of God. Neither those killed by Pilate nor those killed by a freak accident were worse sinners than anyone else. Therefore, we must avoid the tendency to conclude that those who are victims of moral or natural evil in this fallen world are somehow deserving of special judgment.

I have found that a balance between these two perspectives is extremely important as we encounter the multifaceted trials and tragedies that enter our lives. Timothy Keller describes this balance well when he writes: "If we forget the first truth—that, in general, suffering is just—we will fall into proud, resentful self-pity that bitterly rejects the goodness or even the existence of God. If we forget the second truth—that, in particular, suffering is often unjust—we may be trapped in inordinate guilt and the belief that God must have abandoned us. These teachings eliminate what could be called both the "I hate thee" response—debilitating anger toward God—and the "I hate me" response—devastating guilt and a sense of personal failure."[130]

In the throes of adversity, many struggle with one or both extremes. Following the death of my son, the tendency was to fall into the "I hate me" response. The debilitating, incessant stream of "if only . . ." questions proved to be emotionally paralyzing, ultimately hindering the process of healing. On one occasion, an insensitive remark by a fellow believer heightened my sense of guilt. We had just explained the circumstances surrounding Jonathan's death and the high rate of accidental carbon monoxide poisoning in South Korea due to the use of coal briquette for heating. His response was cutting: "Don't you think you should have considered that potential danger before your son left?" While wisdom is always indispensable, the "I hate me" response often springs from the unrealistic assumption that we can ultimately control the unpredictable circumstances of life, such as "falling towers."

It is in the context of different kinds of trials that we often experience a specific kind of trial—*temptation*. This is what James refers to when he writes:

> When tempted, no one should say, "God is tempting me." For God cannot be tempted by evil, nor does he tempt anyone; but each person is tempted when they are dragged away by their own evil desire and enticed. Then, after desire has conceived, it gives birth to sin; and sin, when it is full-grown, gives birth to death. (James 1:13-15)

James writes, "*When* tempted . . ." (v. 13). Just as trials are inevitable and assumed to be a commonplace occurrence in life, so also are temptations. We don't grow out of temptation any more than we grow out of difficulty. In fact as we grow in Christ, we may experience an even stronger assault on our faith through temptation. Jesus himself encountered the most severe temptation in the wilderness (Matthew 4:1-11). As we will see, it is our *response* to temptation that will determine whether a trial will develop or destroy our faith. Martin Luther states it well: "You cannot keep birds from flying over your head, but you can keep them from nesting in your hair." To encounter temptation is *not* sin; to be enticed by temptation *is* sin.

Such close association between trials and temptation helps us understand why James employs the same word to describe both. Testing and temptation are two sides of the same coin.

The word translated "trials" in James 1:2 is also translated "temptation" in verse 13.[131] James uses a similar term in verse 3 when he writes "the *testing* of your faith produces perseverance." According to first century usage, such testing determined the true quality of something, such as the process of testing coinage to determine if it was genuine. The metallurgist would pass metal through the fire to ascertain whether or not it contained any foreign substances. If so, he would remove them, purifying the metal. That is the purpose of spiritual testing. God desires to remove the dross and purge the impurities from our lives, making us more Christlike. However, the very trials, difficulties, and suffering that can potentially draw us closer to God are often co-opted by Satan to move us away from God. God tries, Satan tempts (Fig. 1).

 Test: Used by God to develop our faith

Trial or Temptation?

 Temptation: Used by Satan to destroy our faith

Figure 1

Just as our trials are multifaceted, so also is God's all-sufficient grace in its various forms (1 Peter 4:10). Humility, springing from brokenness before God, helps us to respond positively rather than negatively to the trials of life. Why? Because God resists the proud, but gives more and more grace to the humble (James 4:6). Indeed, grace tastes the sweetest in suffering. Suffering reveals our human weakness, and human weakness and divine grace always go hand in hand. The pain we experience in the multifaceted trials of life is only a pathway to lead us into new dimensions of the experience of God's multidimensional grace.

FACT #4: TRIALS CAN BE PROFITABLE

Trials and subsequent suffering in life are inevitable, unpredictable, and variable. And while never pleasant, they become purposeful and profitable when responded to correctly. While living in Oregon, one of my favorite sports was alpine skiing. Growing up as a boy in the southern state of Tennessee, the only downhill slopes readily accessible were bunny slopes with artificial snow. But Oregon is exceptional, offering multiple opportunities for alpine and cross-country skiers, including year-round skiing for the most fanatical. After a day of skiing (and falling!), I craved the hot, soothing waters of our backyard Jacuzzi. I would turn the water temperature up to 103 degrees Fahrenheit and then hesitantly step into the hot, bubbling liquid. Ouch! An initial, stinging shot of pain would cause me to question my sanity. Withdrawing my leg, I would pause, then try again. As I stepped gingerly into the Jacuzzi, the stinging, steaming water gradually transformed the initial unwanted pain into a calming, soothing balm.

Suffering is often a necessary prelude to a deep sense of enduring happiness—a different kind of happiness. There is even empirical support for the ancient view that "people need adversity, setbacks, and perhaps even trauma to reach the highest levels of strength, fulfillment, and personal development."[132] Therefore, the key to happiness is not avoiding suffering at all costs, but rather learning to harness it to work on your behalf. While secularism denies that suffering is meaningful, Christianity teaches that there "is a purpose to it, and *if faced rightly*, it can drive us like a nail deep into the love of God and into more stability and spiritual power than you can imagine."[133] Our western, domesticated culture has a hard time embracing this truth. Our preoccupation with safety, security, comfort, and convenience often holds us back from raw, radical commitment to Jesus Christ in the face of suffering. After all, who wants to suffer? So we opt for a tame, domesticated faith that runs from risk and shuns suffering.

It is here that the message of the martyr Camel Knees is so pertinent to our lives. He reminds us that God, the giver of every "good and perfect gift," is not just kind, but he is also good. Kindness "cares not whether its object becomes good or bad, provided only that it escapes suffering."[134] But in his unfathomable goodness, God orchestrates the raw realities of this fallen world to provide us the opportunity for growth toward an enduring happiness that he longs for us to taste and enjoy.

Only as our minds are renewed with a growing knowledge of God's providential care will we be able to discern the ways in which he can leverage adversity to shape our character. Missionary and theologian E. Stanley Jones has written: "Take whatever happens—justice and injustice, pleasure and pain, compliment and criticism—take it up into the purpose of your life and make something out of it. Turn it into testimony."[135] That is precisely what James the Just, who was faithful to death, describes for us in the first chapter of his letter to suffering believers. He tells us how to turn our trials into testimony by detailing the roughshod and perilous journey toward a different kind of happiness (Figure 2).

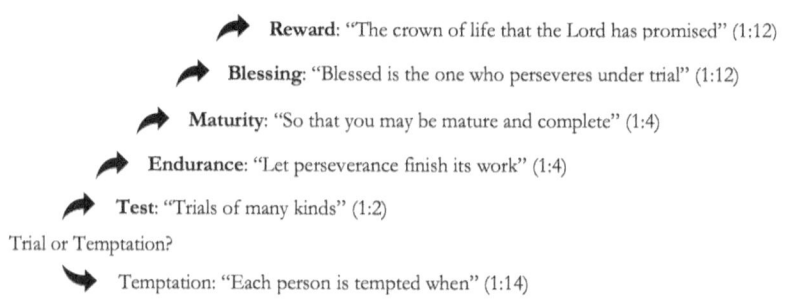

Figure 2

In the following chapters, I'll address each of these aspects in greater detail. But here, as we compare what James says concerning the "trials of many kinds" with other portions of Scripture, we discover several ways in which adversity—when responded to in faith—can prove to be profitable in our lives, spurring us on to endurance, maturity, blessing, and ultimate reward.

THE GRACE OF DISCIPLINE

Certain trials we encounter are corrective in nature. As an expression of the multifaceted grace of God, divine discipline is one of the "good and perfect gifts" that comes down from our "Father of heavenly lights" (James 1:12). The psalmist David declares: "Before I was afflicted I went astray, but now I obey your word" (Psalm 119:67). This is the grace of discipline. As did Jacob in his brokenness, the humble heart is receptive to God's loving discipline and receives it as an expression of grace.

The author of the New Testament letter to the Hebrew Christians writes in detail concerning God's use of adversity in this way:

> Endure hardship as discipline; God is treating you as his children. For what children are not disciplined by their father? If you are not disciplined—and everyone undergoes discipline—then you are not legitimate, not true sons and daughters at all. Moreover, we have all had human fathers who disciplined us and we respected them for it. How much more should we submit to the Father of spirits and live! They disciplined us for a little while as they thought best; but God disciplines us for our good, in order that we may share in his holiness. No discipline seems pleasant at the time, but painful. Later on, however, it produces a

harvest of righteousness and peace for those who have been trained by it. (Hebrews 12:7-11)

Motivational author and speaker Zig Ziglar once noted: "A child who is not disciplined in love by his little world—his parents—will be disciplined without love by the big world." God's loving discipline is always to be preferred over the ruthless, loveless consequences of being in the grip of our adversary who comes only to "steal, kill and destroy" (John 10:10). When we experience God's fatherly discipline, it is never to condemn us, but always to correct us. God cannot and will not condone sin in the lives of his children. That is why the writer to the Hebrews exhorts us in the same chapter to not "miss" the grace of God's discipline in our lives: "See to it that no one misses the grace of God . . ." (Hebrews 12:15). We prefer other demonstrations of God's grace—daily provision, family, friends, forgiveness, and the promise of eternal life. Such things are more palatable to our taste. But discipline? No way! That's probably why it's so easy for you and me to "miss" this expression of God's grace. Literally, we "come up short" of God's grace. When we do, it's not because God is not *giving* us his grace. It's because we are not *receiving* his grace by drawing near to his "throne of grace" in time of need (Hebrews 4:16).

A THORN IN THE FLESH

Sometimes God uses trials in our lives not only to make us into something, but also to keep us from something. In this sense, certain trials are preventative in nature. We see this illustrated in the life of the Apostle Paul. In writing to the Corinthian believers, he says: "Therefore, in order to keep me from becoming conceited, I was given a thorn in my flesh, a messenger of Satan, to torment me. Three times I pleaded with the Lord to take it away from me. But he said to me,

'My grace is sufficient for you, for my power is made perfect in weakness'" (2 Corinthians 12:7-9).

If brokenness is the prerequisite to God's rich blessing, pride is its greatest obstacle. In a recent discussion with my wife, she noted that sometimes I am too proud to admit that I am proud. She's right. In my own life, I've noticed that pride feeds on the ever-persistent tendency to think that my personal worth is determined by what I have or do *apart from* Christ rather than simply by who I am *in* Christ. Even in service to God, my greatest danger is not from the pharisee beside me, but from the pharisee within me who praises and honors himself. My limp in life is gradually helping me avoid that tendency.

The Apostle Paul had a limp—a "thorn in the flesh"—that protected him from himself by puncturing his pride. While no one knows the precise identity of this "thorn,"[136] we do know that thorns are painful. We also know that Paul prayed three times for God to take it away! Furthermore, we know its purpose. Humbly referring to himself simply as "a man in Christ," Paul describes his experience of being caught up into the very presence of God where he heard inexpressible things that others are not permitted to hear (2 Corinthians 12: 2-5).[137] Such a revelation, as well as the other evidences of Paul's apostleship, potentially could have become a source of pride for the apostle. Raised in the pharisaical tradition, his natural tendency was to boast in his religious accomplishments. The deeply ingrained residue of this mentality likely came back to haunt Paul even after his conversion.

Apparently, Paul's greatest temptations in life were not women and wine, but pride. To prevent this, God in his grace gave Paul a very specific trial, a "thorn in the flesh," as a constant reminder that the way up is not up, but down. As a result, Paul's boasting was no longer in his strengths, but in his weakness (2 Corinthians 11:30). Paul learned to walk with a limp: "Therefore I will boast all the more gladly about my weaknesses, so that Christ's power may rest on me. That is why, for Christ's sake, I delight in weaknesses, in insults, in hardships, in persecutions, in difficulties. For when I am weak, then am I strong" (2 Corinthians 12:9-10).

Thanks to this "thorn," Paul learned he could not advance his own cause and the cause of Christ at the same time. As a result, humility became an ever-increasing quality in Paul's life. When he wrote to the Corinthians, he said: "I am the least of all the apostles" (1 Corinthians 15:9). About five years later in writing to the Ephesians, he says: "I am the least of all the saints" (Ephesians 3:8). Then at the end of his life, he writes to young Timothy: "I am the chief of sinners" (1 Timothy 1:15). From "least of the apostles" to "least of the believers" to "chief of sinners"—this is not the depressive spiral of a man suffering from an inferiority complex, but the realism of a man profoundly touched by God's grace. As philosophy professor Peter Kreeft reminds us: "It is the saints who say they are the greatest sinners."[138]

Thank God we don't know for certain the precise identity of Paul's "thorn in the flesh!" If we did, we would likely think that such a thorn was for Paul alone and far removed from what we could ever experience. It seems, however, that Paul left his circumstances undefined so we can all think that Paul's thorn was the same as ours. While we all may not have the same thorn, we all have the same tendency to pride. And if some do not struggle with pride as much as others, then there are certainly a host of other sins that a dose of suffering can potentially prevent.

TRIALS THAT TRANSFORM

Believers who humbly admit they are sinners are receptive to another way in which trials are profitable. When we respond positively to our trials, they become instructive, transformative, and ultimately enhance and enlighten our existence. Tests at school reveal what we know; tests in life reveal who we are.

Even temptation, the negative mirror image of God-given tests, can be instructive. Martin Luther once noted: "My temptations have been my masters in divinity . . . Temptation and adversity are the two best books in my library." One of Job's counselors, Elihu, argues along the same lines, contending that we must interpret Job's suffering in light of God's desire to instruct him. He asks: "Who is a teacher like God?" (Job 36:22). In contrast to the counsel given by the other three friends of Job, God does not rebuke Elihu for pointing out the instructive nature of adversity. Though Job's afflictions originate with Satan's malefic intentions, God turns evil back on itself by using that same affliction to instruct his servant in the ways of divine sovereignty (Job 38-41).

Anyone who has lost a child can probably think of no greater test than that faced by Abraham when he was instructed to sacrifice Isaac (Genesis 22:1-19). One of God's purposes in this well-known test was to discern and develop the quality of Abraham's faith. While we tend to focus on the offering of Isaac to the Lord, God was more concerned with the offering of Abraham to the Lord. It is Abraham, the one bringing the victim, who is called to offer himself to the Lord in radical obedience. That being said, I have come to see in this test an instructive element, not only for Abraham, but also for the generations to come.

What is most troublesome in this passage is God's direct command to Abraham to intentionally sacrifice his own son: "Take your son, your only son, whom you love—Isaac—and go to the region of Moriah. Sacrifice him there as a burnt offering on a mountain I will show you" (Genesis 22:2). My initial response when rereading this account following the death of our son was, "OK, God, you've asked me, like Abraham, to 'sacrifice' my son by offering back to you his life and his death as an expression of worship." While that is true—and I did offer our son's life and death back to God as an act of worship—it did not remove the persistently troubling aspects of the Abraham/Isaac narrative. While I lost a son due to involuntary manslaughter on the part of a hotel owner, here God commands Abraham to commit the grisly, atrocious act of slaughtering his own son. To top it off, this is to be an act of worship! It's been hard enough for me to reconcile our son's accidental death with what I know of the all-loving God in whom I've placed my trust. But how would I respond if God told me to take my son, place him on an altar, mercilessly run a knife through his body, and sacrifice him as a burnt offering? I would certainly question my sanity or the sanity of God himself! Furthermore, what was going on in the mind and heart of Abraham when God gave him such a barbaric command? Additionally, would not this narrative demonstrate that God indeed *does* tempt to sin (cf. James 1:13)?

Leaving aside for the moment the question of child sacrifice, Abraham was undoubtedly shocked by the idea of *whom* he was to sacrifice. God's command is very precise: "Take your son, your only son, whom you love—Isaac—and go . . . sacrifice him there as a burnt offering . . . " (Genesis 22:2). Is God contradicting God? After all, Isaac was the embodiment of all that God had previously promised Abraham, the one through whom the covenant promises would ultimately be fulfilled (Genesis 15:4-6; 17:15-22; 21:1-6). Is God playing bait and switch? How could God maliciously take back what he had already so graciously provided?

The details of the narrative provide little in terms of what must have been Abraham's inward struggle as he carried out the Lord's request. We are simply told that Abraham "got up," "saddled his donkey," "took two of his servants," "cut wood," and "set out for the place" where God had told him to go (Genesis 22:3). Admittedly, what Abraham does say in the narrative seems to depict a man who believes firmly in God's faithful provision. As the climactic moment approaches, he explains to his servants: "Stay here with the donkey while I and the boy go over there. We will worship and then *we will come back to you*" (v. 5). Furthermore, in response to Isaac's probing question concerning the provision of a lamb, Abraham states confidently and explicitly: "God himself will provide the lamb for the burnt offering, my son" (v. 7). Abraham's response already anticipates what the entire narrative is teaching: "The Lord will provide" (v. 14). It is such faith-filled statements that lead the writer to the Hebrews to state:

> By faith Abraham, when God tested him, offered Isaac as a sacrifice. He who had embraced the promise was about to sacrifice his one and only son, even though God had said to him, "It is through Isaac that your offspring will be reckoned." Abraham reasoned that God could even raise the dead, and so in a manner of speaking he did receive Isaac back from death. (Hebrews 11:17-19)

Nevertheless, the lack of description of the emotional turmoil in Abraham's heart and mind as he journeyed to Mount Moriah makes it all the more palpable. Certainly, a multitude of agonizing questions must have overwhelmed the aged patriarch: Am I going to disobey God's command against murder (Genesis 9:6)? How can I commit such an atrocious act? Why did God not give me further explanation for this command? How will God fulfill his promises to me if I kill the very one who embodies them? How will I ever explain this to Sarah? What will the unbelievers around me think of this murderous act?

Particularly on this level, every reader can identify with Abraham's experience. Often in times of testing, what I think I *know* of God and what I know I *feel* about God are out of sync. This tension precisely describes the essence of any test we might encounter. Thus the importance of faith, for it is faith that enables us to obey on the basis of what we know rather than on the basis of what we feel. As we've already seen from

Psalm 22, *whatever we may encounter in life, we must settle in our minds that God is faithful and good, holy, and without sin.*

It is clear from the opening verse of the narrative that this is a test to grow Abraham's faith and not a temptation to lead him into sin: "Some time later God *tested* Abraham" (Genesis 22:1). This introductory statement dispels any thought or suspicion of an actual sacrifice, despite the fact that the sacrifice of Isaac is what was uppermost in Abraham's mind. God's real intentions were not only to find out if Abraham truly trusted God to the point of radical obedience, but also to further *instruct* Abraham as to the true character of Yahweh in contrast to the perceived nature of the Ancient Near Eastern deities that so influenced the culture of the day. In spite of his command to the contrary, God wanted Abraham to trust that he would *not* destroy his son. In fact, it is precisely this point that transforms the entire scenario into an educative experience for Abraham.

The pagan perspective in which Abraham was raised taught that child sacrifice was the ultimate expression of devotion to a deity. Given this background, it is not unreasonable to conclude that Abraham was in need of a profound paradigm shift that would dispel any suspicion that Yahweh was like the child-devouring gods of his past. Certainly, the emotional turmoil in Abraham's heart and mind reached fever pitch as he wielded his knife to slay his son Isaac in the same way that he had witnessed such barbaric sacrifices in his idolatrous past. But at that horrific, climactic moment, the full splendor of Yahweh's gracious character breaks through. Author Ty Gibson states it well when he writes:

> In that cathartic moment of bright epiphany, Abraham underwent a kind of spiritual shock treatment that jolted him into the beautiful realization that God, so far from being an appeasable deity whose favor must be earned, is a God of infinite love who has pledged

Himself to undergo the only sacrifice necessary to save fallen humanity. As Abraham lifted the knife over Isaac, he tasted, ever so slightly by comparison, the pain that God alone would endure in giving His only Son for the salvation of this lost world so lost to love.[139]

With this radical transformation of Abraham's conception of God, the patriarch came to understand that, in stark contrast to the deities of his pagan background, the true God is *Jehovah-Jireh*, the one who abundantly provides rather than capriciously takes. Abraham, therefore, named the place where he had bound Isaac, "The Lord will provide" (Genesis 22:14).

This lesson is also instructive for us today, as we look back on God's most abundant provision in his Son, Jesus Christ. "For everything that was written in the past was written to teach us, so that through the endurance taught in the Scriptures and the encouragement they provide we might have hope" (Romans 15:4). On the very mountain where Abraham learned this lesson, God's angel later appeared to David, who built an altar and worshiped the Lord (2 Samuel 24:16-25). Here Solomon also built his temple (2 Chronicles 3:1), and here, also, is the probable location of Jesus' crucifixion. In fact, the Apostle Paul makes an indirect reference to the offering of Isaac when he writes concerning Jesus Christ: "He who did not spare his own Son, but gave him up for us all—how will he not also, along with him, graciously give us all things?" (Romans 8:32). Indeed, the Lord does provide—even in the moment of our most severe trials (1 Corinthians 10:13).

Not only was this test instructive for Abraham, it was also transformative. At times, God allows us to be tested in such a way and to such a degree as to experience an emotional paradigm shift in our view of God's character. This instructional strategy stretches our faith by pushing us to the edge. As Warren Wiersbe states: "Our faith is not really tested until God asks us to bear what seems unbearable, do what seems unreasonable, and expect what seems impossible."[140] In obeying God's command to sacrifice his own son, Abraham demonstrated the same loyalty to God that the pagan gods demanded.

Such radical faith was not developed overnight. Abraham "passed the test" on this occasion because he had already "passed the test" on multiple occasions. Abraham first enrolled in the school of faith at the age of seventy-five when God called him to leave his loved ones and step out in faith to a new land (Genesis 12:1-9). Now, well over one hundred years old, he faces the ultimate test of his life, the call to sacrifice his much-loved son, Isaac. In the intervening years, however, the patriarch had already made three other great sacrifices. He sacrificed his extended family (Genesis 12:10-20), his nephew Lot (Genesis 13:2ff), and his son Ishmael (Genesis 16:1-16). Each sacrifice involved something or someone extremely precious to Abraham. Furthermore, each test in Abraham's life prepared him for the next test of faith.

Remember, the way you respond to testing today is in some way strengthening or weakening you for the task God has for you tomorrow. I've often remarked to my wife that if I had not experienced the emotional tsunami of my depression earlier in life, God alone knows how I would have responded to the heart-rending grief I encountered in the death of my son. Phillips Brooks, a nineteenth-century pastor who also endured a prolonged period of depression, once wrote: "Some day, in the years to come, you will be wrestling with the great temptation, or trembling under the great sorrow of your life. But the real struggle is here, now . . . *Now* it is being decided whether, in the day of your supreme sorrow or temptation, you shall miserably fail or gloriously conquer. Character cannot be made except by a steady, long continued process."[141]

No one knows the temptations and sorrows that lie ahead in life and how we will respond at that moment in time. As we have seen, they are variable and often unpredictable. However, how we respond today, *right now*, to each trial—whether it be the "dirty diaper" type or the "death and depression" type—will largely determine our trajectory in facing suffering in the future. Furthermore, each positive response to testing brings *blessing*—the blessing of a different kind of happiness. This was true in Abraham's experience. When Abraham left his homeland, God gave him a different homeland. When he left his extended family, God granted him a different and much larger family. When he offered the preferred land to his nephew Lot, God gave him a different and even better land. When he gave up the King of Sodom's reward, God entrusted him with even more wealth. When he gave up his son Ishmael, God made Ishmael the father of a multitude of Abraham's posterity. When he was willing to sacrifice Isaac, God allowed Isaac to live, and through him, multiplied Abraham's seed. While God does not promise believers today material wealth, he does promise transformative growth leading to spiritual blessing in this life and ultimate eternal reward for those who persevere.

⸺⚬⚬⚬⸺

The trials of life help us weed the garden of our spiritual lives. Seventeenth-century French Catholic mystic François Fénelon writes: "Slowly you will learn that all the troubles in your life—your job, your health, your inward failings— are really cures to the poison of your old nature."[142] That describes well my experience in the weeks, months, and years following Jonathan's death. It reflects my experience today. Initially, I tended to obsess over the "poison" that took my son's life. I did extensive research on carbon monoxide poisoning. I mentally lamented the lack of maintenance that led to deadly gases infiltrating his room. And I struggled to reaffirm the forgiveness already extended to those responsible for his death. Gradually, however, my focus turned from the poison that took *his* life to the poison that still remained in *my* life.

As we have seen, this poison is called *evil*—the absence or deprivation of all that is good as defined by God. The seeds of evil produce the weeds of sin that so often pervade our spiritual garden. Though watered by the influence of the world around us and the sinful nature within us, these seeds are ultimately sown by Satan who wants to destroy us and everything that is good (Matthew 13:36-43). But God opposes evil, is constantly at work to restrain evil, and will one day abolish evil (cf. 2 Thessalonians 4:7). What is more, in his stupendous wisdom, he is presently able to work in the midst of evil and all the sin and suffering it entails in order to rid us of evil and bring us into all that is good.

But the pathway is strewn with critical mileposts. Each trial, suffering, and heartache brings a crucial choice. We can, in brokenness, turn to God crying, "Bless me, whatever the cost!" Or we can, in hardness, turn from God in our own misguided attempts to find some kind of superficial relief from our pain. The latter is the downward path that ultimately leads to death. The former is the upward path that ultimately leads to life.

How do we take the upward path through adversity into greater maturity resulting in God's rich blessing and ultimate reward? That is the subject of the following chapters.

CHAPTER 7

Staying Under While Living Above

Jesus was patient under even greater suffering for us,
so we can be patient under lesser suffering for him.
—Timothy Keller

You know that the testing of your faith produces perseverance.
—James the Just (James 1:3)

The upward path of patient endurance through adversity is indeed long and arduous. It is not for sprinters who, with a magnificent burst of momentary energy, smash records and impress crowds. The path through suffering is more like the legendary Heartbreak Hill of the Boston Marathon. What makes the iconic landmark so difficult is not its height, but the fact that world-class runners normally "hit the wall" around mile nineteen. Heartbreak is the last and most grueling of four hills that begin at mile seventeen in the marathon. At this point, the depleted glycogen stored in the runners' muscles is replaced with lactic acid, a phenomenon that tests the strength and determination of the competitors to the very core. But it is not simply the feeling of total cardio-respiratory exhaustion that identifies this stretch of the race as Heartbreak Hill. The popular designation dates to the 1936 Boston Marathon when runner Ellison "Tarzan" Brown set a blistering, unequaled pace in the first twenty miles. On the last hill, however, fellow competitor Johnny Kelley, who had won the marathon the previous year, wiped out a half-mile deficit to catch Brown, patting him on the shoulder as he glided into the lead. The mocking gesture only served to fuel Brown's adrenaline, enabling "Tarzan" to subsequently surge past Kelley and win the marathon in a record breaking time of 2:33:40. The loss broke Kelley's heart and gave rise to the naming of Heartbreak Hill.

While our races in life differ, no one can avoid reaching Heartbreak Hill sooner or later. It's inevitable in such a world as ours. I had already navigated several difficult "hills" in my life, but nothing was as heart wrenching and emotionally devastating as the death of my son. If losing a race, pet, friend, or life's dream feels like a broken limb, the loss of a child feels like an amputation. According to one study, the devastating experience sometimes results in a phenomenon known as broken heart syndrome—a condition that oddly resembles a textbook heart attack with crushing chest pain and elevated cardiac enzyme markers on lab results. Moreover, the emotional and psychological impact, though lessened over time, does not go away. Deborah Carr, Chair of the Sociology Department at Boston University, writes, "Parents and fathers specifically feel responsible for the child's well-being. So when they lose a child, they're not just losing a person they loved. They're also losing the years of promise they had looked forward to." Studies also have shown that even eighteen years after losing a child, bereaved parents reported "more depressive symptoms, poorer well-being, and more health problems and were more likely to have experienced a depressive episode and marital disruption."[143]

It's true—though lessened over time, the devastating impact of losing a child does not go away. My wife recently stated what I feel every day but voice less frequently: "I don't think I'll ever get completely beyond the pain of our loss." In the months and years since the death of my oldest son, I've often wanted to escape the suffering, not endure it. Just throw in the towel and quit . . . *for good*.

However, we are not called to escape, but to endure.

STAYING UNDER

The Scriptures speak frequently of suffering in this life, especially for the Christ follower. Jesus once said: "In this world you will have trouble. But take heart! I have overcome the world" (John 16:33). The Apostle Paul wrote: "For it has been granted to you on behalf of Christ not only to believe in him, but also to suffer for him" (Philippians 1:29). And Peter penned these words: "Dear friends, do not be surprised at the painful trial you are suffering, as though something strange were happening to you" (1 Peter 4:12-13).

The Bible also speaks frequently of endurance in the face of suffering. Paul wrote to the Roman believers suffering severe persecution under the oppressive rule of Nero: "We can rejoice, too, when we run into problems and trials, for we know that they help us develop endurance. And endurance develops strength of character, and character strengthens our confident hope of salvation" (Romans 5:3-4, NLT). James—the one called "Camel Knees" because of his perseverance in prayer—penned similar words to believers experiencing adversity:

> Consider it pure joy, my brothers and sisters, whenever you face trials of many kinds, because you know that the testing of your faith produces perseverance. Let perseverance finish its work so that you may be mature and complete, not lacking anything. (James 1:2-4)

James' words summon us to the perilous but extremely rewarding upward path we are to pursue as Christ followers (Figure 2, page 150). As we respond positively by faith to the varied trials of life, our endurance grows. As our endurance grows (perseverance must finish its work), so does our maturity, resulting in blessing in this life and reward in the next.

ENDURANCE: THE UNROMANTIC VIRTUE

Imagine swimming underwater the full length of an Olympic-size pool. Your friend has bet that you can't make it, but you're certain that you can. Full of confidence and bursting with energy, you take that initial dive and under the water you go. About halfway to your goal, the increased external pressure on your lungs along with the accumulation of carbon dioxide in your arteries demand that you come up for air. Nevertheless, your determination—or maybe your pride—keeps you under the water all the way to the other end of the pool.

That's the meaning of endurance. The New Testament word comes from two words meaning to "stay under." The term as used in the first century also described the quality that enabled a person to remain on his or her feet during a storm. The English term, sometimes translated "perseverance," is derived from the prefix *per*, meaning "through," coupled with the word "severe." Perseverance is to keep pressing *through* adversity, through *severe* circumstances (cf. Acts 14:22).

If we don't learn endurance, we will learn little else. The commentator William Barclay states it well when he writes: "Perseverance is one of the great unromantic virtues. Most people can start well; almost everyone can be fine in spasms. Most people have their good days. Most men have their great moments. To everyone it is sometimes given to mount up with wings as eagles; in the moment of the great effort everyone can run and not be weary; but the greatest gift of all is to walk and not to faint."[144]

Such perseverance demands patience, another word of which the biblical writers are quite fond. This word is also formed from two words in the language of the New Testament, *makros* meaning "long," and *thumos* meaning "passion" or "heat." To be patient, then, is to have a long fuse, a long wick. In older English it is translated "long-suffering." Such patience is a rare commodity in a high speed world. How can a society that exists on fast food, high speed internet, and packaged cake mixes teach us anything about patience? We have a hard time patiently waiting for what we do want and an extremely difficult time patiently enduring what we do not want. Yet patience in suffering is an indispensable ingredient if we are to finish well.

Far too many die long before they are buried. This is true even in the Bible. Noah was a hero at the age of 600 when he built the ark. Then he got drunk and pretty much wasted the last 350 years of his life. Eli, at the age of 98, died fat and inactive. While Solomon wrote much of the wisdom of the Proverbs in his younger years, his only legacy in his later years was 1,000 widows. Of the approximately 100 individuals in the Bible for whom we have sufficient information, only about one-third finished well.[145]

While perseverance does not exclude laying our soul bare before God in the midst of adversity, it does mean finishing the race in spite of adversity. Paul writes to Timothy, his young protégé, stating, "I have finished the race" (2 Timothy 4:7). God is looking for marathoners, not sprinters. God looks for those who, recognizing their weakness, depend entirely on him in order to finish the race—and to finish with their torch still lit. The ancient Greeks had a specific long distance race filled with obstacles, sort of like our modern day steeplechase. They ran these races holding a torch. The winner of this race wasn't the runner who finished in the least amount of time, but the one who finished the race with his torch still burning bright. Such demands careful endurance.

THE SPIRAL OF TEMPTATION

One of the greatest obstacles to endurance in suffering is temptation. When responded to correctly, trials refine our moral character. On the other hand, temptation is outright solicitation to evil, originating in three sources: the world, the flesh, and the devil. According to James, the *world* speaks of everything in our culture and mentality that opposes God and pollutes the believer (James 1:27; 4:4). The second source of temptation is the *flesh*. If the world is external to us, the flesh is internal, referring to our human nature that has been corrupted by sin (James 4:5). The final and ultimate source of temptation is the *devil* himself who stands behind the external world system and our internal fallen human nature (James 4:7). Together, the world, the flesh, and the devil are like a threefold cord that can "lasso" us into the noose of sin with all of its devastating consequences. James' depiction of this downward spiral is insightful (James 1:14). Universally and irrevocably, any pursuit of happiness by taking this path has only death as its ultimate outcome (Figure 3).

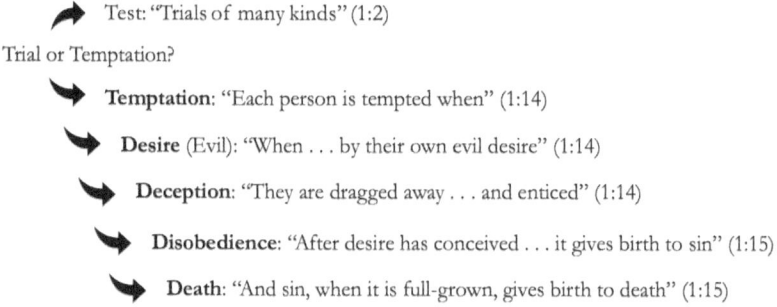

Test: "Trials of many kinds" (1:2)

Trial or Temptation?

Temptation: "Each person is tempted when" (1:14)

Desire (Evil): "When . . . by their own evil desire" (1:14)

Deception: "They are dragged away . . . and enticed" (1:14)

Disobedience: "After desire has conceived . . . it gives birth to sin" (1:15)

Death: "And sin, when it is full-grown, gives birth to death" (1:15)

Figure 3

As we have already seen, some of our greatest temptations come at moments of trial or suffering in our lives. In relation to God, we may be tempted toward unbelief, particularly if we believe God is to blame for our suffering. In relation to others—those we perceive as being responsible for our suffering—we may be tempted toward bitterness or lack of forgiveness. In relation to the circumstances of life, which are often unpredictable, we may find ourselves tempted to fear that which we cannot control. But we face some of our greatest temptations in relation to ourselves. Pleasure (albeit illicit), we reason, is the perfect antidote to pain and an attractive means of escape. Here temptation finds its cutting edge. It was *after* Jesus' fasting forty days and forty nights in the desert that the Devil came to him and said: "If you are the Son of God, tell these stones to become bread" (Matthew 4:2). In pain, there is often the temptation to escape, rather than endure. Some die trying to escape.

Desire

Every temptation begins with *desire*—a desire for happiness or personal pleasure. Desire itself is not evil. God has desires. God *desires* to uphold his people Israel forever (2 Chronicles 9:8). God *desires* mercy rather than mere religious routine (Hosea 6:6). Furthermore, God *desires* that all be saved and come to the knowledge of the truth (2 Peter 3:9). Therefore, desire is a characteristic of who we are as image-bearers of our Creator. The psalmist, David, prays, "May he give you the *desire* of your heart and make all your plans succeed" (Psalm 20:4). This same emphasis on the positive aspect of desire is seen in the New Testament as well. Paul says, "I *desire* to depart and to be with Christ" (Philippians 1:23).

Our real problem with temptation is not that our desires are too strong, but that they are misplaced. No one states it better than C. S. Lewis in his sermon, "The Weight of Glory": "Our Lord finds our desires not too strong, but too weak. We are half-hearted creatures, fooling about with drink and sex and ambition when infinite joy is offered us, like an ignorant child who wants to go on making mud pies in a slum because he cannot imagine what is meant by the offer of a holiday at the sea. We are far too easily pleased."[146] That is why the translators of James 1:13 specify that our real problem is not desire itself, but rather "*evil* desires." James elaborates on this later in his letter when he writes, "Or do you think the scripture means nothing when it says, 'The spirit that God caused to live within us has an envious yearning'"? (James 4:5-6, NET).[147] Like an antenna that transmits and receives signals between multiple wireless points, the human spirit fashioned by the "breath of God" was created to facilitate satisfying communication and communion with God resulting in indescribable happiness. But due to sin, our human spirit directs us with "envious yearning" toward counterfeit "signals" as we seek to satisfy our deepest longings. This even leads to fights, quarrels, wars, and inestimable suffering in the world, all in the passionate pursuit of happiness (James 4:1-3). We desire relief from the deep ache in our soul that comes from living in a fallen world. But rather than letting that ache draw us closer to God, we devise selfish, sinful strategies for relieving it ourselves.

Deceit

The next step in the downward spiral leading to death is *deceit*. Sin is birthed in the explosive connection between desire and deceit. As James states it, we are "dragged away . . . and enticed" (James 1:14).

I'm not much of a fisherman, but it's common knowledge that the secret of successful fishing is in the type of bait you use. Picture what takes place under water. The fish, appearing somewhat timid and fearful, stays close to a rock on the seafloor. The fisherman's bait is cast into the water. Eyeing it, the fish is enticed from its position of relative safety, swimming around it as if to evaluate what appears to be too good to be true. Suddenly, the fish bites, only to discover the dreadful hook hidden within, and is dragged into the fisherman's possession. The fisherman's choice of bait makes all the difference. After all, when was the last time you caught a fish with a bare hook? So also, the deceitfulness of temptation is not so much in the hook, but in the bait—which is why we never ultimately find in sin that which we enter sin to find. Satan knows exactly what bait is best for our points of vulnerability. That is why we must make decisions before the moment of temptation arrives. Paul says: "We take captive every thought to make it obedient to Christ. And we will be ready to punish every act of disobedience . . ." (2 Corinthians 10:5-6).

Disobedience and Death

Evil desire coupled with malevolent deception leads to *disobedience*: "It gives birth to sin" (James 1:15). Satan—most often indirectly through the influence of the world and the flesh—captures our attention through our desires. He then manipulates our attitude by means of deception, leading us to believe that a step of disobedience will bring the lasting happiness our hearts crave. But it doesn't. To illustrate this, James takes us from the fishing industry to the maternity ward where a woman called *Evil Desire* conceives and gives birth to a daughter named *Sin*. This child then grows, finally reaching adulthood (when it is full-grown)—a dark mirror image, the antithesis of the genuine maturity that characterizes the one who endures temptation (cf. v. 4). At this point, she herself gives birth. The tragic paradox, however, is that this birth is a stillbirth—*death*. This is always the case with *sinful* desire—ultimately, inevitably, and universally.

THE SOURCE OF TEMPTATION

Satan, sin, and sinners, *not God*, are the cause of the greater part of tragedy and suffering in life (James 1:13-14). However, some Jews in the first century reasoned that since God was the creator of all that exists, he must have also created the evil impulse. Since the evil impulse is what tempts man to sin, then God is ultimately responsible for evil. Their reasoning was remarkably similar to that of Adam who sidesteps responsibility for his sin by cunningly tracing it back to the woman whom *God* had given him. Today, we can find all kinds of excuses for our sin, even claiming that God made us with a particular personality, sexual bent, or propensity or that he has placed us in such difficult circumstances that we have no choice. We might even reason: "If God has allowed these trials in my life, then he is also responsible for the temptations in my life." How easily we subtly blame God for our sin. We tend to forget the wisdom of Solomon who himself was well versed in wrong choices and the suffering they entail: "People ruin their lives by their own foolishness and then are angry at the LORD" (Proverbs 19:3, NLT).

James goes out of his way to emphasize that God is *never* the source of temptation: "God cannot be tempted by evil, nor does he tempt anyone" (James 1:13). To the contrary, he is the source of all that is good. James underscores that point when he writes, "Don't be deceived, my dear brothers and sisters. Every good and perfect gift is from above, coming down from the Father of the heavenly lights, who does not change like shifting shadows" (James 1:17). My wife and I both had this verse engraved inside the band of our wedding rings. When we first chose this verse, we were thinking of the good gift God had given to us in each other (I'm convinced I got the far better deal!). However, God's good gifts include far more than the tangible blessings of which we immediately think, such as the people we love and daily provision. God's good gifts include the transforming work he patiently and lovingly performs in our lives as he points the way to a different kind of happiness. They include the character God develops in our lives through adversity, the wisdom he gives in adversity, and the unspeakable blessing and reward that awaits those who persevere in spite of adversity.

While sin and Satan give "wages" that ultimately lead to death (Romans 6:23), God gives good gifts that reflect his character of light and goodness and ultimately lead to life.

While sin and Satan deceive, God enlightens. While the stars and planets change and are in constant movement, God never changes. The heavenly bodies to which James refers indicate the change of the seasons, and the variation in length of days and in light. Change is a good and common feature of all created things. But God is not like "shifting shadows." God is *not* capricious. He does *not* change. He *is* dependable. He does *not* tempt us to evil.

If God does not tempt, why did Jesus teach his disciples to pray, "Lead us not into temptation"? Does not that prayer imply that sometimes God *does* lead us into temptation? Furthermore, how do we explain Jesus being led into the desert to be tempted by the devil? Matthew states it clearly: "Jesus was led by the Spirit into the desert to be tempted by the devil" (Matthew 4:1). Who did the leading? The Holy Spirit. Who did the tempting? The devil. Did God know what would transpire during this encounter between his Son and Satan? He did. But he also knew this was an important ingredient in his Son being "made perfect" by resisting the temptation of Satan and thus being fully qualified as the compassionate Savior of the world (Hebrews 2:10; 4:15-16; 5:8-9). God the Father led his Son into a *test* (Jesus was led *by the Spirit* into the desert) that Satan turned into a *temptation* (to be tempted *by the devil*). Similarly, while God graciously and redemptively uses the adversity and attractions of this fallen world as tests to develop our faith, Satan maliciously uses the same adversity and attractions as temptations to destroy our faith.

We can better appreciate the difference between testing and temptation when we think of God as our Father. When my children were young, I would never have deliberately enticed them to sin. To the contrary, as their father I desired their very best. However, I did allow each of our children to enter into situations in which they were obligated to make moral choices. For example, in attending public school both in Europe and in the United States, our children were confronted with moral choices that tested their strength of character. To the degree that they chose appropriately, it resulted in greater growth toward maturity. From my standpoint as their father, it was a test. At the same time, plenty of opportunity existed for Satan to use it as a temptation, which he did in several situations. Was I as their father responsible for the occasions when my children gave into temptation? Not unless I had acted unwisely, which our Heavenly Father never does. I did the *leading* in order to build moral character. Satan did the *tempting* in order to destroy moral character.

Immediately after speaking of the "envious yearning" that so often misdirects our fallen human spirit toward the pathway that leads to death, James reminds us, "But he gives greater grace. Therefore it says, 'God opposes the proud, but he gives grace to the humble'" (James 4:5-6, NET). Yes, God grants a "greater grace" to those who humbly receive it. This "greater grace" enables us to stay under by living above.

LIVING ABOVE

When Jesus taught his disciples to pray, he requested of the Father that the realities of heaven become realities on earth—"Your will be done *on earth* as it is *in heaven*." Randy Alcorn correctly observes, "We tend to start with Earth and reason up toward Heaven, when instead we should start with Heaven and reason down toward Earth."[148] While on earth— with all its trials and temptations—we are called to patiently stay under. But we can only *stay under* to the degree that we *live above*. Only by starting with heaven and reasoning down toward earth can we consider it pure joy to encounter affliction.

What does it mean to "start with heaven" and "reason down toward earth"?

Living above begins with understanding who we are— *our true identity*. As individuals, whether believer or unbeliever, the single most important element in our emotional and mental health is a sane self-image. This includes a proper understanding of who we are as the image of God. Whatever may be your strengths or weaknesses, your positive personality traits or handicaps, you are of eternal value in God's eyes—created to to resemble your Maker, and to enjoy harmonious relationship with God and with fellow humans, and to rule on this earth. The incessant call of the New Testament writers is, "Be who you are!" But if we don't know who we are, it is impossible to *be* . . . and to endure. Our failure to "stay under" in suffering—whether it be trial or temptation—can ultimately be traced back to this one issue: *a crisis of identity*.

For some years following Jonathan's death, I kept on my desk an analytical balance. It's the old fashioned kind, with a weighing pan suspended from each arm of the scales. These balances have been used for centuries to determine precision mass measurement. A known weight is placed in one pan, which is then compared to an unknown sample placed in the other pan. The objective is to tip the scales, bringing the two objects into balance. This analytical balance reminded me daily of the spiritual resources God had provided enabling me to move through my suffering.

The apostle Paul may well have had in mind such an analytical balance when he wrote these words to the Ephesian believers: "I urge you to live a life *worthy* of the calling you have received" (Ephesians 4:1). The term "worthy" (*axios*) literally means "bringing up the other beam of the scales." Paul is telling us that our *lifestyle* (practice) as believers is to be brought into balance with our *identity* (position) as believers. To the degree that we do, we will "tip the scales," bringing our earthly experience into balance with our heavenly vocation. Furthermore, whom we believe ourselves to be in Christ will profoundly influence how we behave in suffering. That is why Paul begins his letter to the Ephesians by reminding us of our heavenly position that should necessarily shape our earthly practice. Having described our salvation as an inheritance planned by the Father (vv. 3-6), purchased by the Son

(vv. 7-12), and protected by the Holy Spirit (vv. 13-14), he then proceeds to pray these realities into our experience (vv. 15-22):

> I keep asking that the God of our Lord Jesus Christ, the glorious Father, may give you the Spirit of wisdom and revelation, so that you may know him better. I pray that *the eyes of your heart may be enlightened in order that you may know* the hope to which he has called you, the riches of his glorious inheritance in his holy people, and his incomparably great power for us who believe. (Ephesians 1:17-19)

We all have physical eyes with which we see (some more easily than others) what is around us. We also have mental eyes with which we perceive and process information. But we also have "heart eyes" with which we grasp spiritual truth. Paul here prays that we would know and grasp with the eyes of our heart the full significance of our identity in Christ "in the heavenly realms" (Ephesians 2:6). What are the heavenly realms? It is the realm in which Christ reigns (1:20) and where his people are blessed and reign together with him (1:3; 2:6). The heavenly realms is that sphere of reality in which we as believers live as a result of being enlivened together, raised together, and seated together in Christ (2:5-6). In Ephesians, the heavenly realms are not described in contrast to the earth; rather, they encompass our everyday lives on this earth. To live in the heavenly realms is to engage in a process of identity formation. Paul is referring to the inner realities of our lives: our thought life, our attitudes, our way of viewing ourselves and others.

In facing trials, our identity as believers is foundational to our behavior as believers. It is only with the eyes of the heart that we can learn to *stay under* all the while *living above*. We must put on a new way of thinking before we can put on a new way of acting. James explains that the reason we can consider suffering from such a perspective is because we *know* something: "Consider it pure joy, my brothers and sisters, whenever you face trials of many kinds, because *you know* that the testing of your faith produces perseverance. Let perseverance finish its work so that you may be mature and complete, not lacking anything" (James 1:2-3). How would you like to get a letter like that? Got problems? Well, be happy! I tend to "consider it pure joy" when I escape trials and "consider it all grief" when I encounter trials. Have you ever heard of someone else's severe trial and breathed a sigh of relief, "Whew, so glad that's not me!" James, however, is insistent. He literally says, "Pure joy . . . consider it, my brothers, whenever you fall into various trials." By describing this attitude in the first two words of the verse, James underscores the contrast between joy in trial with despondency in trial.

What amazing advice for a society so obsessed with eliminating all difficulty, danger, and discomfort. The difference between trials making us bitter or better is just one letter, "i." *I* make the difference. Life is really 10 percent circumstances and 90 percent my *attitude* toward those circumstances. That is why James goes on to exhort us to *consider*, to take a deliberate look at the trials of life from God's perspective. I cannot control many of the circumstances of my life, but I can—with God's grace—control my perspective on those circumstances.

Notice that James does *not* say that trials are all joy. It is not the evil or difficulty at the heart of the trial that produces the qualities of Christlike character. These qualities are rather produced by the work of the Holy Spirit who brings forth the fruit of the Spirit in the life of the suffering believer. We are never encouraged in Scripture to give thanks for the sin or evil that may stand behind any particular trial. Rather, we give thanks for the assurance of God's providential way of turning evil back on itself by granting us the grace to embrace more and more of his goodness.

In both of the above verses, the phrase, "We know that . . ." or "You know that . . . " looks forward, not backward (James 1:2-3; Romans 5:3-4). What we are to *know* has nothing to do with God planning the suffering. It has everything to do with how God dynamically works with us *in* and *through* the suffering to accomplish his good purposes in our lives. The question to ask in suffering is not *Why* (Why did God bring this about?)? But *What now* (How can God use this in my life?)?

RETHINKING ROMANS 8:28

One of the verses I have tenaciously clung to over the years following the death of my son is Romans 8:28, a verse that R. A. Torrey (1856-1928) once called, "a soft pillow for a tired heart." The King James Version (KJV) reads: "And we know that all things work together for good to them that love God, to them who are the called according to his purpose."

While bringing a certain degree of comfort to my heart, this verse has also brought probing questions to my mind. During World War II, one prominent preacher described this verse as "the hardest verse in the Bible to believe."[149] The Old Testament patriarch, Jacob, certainly would have had a hard time believing it! Fearing that Joseph was dead, that Simeon was held hostage, and that Benjamin must also go to Egypt, he cries out in his crucible of suffering: "All these things are against me!" (Genesis 42:36, KJV).

I, at times, feel like Jacob. Maybe you do, too.

Not only is this well-known verse difficult to believe, it is difficult to understand. For sure, Paul wants us to *know* something. But the multiple and divergent translations of this verse leave us in doubt as to exactly what we are to know. Beyond the above cited version, here are two other popular translations of this verse:

And we know that God causes all things to work together for good to those who love God, to those who are called according to His purpose. (NASB)

And we know that in all things God works for the good of those who love him, who have been called according to his purpose. (NIV)

So which is it? Are *impersonal things* somehow working together for good (KJV)? Or is God *causing* all things to work together for good (NASB)? Or is God simply working *in* all things for good (NIV)? Or is there another way to understand this verse?

While some aspects of this verse are not clear, a few are crystal clear. For example, Paul's words concern *believers*—those who love God and are called according to his purpose. Believers are described from both a human and divine perspective. From the human perspective, believers are those who "love God" (1 Corinthians 2:9; 1 Peter 1:8). From the divine perspective, believers are those who are called for a specific purpose as further defined in the following verse—conformity to the image of Christ (Romans 8:29). Moreover, from the first verse of this chapter, Paul is speaking about "those who are in Christ Jesus" (vs. 1) and as a result are "brothers and sisters" in Christ (vs. 12).

The second indisputable aspect of this verse is that "things," "all things," or "everything" (depending on the translation) refer to "our present sufferings" (Romans 8:18). Paul specifically mentions some of these sufferings later in this chapter, things like troubles, pressures, persecutions, deprivations, dangers, death threats, or even demons and death itself (vv. 35-39). It's fair to say that today these "things" could include the events of 9/11, the tragic drowning of a child, or the diagnosis of brain cancer in a family member.

Finally, suffering in the believer's life can result in "good." Just what that "good" entails and how it is experienced can only be understood from the immediate context. More about that in a moment.

Beyond the fact that Paul's words pertain to believers facing suffering that can somehow result in their good, the translations, interpretations, and practical applications of this verse vary widely.[150] Our traditional understanding of this verse comes from three of our most popular translations. According to the KJV, "all things" is the subject: "And we know that *all things work together* for good . . ." On the other hand, the translators of the NASB understood God to be the subject: "And we know that *God* causes all things to work together for good . . ." This is followed closely by the NIV that also understands God to be the subject, but with a slightly different nuance: "And we know that *in all things God* works for the good . . ."

So, do *things* work or does *God* work things or does God work *in* things?

Does it mean (as some would say) that there are no accidents in God's providence? Or that, if I just believe, everything will turn out OK?

Or is there a better option for understanding this often-cited verse?

Though all three of these translations are grammatically possible, they are not preferred. Below I'll explain why. But first, we must consider the implications of our traditional understanding of this verse. In particular, the translations of the KJV (all things work together) and the NASB (God causes all things to work together) leave us with this impression: God has a detailed blueprint of our individual lives by which he is intentionally weaving together the good, the bad, and the ugly—all the circumstances, events, blessings, and tragedies of our lives—into a beautiful tapestry that reflects a higher good. Just as an apothecary can skillfully mix together several poisonous ingredients in view of making an appropriate medicine, or as a baker can mix together several distasteful ingredients (if eaten individually) to cook something delicious, so God intentionally "mixes together" all the circumstances of our existence in such a way that *only* good results in the life of the believer.

Following the murderous events of 9/11, one well-respected theologian wrote an article entitled, "Why I Do Not Say, 'God Did Not Cause the Calamity, but He Can Use It for Good.'"[151] Based on a rigid blueprint interpretation of verses like Romans 8:28, the author concludes that God indeed *did* cause that horrendous event (just as he also brought about the Holocaust). According to the author, just how God did this without negating human responsibility or compromising his own holiness remains a mystery! Some conclude that this "divine tapestry" understanding of Romans 8:28, not unlike the Islamic view of *kismet*,[152] should increase our trust in God's providential protection over our lives.

I understand the desire to adopt a narrative of life that helps take the cutting edge off the harsh realities that come our way. Nevertheless, I have not found such an understanding of this verse to increase my trust in God in the face of suffering. Nor have many others. To "live above" does not entail adopting a pollyannaish view of the stark and dark realities of life. Does the believer have the guarantee that impersonal *things* always work together for good (KJV) or even that a personal God always *causes things to work together* for good (NASB) apart from the active participation of the one who loves God? Are we to believe that God, as the divine "puppet master," pulls the strings behind every demonic debacle that brings inexpressible tragedy and suffering into the lives of his children in order to bring about good for them and glory for himself? Just because we as finite humans would need to meticulously control everything to bring good out of evil does not mean that the all-wise and sovereign God is under the same limitations.

Not only does such an understanding of this verse discourage confident trust in God, it furthermore encourages a passive response to evil and suffering in the world. If I believe that God is automatically working together all the evil and suffering that enters my life in a neat *quid pro quo* way in view of a greater good, then why should I intervene to change the course of events? After all, God wills it! In this case, I am simply called to be the passive recipient of the good that God is weaving into the tapestry of my life. But as we have seen, the believer is called to aggressively fight evil as a foe, not to passively accept evil as a friend by believing that it somehow comes from the hand of God. Otherwise, we could end up accepting things that come from Satan as coming from the hand of God! For example, does the previously mentioned downward spiral of temptation (evil desire, deception, and disobedience) work together for good? No! Apart from the believer's active participation with God in resisting Satan, sin, and self, it results in death!

Other than these observations, we must consider several grammatical considerations that point us toward a different and fresh understanding of this verse. The English expression "working together" translates the Greek word *sunergeo* (*sun* = with + *ergon* = work) from which we get our English word "synergy." Synergy speaks of the interaction or cooperation of two or more individuals to produce a combined effect greater than the simple sum of its parts. According to the KJV translation, it is impersonal "things" that are somehow (under God's direction?) synergistically working together for good in the believer's life. On the other hand, the NASB depicts God as synergistically working with impersonal things for the believer's good. However, the problem with both of these translations is that in the vast majority of cases where this word appears in the New Testament, it specifically refers either to God working in partnership with believers (not with impersonal things) or with believers working together. Here are just three examples among the more than forty in the New Testament:

> Then the disciples went out and preached everywhere, and *the Lord worked with them* and confirmed his word by the signs that accompanied it. (Mark 16:20)

> For we are *coworkers in God's service;* you are God's field, God's building. 1 (Corinthians 3:9)

> As *God's coworkers* we urge you not to receive God's grace in vain. (2 Corinthians 6:1)

When we interpret Romans 8:28 in light of how this term is consistently used throughout the New Testament, we conclude that (1) impersonal things and circumstances are not necessarily working together for good on our behalf; nor is (2) God working primarily with impersonal things and circumstances in view of our good; but rather (3) God is personally, dynamically, and lovingly working in partnership with *people* who love God in order to advance his good purposes in and through their lives. In other words, what happens *in* us is far more important than what happens *to* us.

This understanding of God working with believers (not things) is further supported by the use in this verse of what is called the dative case in the Greek language. The dative expresses the idea of personal interest, accompaniment, and means. For example, on my granddaughter's birthday, I might buy a book *for* my granddaughter, give that book *to* my granddaughter, and read the same book *with* my granddaughter. If expressed in the language of the New Testament, each of these phrases—"for/to/with my granddaughter"— would require the dative case. The difficulty, however, is that the little preposition ("for," "to," or "with") is often not present in the text. The specific nuance must be determined by other factors in the context. This helps explain why we have different translations of the dative in Romans 8:28 such as ". . . *for* those that love God" (ESV), ". . . *of* those that love God" (NLT), or ". . . *to* them that love God" (KJV). However, many translations overlook the fact that the verb "work together" (*sunergeo*) most frequently takes the dative of accompaniment ("with") in order to indicate two partners working alongside each other with the same objective in view. The question then is not "*what* does God work together?" but rather "*with whom* does God work together?" Fortunately, it is here that the translations of the Revised Standard Version (RSV), the Good News Translation (GNT), and a small footnote in the New International Version get it right!

> We know that in everything God works for good *with those who love him*, who are called according to his purpose. (RSV)

> We know that in all things God works for good *with those who love him*, those whom he has called according to his purpose. (GNT)

> And we know that God works together *with those who love him* to bring about what is good—with those who are called according to his purpose. (NIV, marginal note)

As the church father Athanasius of Alexandria once said, "To all who choose the good, God works with them for the good."[153] With this understanding of the verse, the focus moves from what God is doing in *things* to what God is doing in and through *me*.

But there is more. The majority of Greek manuscripts do not specifically state that it is *God* who is working together with believers to bring about what is good.[154] Given that the preceding verses speak of the ministry of the Holy Spirit toward the believer in the midst of suffering, it seems preferable to understand the third person of the Trinity to be the implied subject of verse 28. F. F. Bruce calls this an "ancient and attractive interpretation" that, unfortunately, has been ignored by many translators and commentators. Citing the translation of the *New English Bible,* he suggests that Romans 8:27-28 could read: ". . . he (i.e. the Holy Spirit) pleads for God's own people in God's own way; and in everything, as we know, he co-operates for good with those who love God . . ."[155] As God lovers, we can be assured that the Spirit of God who lives *in* us (v. 23) and intercedes *for* us (vv. 26-27) is also desirous of cooperating *with* us to bring ultimate good out of every suffering we experience in life.

THE COMPLEX GOOD

One of the best examples of the truth of Romans 8:28 is seen in the Old Testament account of the life of Joseph (Genesis 37-50). The entire account is replete with examples of how God by his Spirit actively and lovingly works with people in the context of their everyday life circumstances to accomplish his good purposes. With the little that he knew, Joseph did start with heaven and reasoned down toward earth. Therefore, he was able to "stay under" in the most severe trials and temptations. Joseph's brothers saw only with their physical eyes. Joseph saw with the eyes of the heart (Genesis 50:19-20). Though he didn't have the additional revelation of the New Testament teaching concerning the believer's joy in trials, his life is a testament to how God works with us and in us through suffering to accomplish his good purposes.

A multitude of "accidents" or "coincidences" took place that resulted in Joseph becoming a prince in Egypt. It began when Jacob decided to send Joseph to see how his brothers were doing while grazing their sheep (Genesis 37:13). Jacob believed his sons were in Shechem (v. 12). If he had known they were in Dothan, a town much further away, he most likely would not have sent him (v. 17). When Joseph arrived in Shechem, he happened to run into a stranger who knew where his brothers were (v. 15). However, the stranger knew this because he had just overheard a conversation by men in a nearby field (v. 17). When the brothers plotted to kill Joseph, Reuben intervened, convincing them to throw him into a cistern (v. 23). But Reuben just happened to be away when the Egyptian traders came by, enabling Judah and the others to sell Joseph into slavery (vv. 26-28). Once Joseph arrived in Egypt, he encountered the enticement of Pharaoh's wife along with the false accusations that led to his imprisonment. Yet it was in prison that Joseph met Pharaoh's cupbearer whose dream he interpreted (Genesis 40). All this eventually led to Joseph's reinstatement as an attendant in Pharoah's government (Genesis 41) and paved the way for the arrival of Jacob's family in Egypt (Genesis 42-46). In his infinite, matchless wisdom God knew, in every circumstance and situation, not only what *was* and what *would be*, but also what *might be* and what *could be* . . . depending on the free choices made by Joseph, his family members, and others. And through it all, God was working to accomplish good in the lives of those involved.

But what about the sinful choices made by those in this narrative? This patriarch's "bio" is full of some of the most devastating suffering and injustices imaginable (Genesis 35-39). Following the death of his mother, Joseph's brothers threatened him with death, mercilessly threw him in a pit, and eventually sold him to Egyptian merchants as a slave. In Egypt, Joseph felt the loss of home and family, endured sexual propositions from his master's wife, and was finally imprisoned under false pretences. Nevertheless, when his brothers finally confessed the wrongs they committed against him, Joseph redirects their focus away from their sin to God's overriding redemptive design: "Don't be afraid. Am I in the place of God? You intended to harm me, but God intended it for good to accomplish what is now being done, the saving of many lives" (Genesis 50:19-20). Joseph's declaration to his brothers certainly reflects what it means to "live above" the suffering and injustices of this life. But how are we to understand Joseph's words to his brothers in light of Romans 8:28?

Some take Joseph's statement to mean that God sovereignly planned (even *predestined*) the evil that was in the brothers' hearts in order to transport Joseph into Egypt. However, such a view poses insurmountable problems. Earlier, Joseph tells his brothers, "And now, do not be distressed and do not be angry with yourselves for selling me here, because it was to save lives that God sent me ahead of you" (Genesis 45:5). Are we then to conclude that each murder, kidnapping, incident of sexual abuse, and robbery is ultimately designed by God in view of his redemptive plan? And should the perpetrators of such crimes not be distressed or angry with themselves because they are unwittingly playing a key role in the realization of God's will? Would not such a conclusion only "insult the pain of the victims by providing the criminals with excuses"?[156]

I believe that God no more planned the sinful reactions of Joseph's brothers than he planned the negligence of the owner of the hotel where my son died. Evil intentions on the part of Joseph's brothers were "evil" precisely because they were *not* according to the will of God. To say that God ordained the brothers' evil acts to accomplish a higher good is to say that God wills what is contrary to his will. Yet Jesus' declaration is unequivocal: "Every kingdom divided against itself will be ruined . . . " (Matthew 12:25-28). It is one thing to say that God brings good out of evil once evil is present as the result of the choices of free moral agents. It is quite another to say that

God plans it in order to accomplish good. The former places before us the wonderment of God's infinite, unfathomable wisdom, whereas the latter impugns the character of God in whom there is no darkness. French theologian Henri Blocher is correct when he writes: "When evil is already present, if God makes use of that hostile reality as an opportunity to act, and even as a means to punish and to warn, the fact in no measure lessens the malignity of evil, and in no way allows for any insinuation that God might be its accomplice."[157]

While God is always at work to bring good out of evil, he never works the evil out of which he brings good. And the good that he does bring about is, what C. S. Lewis has termed, a "complex good." In our fallen and chaotic world characterized by unimaginable suffering, we can distinguish (1) the simple good which comes from God (James 1:17); (2) the simple evil produced by Satan, sin, and sinners (James 1:14-15); (3) the exploitation of that evil by God for his redemptive purpose (Psalm 76:10); and (4) the resulting "complex good" experienced by lovers of God who cooperate with him in his loving intentions (Romans 8:28). In this case, Joseph pursued God's will, consciously and deliberately cooperating with the "simple good." On the other hand, Joseph's brothers opposed God's will by intentionally carrying out "simple evil." Nevertheless in doing so, they contributed, albeit unconsciously and without their consent, to the "complex good." Joseph served God as a son, freely and deliberately. His brothers served God as a slave, unconsciously and unwillingly. All will ultimately contribute to God's good purposes. The question is whether we will do so like Joseph or like Joseph's brothers.[158]

Joseph's words to his brothers are best understood as, "You had thought evil, God thought it for good." God, in his matchless wisdom, was able to anticipate a response to every motivation and decision conceived in the heart of Joseph's brothers. As the divine chess master, he was able to take the malevolent intentions and actions of Joseph's siblings and turn evil back on itself by accomplishing his good and perfect will. Joseph's brothers intended his suffering for evil; God *used* it for good. Satan intended Job's suffering for evil; God *used* it for good. Satan intended Paul's suffering for evil; God *used* it for good. In each case, God's purpose prevailed. Satan intends your suffering for evil; God can use it for good to the degree that you "live above" by cooperating with the work of his Holy Spirit in the midst of your suffering.

Whose purpose in your suffering will prevail?

Remember Claire, whom I mentioned in Chapter 1? One day I asked her, "How did God work with you to bring about good from the pain of your childhood sexual abuse?" The setting of the question was idyllic, a crisp spring day in Tennessee. The sun's rays breaking through the forest provided a reminder of God's all-embracing love that warms the heart. The pointed question, however, brought back cold, dark memories that one would rather forget . . . *forever.* However, after a moment's reflection, but more than fifty years of reckoning with one of the most painful injustices in this life, she said, "God used it to bring me to himself." She went on to share how in the ensuing years her Heavenly Father wisely and lovingly used the sting of that evil act to sensitize her young heart to her need of the Savior and of his perfect, unfailing, life-giving love in a cruel and confusing world. Yes, God can even use what he hates to accomplish what he loves.

With those who choose the good in the face of suffering, God by his Spirit works with them for good. God is good to all in some ways, by giving rain from heaven and food from the earth (cf. Acts 14:17; 17:24-28). But he is particularly good to some in all ways, the "some" being those who love him and are called according to his eternal purpose. In the crucible of suffering, we can be assured that God's Spirit is at work *with us*—relationally, personally, intimately—to bring redemptive meaning out of every circumstance of life, whether sweet or bitter, bright or dark, good or bad, happy or sad. That means I can persevere through the tears and heart-aches, the hurts and disappointments, the horror and the nightmares, the losses and sleepless nights and, at the end of the day, stand on top of Heartbreak Hill and boldly declare, "In all these things I am more than a conqueror through him who loves me!" (Romans 8:37).

Just as a spiritually hardened heart can be further hardened by heaven's blessings, a spiritually soft heart can be further softened by earth's sufferings. God lovers are made better by some of the worst things imaginable.

That was Jacob's experience. It was also Joseph's. It, too, can be ours. It all depends upon how we view our suffering. Furthermore, the way we experience suffering depends upon what we know about suffering with the eyes of our heart. We must start with heaven and reason down toward earth. In fact, this is the *only* way that perseverance in suffering will "finish its work." What is that "work"? And how does God accomplish it in our lives? To answer those questions, we must return to God's original and ultimate intentions for humanity.

CHAPTER 8

The Image Restored

*It is always true to some extent that we make our images
of God. It is even truer that our image of God makes us.
Eventually we become like the God we image . . .
Healing our image of God heals our image of ourselves.*
—Brennan Manning

*Let perseverance finish its work, so that you may be mature
and complete, lacking in nothing.*
—James the Just (James 1:4)

To produce *David*, a masterpiece of Renaissance sculp-
ture, the Italian artist Michelangelo salvaged a block
of marble that had been damaged in the hands of Simone
da Fiesole, a less-skilled sculptor who had given up on the
project. Seeing the hidden potential in the massive, marred
block of marble that for years had been abandoned to the
elements, Michelangelo began to painstakingly chip away
everything that *wasn't* David. The master artist worked diligently over a period of several years to transform that flawed
block of marble into a statue of exquisite beauty.

Humanity is God's *chef d'oeuvre*—his masterpiece! As
we have seen, God created mankind *as* his image; all the rest
of the Bible is simply a commentary on that truth (Genesis
1:26-27; 5:1; 9:6). As such, we were created to *resemble* our
Creator, to live in loving *relationship* with God and fellow
humans, and to *rule* over his creation as authoritative vice-regents. However, the intrusion of Satan and sin into the idyllic

conditions of Eden brought about catastrophic consequences for humanity. Though ever remaining the image of God, we must now live in a world alienated from God. Evil defaced God's priceless masterpiece, bringing inestimable suffering into our human experience.

Thankfully, that is not the end of the story. "God is the ultimate salvage artist," writes author Randy Alcorn. "He loves to restore things to their original condition—and even make them better."[159] Jesus Christ, the "second man" and "last Adam," more than replaced what Adam erased! Nevertheless, if we who are *in* Christ are to become *like* Christ, a long, painstaking apprenticeship is required. We must let perseverance in affliction "finish its work" (see Figure 2, page 150). The result of such patient endurance through suffering is what James terms *maturity*—"so that you may be *mature* and complete, not lacking anything" (James 1:4).

What is maturity? How do we know when we've arrived?

DEFINING MATURITY

Some associate maturity with age. However, many grow old without ever growing up. Others define maturity in terms of personality, assuming the extroverted, accomplishment-oriented leader is more mature than the reserved, quiet follower. Sometimes maturity is associated with knowledge. Yet some of the most brilliant individuals intellectually may demonstrate great immaturity socially, relationally, or spiritually.

For James and the other biblical writers, maturity has little to do with age, knowledge, or personality. It has everything to do with soundness, completeness, and integrity. The Greek term for maturity (*teleios*) is sometimes translated "perfect," referring to wholeness, not sinlessness.[160] In the above verse, James employs the word twice: "And let endurance have its *perfect* effect, so that you will be *perfect* and complete, not deficient in anything" (James 1:4, NET). Paul uses the same word to describe his own arduous and single-minded journey toward spiritual maturity: "Not that I have already attained this—that is, I have not already been perfected—but I strive to lay hold of that for which Christ Jesus also laid hold of me" (Philippians 3:12-14, NET).

None of us has attained *absolute* maturity—"*I have not already been perfected.*" As seen in the preceding context (vv. 10-11), our journey toward maturity includes intimate knowledge of Christ, the righteousness that comes by faith, the power of Christ's resurrection, the fellowship of Christ's sufferings, becoming like Christ in his death, and finally the resurrection from the dead at which moment we shall "bear the image of the heavenly man," Jesus Christ (1 Corinthians 15:49).

But that moment has not yet arrived.

We live in the "already/but not yet"—between Christ's finished work of salvation and his future work of reconciling all things when sin and suffering will be no more (Ephesians 1:19). Today we know only partially what one day we will experience fully. For this reason, Paul affirms in Philippians 3:15, "Therefore let those of us who are 'perfect' (*teleios*) embrace this point of view" (NET). With a hint of sarcasm, Paul reminds us that if we think we've "arrived," we haven't! It is only those who acknowledge their need of further maturity who are truly growing in maturity.

What is maturity? The Bible defines maturity as *being like Christ.* Christ is the perfect representation of all that God intends for you and me. As such, he is the quintessential image of God into whose likeness we as believers are being transformed (Colossians 1:15; 3:10). We have seen that God by his Spirit cooperates with those who love God to bring ultimate good out of every suffering experienced in life (Romans 8:28). Furthermore, ultimate good is defined as being "conformed to the image of his Son" (v. 29).

God's Son became like us so that we might become like him.

We cannot count on God to make our lives happy, stress-free, relatively comfortable, and enjoyable. We can count on him to work with us in our suffering in such a way that we become more and more like Christ.

This is God's supreme desire for his children.

The question is—"*How* does God fashion us into the image of his Son?"

THE CRUCIFORM LIFE

In *The Voyage of the Dawn Treader*, C. S. Lewis tells of a young boy named Eustace who, motivated by his greed, steals a gold armband. When he puts it on, however, he discovers that his greed turns him into a dragon. To make matters worse, the armband becomes painfully tight on his dragon foot. One night, Eustace the dragon encounters a huge lion who offers a solution to his predicament. The lion tells Eustace to follow him to a high mountain well resembling a round bath. Upon arriving, Eustace longs to bathe his aching foot in the crystal-clear water, but the lion tells Eustace that he must first undress. At first, Eustace objects, reasoning that dragons don't wear clothes. Then he remembers that dragons—being "snaky sort of things"—shed their skins.

As Eustace starts scratching, the scales tumble to the ground. Like the peeling of a banana, the dragon's whole outer skin falls away. When he puts his foot into the water, however, he observes that it is just as tough, wrinkled, and scaly as before. So he continues scratching at the skin underneath only to realize that there is yet another layer of skin underlying that one. Finally the lion, named Aslan, says, "You will have to let me undress you." Though fearful of the lion's claws, Eustace is desperate to be free from his dragon character. As Aslan begins to peel away the skin, layer by layer, Eustace feels as though he is about to die. Finally, with the thick, gnarled mess of dragon skin lying on the ground, Aslan takes hold of Eustace and throws him into the crystal-clear water. Initially, the water stings; but it soon becomes perfectly delectable. Eustace begins to swim, splash, and laugh without pain. Eustace is a boy again![161]

In this story, Lewis vividly and masterfully illustrates the profound biblical truth of the effects of evil upon our most essential identity as the image of God. Like it did for Eustace, the primeval deceit of sin only led to enslavement. In desiring to become more than God intended, humanity became far less than God intended. We became a "dragon" of sorts. Upon discovering our nakedness we hid, attempting to conceal our shame from an all-knowing God. The effort proved futile. Makeshift garments were put on as an attempt to regain some measure of respectability and righteousness. This, too, proved to be inadequate. The transparency and intimacy initially characteristic of our identity as the image of God degenerated into shame, blame, and suffering.

Like Eustace, we must strip off the clothes of the Old Man and put on the clothes of the New Man if we are to become more like Christ (Ephesians 4:22–24; Colossians 3:9–11). Also like Eustace, *we cannot do it on our own*. We scratch and peel away, layer after layer, only to discover that we are as rough and scaly as before. Indeed, the more we scratch and attempt to shed in our own strength the tattered garments of the Old Man, the more we discover our inadequacy. Dragon skins are not easily discarded.

That is why Jesus says, "You will have to let me undress you!" That he does—*when we embrace the cross*. The old garments of selfishness and self-righteousness are only stripped away by a "circumcision done by Christ" (Colossians 2:11). Such "undressing" is painful, penetrating, and profoundly transforming. It strips off the gnarled mess of the Old Man and makes all clean and fresh in the New Man (2 Corinthians 5:17). Now, "buried with him in baptism and raised with him through . . . faith" (Colossians 2:12), we discover ourselves fully human once again. This is the cruciform life—a life shaped into the image of Christ by the cross of Christ.

DEATH, BURIAL, AND RESURRECTION

We cannot reflect deeply on suffering without contemplating the believer's relationship to the ultimate cause of suffering—Satan, sin, and self.[162] At Calvary, the Son of God experienced the most horrendous manifestation of suffering imaginable. Nevertheless, by the cross of suffering he conquered suffering. Therefore, the cross of Christ holds great significance for our perspective on every trial and temptation we face in life, speaking not only of our victory over sin, but also of our ultimate victory in and through suffering.

On one occasion, Jesus told his disciples, "The Son of Man must suffer many things . . . be rejected . . . killed and on the third day be raised to life" (Luke 9:21). Following this prediction of such intense suffering, he then adds, "Whoever wants to be my disciple must deny themselves and take up their cross daily and follow me" (v. 23). We take up our cross as we recognize and experience our intimate and inseparable association with Christ on his cross (Romans 6:1-11). Only as we know and experience who we are in Christ can we boldly and successfully face the remnants of who we were in Adam, including suffering. Having spoken of his own suffering on behalf of other believers, Paul reminds the Colossians believers:

> Since, then, you have been raised with Christ, set your hearts on things above, where Christ is, seated at the right hand of God. Set your minds on things above, not on earthly things. For you died, and your life is now hidden with Christ in God. When Christ, who is your life, appears, then you also will appear with him in glory. (Colossians 3:1-3; cf. 1:24)

All believers know that Christ died *for* their sin. Far fewer know that they died with Christ *to* sin. Knowing and believing that *Christ died for us* frees us from the penalty of sin. Knowing and believing that *we died with Christ* frees us from the ongoing power of sin in this life and from its presence in the next. That is why any authentic change of clothes begins with embracing our intimate identification with Christ in his historical death, burial, and resurrection.

The American film director and comedian Woody Allen once quipped, "I'm not afraid to die; I just don't want to be there when it happens!" But according to Paul's words, when Christ died *for* and *to* sin, the believer was there! At the cross, our relation to Adam, sin, and spiritual death was definitively broken. Death means separation. Physical death is the separation of the spirit from the body. Spiritual death is separation from the life of God. Finally, eternal death is separation from God forever. In Adam, we were dead *in* sin; in Christ, we are dead *to* sin—once for all separated from the Old Man and the tattered clothes of our past life.

Not only have we died with Christ to the penalty and power of sin, we have also been "buried with him" (Romans 6:4). Burial says, "This person is dead!" When the casket is closed, lowered into the ground, and covered with dirt, it symbolically marks the end of one's earthly pilgrimage. The deceased is shut out from life as we know it. Our burial with Christ is the sign and seal of our death with Christ, signifying that we have been effectively separated from the penalty and power of the old "dragon life" as those in the grave are shut out from physical life.

If our death and burial with Christ severed us from the old humanity of which Adam is the head, our resurrection with Christ secures us in the new humanity of which Christ is the head—"You have been raised with Christ . . . and your life is now hidden with Christ in God" (Colossians 3:1, 3; cf. Romans 6:8). Paul is speaking not only about the future, bodily resurrection of believers, but also about the fresh, new "clothes" that should characterize our lives as we journey through suffering this side of heaven. Elsewhere, Paul states it like this: "Therefore, if anyone is in Christ, the new creation has come: The old has gone, the new is here!" (2 Cor. 5:17). The old is not merely patched up or refurbished. It is replaced! New wine must be poured into new wine skins.

THE *EX*CHANGED LIFE

A changed life in a world of suffering begins with an *ex*changed life. No truth of Scripture has helped me more in my own journey of grief and suffering than this. The old saying holds true:

> Do this and live, the law demands,
> But neither gives me feet nor hands;
> A better word the gospel brings,
> It bids me fly and gives me wings![163]

Yes, wings to fly even in the face of trials and temptation. However, such liberating flight begins at the cross. At Calvary, God dealt decisively, not only with the fruit of sin (what we do), but also with the root of sin (who we are). That is what Paul means in Galatians 2:20—"I *am* crucified with Christ, and it is no longer I who live, but Christ who lives in me." In other words, the Old Man of Romans 6:6 is the "I" of Galatians 2:20 who no longer lives. The "dragon" was crucified!

Such a change of clothes takes place at the point of personal salvation through faith in Christ's finished work at Calvary. This is the emphasis of Paul's "put off/put on" termi-nology in Colossians 3:9-11: "*Since* you have put off the old man with his deeds, and have put on the new man" (NKJV). No doubt, Paul is referring to the believer's conversion and subsequent baptism into Christ at which moment the "Lion" endows us with a new set of clothes. At the point of salvation, the historic death, burial, and resurrection of Christ are no longer merely historical events of the past, but the experiential new identity of which every believer is now a part. As the nineteenth century French preacher and theologian Henri Lacordaire once said, the believer is "born crucified."[164]

Though born crucified, we sometimes fail to understand the significance of our new wardrobe. Even as Jacob had to be brought to a point of brokenness at Peniel, so we must be brought to the foot of the cross . . . *daily*. Though lacking the same spiritual resources that we have this side of the cross, Jacob also needed this ongoing change of garments after his face-to-face encounter with the God-Man. Still limping from having been broken at his point of greatest strength, he said to his household and to all who were with him, "Get rid of the foreign gods you have with you, and purify yourselves and *change your clothes*. Then come, let us go up to Bethel, where I will build an altar to God, who answered me in the day of my distress and who has been with me wherever I have gone" (Genesis 35:2-3).

While no one will attain sinless perfection until heaven, we must never be content with sinful imperfection while on earth. Christ's once-for-all death for us must become our daily death with him. As Dietrich Bonhoeffer reminds us, "The cross is not the terrible end of a pious, happy life. Instead, it stands at the beginning of community with Jesus Christ. When Christ calls a man, he bids him come and die."[165] When we meditate on the cross and all that Christ accomplished for us at Calvary, we may feel overwhelmed with joy and peace. But such positive feelings are the *result* of the cross, not the cross itself. The cross itself is hard and painful, cutting to the very core of our being. That is why Paul exhorts believers on an ongoing basis to strip off one set of clothes and put on another suit of clothes (Ephesians 4:20-24). That is also why he can say, "I die every day" (1 Corinthians 15:31), and elsewhere, "I am always carrying in the body the dying of Jesus"

(2 Corinthians 4:10-11). In the words of John Calvin, "We must fight throughout life under the cross."[166]

If we are *in Christ*—which is only by grace—we can be assured that God will faithfully complete his work of forming Christ *in us*, which, too, is only by grace. Such transformation takes place as we put off (daily) the dirty, tattered clothes of the Old Man and put on (daily) the fresh, clean clothes of the New Man (Ephesians 4:22-24). In this way, gradually but surely, the "I in Christ" (Colossians 3:1-3) becomes "Christ formed in me" (Galatians 4:19).

THE METAMORPHOSIS

Just as a butterfly goes through four stages of gradual transformation—egg, larva (caterpillar), pupa (chrysalis), and finally the adult butterfly—so we as believers must undergo a similar metamorphosis if Christ is to be formed in us. Paul describes this process of profound transformation in 2 Corinthians 3:18: "And we all, who with unveiled faces contemplate the Lord's glory, are being *transformed* into his image with ever-increasing glory, which comes from the Lord, who is the Spirit."

Our English word "transformation" comes from the Greek term used to describe the process of metamorphosis (*metamorphoō*). The metamorphosis from larvae to butterfly involves significant alterations of the organism's essential nature, including its physiology, biochemistry, and behavior. The process transforms both what is seen and unseen. The metaphor of an iceberg proves helpful in understanding the extent of such metamorphosis.[167] The hidden part of an iceberg can sink a massive ship . . . *and a life*! Like an iceberg, only a small portion of our lives are visible to the human eye (Figure 4). We can compare the portion "above-the-waterline" to the outward moral clothes that we wear. Clothes, however, do not make the man; they merely reveal who the man is. God's work of transformation goes deep, touching not only our outer "clothes" (actions, words, and decisions), but also our inner person (attitudes and motivations).

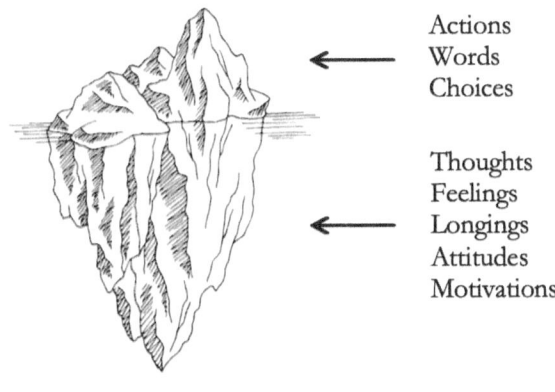

Actions
Words
Choices

Thoughts
Feelings
Longings
Attitudes
Motivations

Figure 4

RESEMBLANCE: CHANGE FROM THE INSIDE OUT

As the apex of God's creation, human beings alone possess the "breath of life" (Genesis 2:7). The breath of life distinguishes us humans *from* all other forms of life and *as* those who resemble God as his "likeness-image." However, since our God-endowed dignity has been severely marred by our moral depravity, God's work of transformation must extend to the deepest parts of our personhood. *There must be change from the inside out.*

We have seen that we share with our Creator certain features that define our essential dignity as persons: reflective *thinking*, emotional *feeling*, deep *longing*, and active *choosing*. It is precisely in these four areas that the Spirit of God now actively works to renew his family members according to the image of God. Because the effects of sin go deep, authentic change effectuated by the cross must also go deep. Such profound change begins in the mind, then touches our emotions and deepest longings, resulting in a gradual metamorphosis of our choices and ultimately our character.

All deep, lasting change begins in the *mind*. That is why Paul describes the renewal of the mind as indispensable to any outward change of moral clothing. In Ephesians 4:23, Paul urges us: "Be made new in the *attitude of your minds*." And in Colossians 3:10, the New Man is "being renewed in *knowledge* in the image of its Creator." Elsewhere, Paul exhorts us, "Let this *mind* be in you which was also in Christ Jesus" (Philippians 2:5, NKJV). For the biblical writers, the "mind" includes not merely the ability to think, but the very seat and sum total of our moral state of being that determines our attitudes, perspective, and orientation in life. Our daily prayer should be that of Kate B. Wilkinson (1859-1928) in her well-known hymn: "May the mind of Christ my Saviour, Live in me from day to day, By His love and power controlling, All I do and say." But such can only take place through a process of ongoing renewal: "Do not conform to the pattern of this world, but be transformed by the *renewing of your mind*" (Romans 12:2). Conform means to press in from the outside. Transform means to change radically from the inside. We will never be able to consistently dress up like Jesus apart from such renewal of our minds.

As our minds are renewed, our *emotions* are reoriented. Since our emotions are the "energy content" of our perceptions and evaluations,[168] they must be considered and evaluated, not simply expressed, repressed, or ignored.

Our emotional problems have a moral root. That is why we must be willing to consider and evaluate our emotions in order to appropriately address the underlying issues responsible for human suffering.[169] Unfortunately, we often want to merely relieve the pain. Christian psychologist and author Larry Crabb describes it this way: "We have become committed to relieving the pain behind our problems rather than using our pain to wrestle more passionately with the character and purposes of God. Feeling better has become more important than finding God. And worse, we assume that people who find God always feel better."[170]

Emotional pain is one of the most severe forms of human suffering. But it can also be an effective tool in God's hands to help us explore its source. Emotions are like the indicators on the dashboard of our car, informing us of a potential malfunction of the vehicle. They are part of who we are as the image of God and to ignore or repress them is to slice off a part of our humanity. For some years in my life, I did just that—I "sliced off a part of my humanity" by failing to allow the Spirit of God to deeply touch my emotional center. I sought to *repress* my emotions rather than *evaluate* and *reorient* my emotions. The result was a severe emotional and endogenous depression during which time God did soul surgery on the deeper, underlying layers of my person. Such surgery is vital to our continued growth in Christ, for growth in emotional maturity is indispensable to spiritual maturity.[171]

When the mind is renewed and emotions reoriented, our deepest *longings*—springing from the innermost part of our person—are redirected. Jesus invites all who are thirsty to come and drink from the water of life. For the one who does, Jesus promises that "out of his *belly* shall flow rivers of living water." (John 7:37-38 KJV). Though the expression "belly" (*koilia*) can refer to the physical stomach, it can also metaphorically signify a hollow cavity in the innermost part of our being that is the seat of thought, feeling, choice, and ultimately our overall orientation in life. It is also from this core of our being that we thirst for what only Christ can supply.

The psalmist David uses a similar term in Psalm 51:6 when he refers to the hidden, covered places of our lives: "Look, you desire integrity in the *inner man*; you want me to possess wisdom" (NET). This came from a man who for days lived in denial by covering up his sin rather than allowing God to uncover his sin (2 Samuel 11:1-12:13). During this time, he came to understand that God does not value the outer "clothes" of religious activity apart from the inner transformation of the heart. He later states, "Going through the motions doesn't please you, a flawless performance is nothing to you" (Psalm 51:16, MSG). Apparently, David learned what we all need to learn. We can unwittingly use God to run from God by creating a flurry of religious activity, all the while ignoring the deeper, hidden areas of our lives that God wants to change. Fortunately, such denial did not last long in David's life, for he continues in verse 17: "I learned God-worship when my pride was shattered. Heart-shattered lives ready for love don't for a moment escape God's notice" (MSG).

What we perceive to be the deepest longings of our heart impacts our active *choices* in life. These, in turn, ultimately fashion our character (Proverbs 12:4; Acts 17:11). The difference between a Judas (John 13:2) and a Joseph (Genesis 39:10) started somewhere with a small decision. Our choices, not our circumstances, ultimately shape our character; circumstances merely reveal and refine it to the degree that we respond positively. Philosopher and author Peter Kreeft writes: "Everyone also creates a character, a person: themselves. God gives us only the raw material; by our choices we shape it into who we are . . . We are always painting our own eternal self-portrait. Each choice is a brush stroke. We are sculpting our own likeness. Each act is a cut of the chisel."[172] That is why our choices eventually choose us.

D. L. Moody once said, "Character is what you are in the dark." Moreover, what we are in the dark—in the "covered places" of our lives—is ultimately shaped by the "under the water line" issues in our lives. That is why our daily prayer must be, "Examine me, O God, and probe my thoughts. Test me, and know my concerns. See if there is any idolatrous way in me, and lead me in the everlasting way" (Psalm 139:23-24, NET).

How does such change from the inside out take place?

The Art of Contemplation

Clothing ourselves with Christ begins with contemplating Christ. Paul could not be more clear: "And we all, who with unveiled faces *contemplate* the Lord's glory, are being transformed into his image with ever-increasing glory . . ." (2 Corinthians 3:18).

In Nathanael Hawthorne's short story, *The Great Stone Face*, he recounts the tale of a young man, named Ernest, who lived in a rural village nestled in the foothills of a nearby mountain. On that mountain, a rock formation resembled the facial features of a human. The local folklore predicted that one day a personage of great and noble character resembling the Great Stone Face would come to that village bringing untold blessing. This legend inspires four wannabe heroes who, out of personal ambition, promote themselves as the fulfilment of the prophecy. Over the years, a merchant of immense wealth, a conquering general, a politician renowned for his skillful oratory, and a brilliant poet successively arrive in the humble glen. Though each briefly revels in the admiration of the populace, their character flaws soon disqualify them as potential candidates to fulfill the prophecy.

All during this time, Ernest was growing into adulthood. He, too, was fascinated by the legend of the Great Stone Face, but in a different way. As a youth, he would often slip away from his daily chores and stand contemplating the majesty and beauty of the Great Stone Face etched on the mountainside. Even as an aged adult, the humble hill farmer turned lay preacher continued his daily practice of gazing upon the renowned image engraved in stone. One evening, Ernest delivered an evening meditation at the foot of the mountain where all could see the Great Stone Face high above. Present in the crowd was one of the would-be heroes, the poet, who alone humbly acknowledged his failure to fulfill the prophecy. Hawthorne graphically describes the climax of Ernest's sermon:

At that moment, in sympathy with a thought which he was about to utter, the face of Ernest assumed a grandeur of expression, so imbued with benevolence, that the poet, by an irresistible impulse, threw his arms aloft and shouted, "Behold! Behold! Ernest is himself the likeness of the Great Stone Face!" Then all the people looked, and saw that what the deep-sighted poet said was true. The prophecy was fulfilled. But Ernest, having finished what he had to say, took the poet's arm, and walked slowly homeward, still hoping that some wiser and better man than himself would by and by appear, bearing a resemblance to the GREAT STONE FACE.[173]

What we contemplate determines what we emulate. Scottish theologian Henry Scougal (1650-1778) wrote that the "worth and excellency of a soul is to be measured by the object of its love."[174] Centuries before, Hosea said that the people of Israel "became as vile as the thing they loved" (Hosea 9:10). As did Ernest before the Great Stone Face, we become like the object of our focus.

The term *contemplate* means to look at something as in a mirror. In contemplating Christ, we contemplate God himself, for the Son is "the radiance of God's glory and the exact representation of his being" (Hebrews 1:4). And since the living Word (the Son) is best reflected in the written Word (the Bible), we contemplate the Lord's glory primarily by meditation upon the Scriptures. The Scriptures always point us to the person of Christ, inform us of who we are in Christ, and give us the encouragement to persevere like Christ in the face of suffering. As we do so, we are progressively transformed by the living Spirit of God into the image of the Son of God.

For this to happen, we must take our cue from Mary who chose the best—*to sit at the feet of Jesus* (Luke 10:38-42).

For many, the greatest hindrance to authentic spirituality is frenzied activity. We've bought into our cultural perspective that the busiest people are the best. We're simply too busy to nurture in our lives the various means of grace that lead to deep transformation of character: prayer, the Scriptures, and moments of quiet meditation. We've forgotten that the "stops" of Jesus are just as important as his steps. Whether in times of suffering or in its absence, God is eager to speak to us and with us . . . if we would just slow down.

God's Sword of Providence
Contemplation of Christ leads to a transformation of our perspective on suffering. As we have seen from Romans 8:28-29, the Spirit of God cooperates with us in the harsh circumstances of life to accomplish his good purpose—to fashion us according to the very image of his Son. As the master sculptor, God wisely uses the suffering intrinsic to this fallen world to chip away all that does not reflect who we *truly* are in Christ. This process is what author L. E. Maxwell (1895-1984) calls God's "sword of providence."

> God's sword of providence may be laid successively to every tie that binds you to self and sin. Wealth and health and friends may fall before that sword. The inward fabric of your life will go to pieces. Your joy will depart. Smitten within and without, burned and peeled and blasted, you may finally, amidst the dreadful baptism, be driven from the sinful inconsistency of living for yourself. You may at length be *disposed* [blessed word—sweet compulsion] to yield self over to the victory and undoing of Calvary. Oh, the glorious power of the cross![175]

That is why we must not waste our sorrows, for they are part of our earthly apprenticeship preparing us for our heavenly vocation (Hosea 6:1). Suffering loosens our grip on all that can keep us from Christ in order to make us more like Christ.

The writer to the Hebrews reminds us that the Pioneer of our faith was himself made perfect (i.e., fully qualified) through suffering: "In bringing many sons and daughters to glory, it was fitting that God, for whom and through whom everything exists, should make the Pioneer of their salvation perfect through what he suffered" (Hebrews 2:10). As Christ followers, how can we expect less?

While the Christ we profess to follow was made perfect through suffering, I find that all too often I prefer to be made perfect through success. But God will not do for us what he did not do for his Son—exempt us from suffering. In writing of his supreme goal in life, the Apostle Paul exclaims, "I want to know Christ—yes, to know the power of his resurrection." But we cannot experience the power of Christ's resurrection apart from what Paul says next: "and [to know] participation in his sufferings, becoming like him in his death" (Philippians 3:10).

Helen Rosevere (1925-2016) was a British medical missionary in the Congo from 1953 to 1974. She came to Christ in her younger years during a Bible study taught by the well-known British pastor and author, Dr. Graham Scroggie. Following the study, Dr. Scroggie wrote Philippians 3:10 in the flyleaf of Helen's Bible and said to her, "Tonight you've entered into the first part of the verse, 'That I may know Him.' This is only the beginning, and there's a long journey ahead. My prayer for you is that you will go on through the verse to know 'the power of His resurrection' as you go out to serve Him." Then, very quietly, looking straight into her eyes, he added, "And also, God willing, one day perhaps, 'the fellowship of His sufferings, being made conformable unto His death.'"

As Helen left for the Congo, her faith was strong and her trust was confident. Yet during the uprising of local rebels, she was raped, assaulted, and brutally beaten. Commenting later, she said, "I must ask myself a question as if it came directly from the Lord, 'Can you thank Me for trusting you with this experience even if I never tell you why?'"[176]

Knowing we are *in Christ* and Christ is being formed *in us* enables us to face suffering with courage. In doing so, the real question we each must ask is not, "Am I successful for God?" but rather, "Am I surrendered to God?" One rarely moves from the first question to the latter apart from suffering. We so often do not move forward and go deeper in our walk with Christ until the pain of remaining the same becomes greater than the pain of change. Pastor and author Timothy Keller reminds us that suffering ". . . is not only the way Christ became like and redeemed us, but it is one of the main ways that we become like him."[177] Even as Christ suffered in his body, and through that suffering conquered sin, so suffering in our lives moves us to reorient our priorities so that we live our earthly lives free from the control of sin (1 Peter 4:1-2).

A Long Obedience
Because our metamorphosis into the image of Christ goes deep, it also takes time. It is more of a process than a crisis. It requires what Eugene Peterson has termed "a long obedience." This was evident in Jacob's life. Twenty-one years expired between the time that Jacob first encountered God at Bethel and when he returned as a different man (Genesis 35:1-15). Even beyond this crucial point, God continued his persevering work of shaping Jacob's character. Jacob's face-to-face encounter with the God-Man at Peniel brought him to a point of humble brokenness. His strongest sinew, his persistent self-confidence, had shrivelled. It was his persistent limp thereafter that kept him leaning into his new identity as Israel, the "God wrestler." When he arrived at Hebron, his mother had already died and his father, Isaac, would soon die

(Genesis 35:9). Then Jacob grieved the supposed death of his much loved son, Joseph:

> Then Jacob tore his clothes, put on sackcloth and mourned for his son many days. All his sons and daughters came to comfort him, but he refused to be comforted. "No," he said, "I will continue to mourn until I join my son in the grave." So his father wept for him. (Genesis 37:34-35)

It was soon after that Jacob said to his remaining sons: "You have deprived me of my children. Joseph is no more and Simeon is no more, and now you want to take Benjamin. Everything is against me!" (Genesis 42:36). Finally, Jacob offers Pharaoh a descriptive summary of his life when he says, "The years of my pilgrimage are a hundred and thirty. *My years have been few and difficult,* and they do not equal the years of the pilgrimage of my fathers" (Genesis 47:7-10). However, Jacob lived and limped for another seventeen years before his death. Finally, at the point of death and while leaning on his staff, he doesn't whine, but worships! According to the inspired insight of the writer to the Hebrews, "By faith Jacob, when he was dying, blessed each of Joseph's sons, and *worshiped as he leaned on the top of his staff*" (Hebrews 11:21). At the end of his life, Jacob was still a cripple, but a cripple who worships!

RELATIONSHIP: THE BOND OF LOVE

Growth in resemblance to Christ inevitably affects our way of relating to others. When our character is transformed, our relationships are reoriented. How could it be otherwise? As we have seen, the loving, intimate oneness of Father, Son, and Holy Spirit is the template expressing God's most cherished intentions for all of humanity—*relational love.* Therefore, a metamorphosis into the "likeness-image" of the great Three-in-One necessarily entails growth in the bond of love, which binds all other virtues together in perfect unity (Colossians 3:14).

Suffering Love

According to early tradition, the Apostle John lived to be nearly 100 years old. When he could no longer walk to the front of his congregation, friends would carry him as he sat in a chair. Each Lord's Day, he only had enough strength to lift his hand into the air, point his finger toward heaven, and say to his church family, "Little children, love one another."[178]

Such love comes at a cost. Evil is a four letter word. So is love. In an evil world, the call to love is a call to suffer. Theologian N. T. Wright states it well, "The call of the gospel is for the church to implement the victory of God in the world through suffering love."[179] Such words echo those of the Apostle Paul, "Love suffers long" (1 Corinthians13:4, NKJV).

It is of such suffering love that Paul also writes to the Colossian believers, "Now I rejoice in what I am suffering for you, and I fill up in my flesh what is still lacking in regard to Christ's afflictions, for the sake of his body, which is the church" (Colossians 1:24). What does he mean? Were Christ's sufferings not sufficient for our salvation? Certainly they were. But many more still need to hear and personally experience the Good News of God's love as demonstrated in Christ's afflictions. It is as if our Lord left behind a bowl called "Christ's sufferings." We help fill that bowl as we suffer on behalf of Christ and his Body. That is why Paul tells his readers not to be discouraged by his sufferings: "I ask you, therefore, not to be discouraged because of my sufferings for you, which are your glory" (Colossians 3:13). This included being in prison, suffering from and persevering through misunderstandings, divisions, and even verbal attacks from other believers. Scottish pastor and author George MacDonald (1824-1905) writes,

"The Son of God suffered unto death, not that men might not suffer, but that their sufferings might be like His."[180] As we suffer *for* Christ, we do so *in* Christ. In a very real sense, we are united together in his suffering as we are members of his Body.

The Arithmetic of Forgiveness

Forgiveness is the purest expression of love and one of the most difficult forms of suffering. Author Peter Kreeft describes it as "the best fruit, the most beautiful flower, of suffering . . . 'the plant that blossoms only when watered with tears.'"[181] That is likely why we as humans struggle so intensely in offering forgiveness to those who have wronged us.

The struggle to forgive is centuries old. On one occasion, Peter asked Jesus, "Lord, how many times shall I forgive my brother or sister who sins against me? Up to seven times?" (Matthew 18:21-35). My own journey in understanding and offering forgiveness is much like that of Peter's. Our son's unexpected death came as a result of negligence. The authorities classified it as involuntary manslaughter. No one intended to harm him. The negligence that caused his death wasn't premeditated. Nevertheless, the excruciating pain of losing my son evoked a question in me much like the question Peter asked: "Lord, how forgiving am I to be?"

Peter tried to impress Jesus and the other disciples by his outward appearance of mercy and generosity. After all, the Jewish rabbis taught that a person should offer forgiveness three times to those who offended them. Amazingly, Peter was willing to more than double the limit proposed by the rabbis, extending forgiveness even up to seven times—the number of perfection. But that was the limit!

Jesus' response took Peter by surprise: "I tell you, not seven times . . ." Perhaps a smile began to flicker across Peter's face. He's certain that Jesus is going to lower the bar, reducing the final count that defines the limits of forgiveness. But no,

Jesus continued: ". . . but seventy times seven." That's ten times the number of divine fullness with another seven added on! Suddenly, all human notions of forgiveness have been dismissed. Divine love far surpasses our human tendency to keep records, coldly calculating the extent of our forgiveness. The kingdom of heaven is a kingdom of incalculable numbers and unlimited forgiveness.

Author William S. Stoddard has written, "Forgiving the unforgivable is hard. So was the cross: hard words, hard wood, hard nails."[182] The cross marked a turning point in my own journey toward forgiveness. It's as if Jesus said to me, "If you want to talk about numbers, let's first talk about your own. If you want to limit your forgiveness of others, let's first calculate your own debt before God!" This is the point of the parable Jesus recounted in response to Peter's question. "I canceled all that debt of yours because you begged me to. Shouldn't you have had mercy on your fellow servant just as I had on you?" (Matthew 18:32-33).

I have come to realize that *no* wrong committed against me—intentional or unintentional—could ever compare with the immeasurable debt I have already been forgiven in Jesus Christ. We each face the inevitable question: As a multiple offender graciously forgiven by God, dare I ever withhold forgiveness *even once* toward another?

Since that initial step of forgiveness—a decision that I have had to reaffirm again and again over the years—I have seen blossom the flower of suffering that was watered with tears. I'll never forget embracing Ms. Lee, the elderly Korean lady who managed the small hotel where our son died, as she wept profusely in my arms. Some months later, our entire family visited South Korea, the "Land of the Morning Calm" that Jonathan had come to love. Though our hearts were not calm, it was an indispensable step of healing for us all. We saw where Jonathan had spent the last months of his life and visited with Ms. Lee. Sitting with her on the very steps that led to the room where Jonathan took his last breath, my wife via translation shared with Ms. Lee the good news of forgiveness freely offered in Jesus Christ: "But God demonstrates his own love for us in this: While we were still sinners, Christ died for us" (Romans 5:8).

Some months later we received a letter from Ms. Lee in which she expressed her own struggle with forgiving herself and embracing the forgiveness offered her in Christ. She wrote:

Oh, dear Jonathan's father and mother! My heart has been touched and moved by something. And so I spoke with someone who knows quite well what has happened. He told me, "The Holy Spirit is working on you now." And he said to me, "This is in answer to the prayers of Jonathan's parents." While he prayed with me, I was drenched with tears. Finally, I made up my mind to go to church with him next week. Thank you very much for your prayer for me—a sinful and defective woman. I earnestly hope to meet Jonathan in heaven with assurance of the resurrection by strong faith in Christ. I looked at the picture you sent of Jonathan's tombstone. According to the inscription, if we believe in Jesus Christ as our Savior and Lord, we shall meet again. I truly want to see him in Heaven.

Sincerely yours,
Jung-ja, Lee
Seoul, South Korea

Corrie Ten Boom (1892-1983), who survived a Nazi concentration camp during the Holocaust, once said, "Forgiveness is to set a prisoner free, and to realize the prisoner was you." Over the years since our son's death, we have been set free . . .

and so, we believe, has Ms. Lee. The plant watered with tears has blossomed.

RULE: OUR MANDATE AS VICE-REGENTS

On June 6, 1944, the Allied forces launched a combined naval, air, and land assault on Nazi-occupied Europe. The massive initiative, called Operation Overlord, took place on the beaches of the Normandy coast in France. There, at great cost of life, the allied forces dealt a fatal blow to Germany, rendering its defeat inevitable. Historians agree that, for all intents and purposes, the outcome of World War II was decided in the Battle of Normandy (known as "D-Day"). Nevertheless, it took another 336 days for Germany to unconditionally surrender (known as "VE Day"). On D-Day, the Allied forces already *in principle* defeated the enemy. But it took nearly another year of ongoing warfare and suffering for that victory to be manifested as actual fact.

Christ's work at Calvary, so graphically described in Psalm 22, marks our spiritual "D-Day." On Friday, April 3, AD 33,[183] Christ's resounding declaration from the cross "It is finished!" *already* dealt a fatal blow to the ultimate source of all suffering in this world—sin and Satan. Nevertheless, our much longed for "victory day" has *not yet* arrived. Today, we live in the "between" times—between the cross and the crown. A tension exists in our lives between the way things should be, how they one day will be, and what we experience today. We know deep inside that we were made for something far better, far more satisfying than what this world has to offer.

In Hebrews 2:5-10, the writer cites Psalm 8 which speaks of our dignity and destiny as the image of God. Wearing a crown of glory and honor, we were and are destined to exercise dominion. Nevertheless, *"we have not yet seen all things put under their* [our] *authority"* (v. 8). In this present world, something is wrong with everything. Toys break, accidents happen, relationships fail, healthy bodies get sick, friends and family members die, wars and terror seem to prevail, and hope can so quickly turn to despair. Beyond that, we face the ever persistent temptation to sin as well as the pernicious attacks of Satan himself.

What gives us hope? *Jesus*—"What we do see is Jesus" (v. 9). Through suffering he was made our "perfect leader," fully qualified to also bring us *through* suffering into a far better world than we could ever imagine. As we await that world, we are engaged in a spiritual apprenticeship as we learn to exercise dominion over sin and Satan. To that end, the Scriptures promise that those who persevere through the temptations and sufferings of this life will reign with Christ in the next (Romans 8:17; 2 Timothy 2:12).

Ruling over Sin and Satan

Before Cain treacherously murdered his brother, Abel, God said, "Sin is crouching at the door; it desires to have you, but *you must rule over it*" (Genesis 3:7). Cain did not. We must. But we can only do so as we take up our cross and follow Jesus.

Such an aggressive stance against sin requires an ongoing struggle, which itself is a form of suffering for righteousness. Paul describes it in these terms: "I do not fight like a boxer beating the air. No, I strike a blow to my body and make it my slave so that after I have preached to others, I myself will not be disqualified for the prize (1 Corinthians 9:26-27).

The New Testament often describes the Christian life in terms of a titanic struggle, a wrestling match, or a boxing match. It's the struggle against the law of sin and death at work in our lives. It's the fight against all that opposes the progress of the Gospel in our own lives and in the world. But as we have seen, in Christ we have all the spiritual resources necessary to daily die to sin and live for righteousness (Romans 6:15-23; 2 Peter 1:3). We exercise our divinely endowed role as God's vice-regents by putting to death the "misdeeds of the body" (Romans 8:13) and by clothing ourselves with the Lord Jesus Christ (Romans 13:14). To the degree that we persevere, we will receive the promised recompense for those who "overcome" (Revelation 2:7, 11, 17, 26; 3:5, 12, 21).

Our union with Christ in his cross work also defines our identity with Christ in his cosmic work, assuring victory over the powers of darkness. The little phrase "Now the serpent. . ." is the Bible's explanation for all the evil and suffering of this world (Genesis 3:1). That is why the apostle John defines in no uncertain terms the reason for Christ's first coming: "The reason the Son of God appeared was to destroy the devil's work" (1 John 3:8). The New Testament makes much of this perspective, often called *Christus Victor*. Paul, looking back on Christ's redemptive work, states, "And having disarmed the powers and authorities, he made a public spectacle of them, triumphing over them by the cross" (Colossians 2:15). We don't wear battle fatigues, drive armored tanks, or fire M16s, but *we are at war*. As scholar R. H. Charles (1855-1931) writes, "It is a warfare from which there is no discharge until the kingdom of this world is become the kingdom of the Lord and of His Christ."[184]

That is why we must daily put on the splendid armor that is ours in Christ (Ephesians 6:10-20), remembering that *we fight from the high ground*. We who are in Christ are seated with him "far above all rule and authority, power and dominion, and every title that can be given, not only in the present age but also in the one to come" (Ephesians 1:21-22). Christ's resounding "It is finished!" once-and-for-all changed our spiritual status and stance. Our intimate union with Jesus in his death, burial, and resurrection has invested us with royal authority over the divisive powers of this age. A lethal leash has been placed around the neck of the adversary and his ultimate doom is guaranteed. Though at times that leash appears long, if not loose, nevertheless, it is there. We can therefore take up our spiritual armor with confidence. One of the primary ways we do that is through prayer.

Ruling through Prayer

It is said that in 1952 a doctoral student at Princeton University asked the visiting lecturer, Albert Einstein, "What is there left in the world for original dissertation research?" Einstein replied, "Find out about prayer. Somebody must find out about prayer."[185] The Scriptures describe prayer as God's favored vehicle for associating us with the accomplishment of his purposes in this world. While the interplay of God's sovereignty and human responsibility remain intact, prayer nevertheless engages believers in both facilitating and accelerating the accomplishment of God's will "on earth as it is in heaven." That is why the prayers that honor God are in the name of Jesus, for the fame of Jesus, and toward the reign of Jesus. Indeed, we *can* and *must* pray in those terms when it comes to exercising our endowed role as God's vice-regents.

Blaise Pascal (1623-1662), the seventeenth century French philosopher and mathematician, once said, "God instituted prayer in order to lend His creatures the dignity of causality."[186] Epaphras certainly understood the vital role of prayer in the believer's journey towards maturity. Paul writes, "Epaphras, who is one of you and a servant of Christ Jesus . . . is always wrestling in prayer for you, that you may stand firm in all the will of God, mature and fully assured" (Colossians 4:12). Metamorphosis into the image of Christ swings on the hinge of prayer. It is through prayer—individually and collectively—that we deploy our spiritual armor and demolish spiritual strongholds (Ephesians 6:18-20; 2 Corinthians 10:4-5). Prayer is the starting point for bringing heavenly realities into our earthly experience. We can do more than pray *after* praying, but we can never do more than pray *before* praying.

Not only is prayer indispensable in ruling *over* sin and Satan, it is also the primary means of ruling *in* suffering. God is never the ultimate cause of the sin and suffering of this fallen world. However, he does make wise use of these cruel realities to fashion those who belong to him into the very image of his Son. So while we must always embrace God's use of suffering in our lives to bring us to maturity, we must at the same time firmly oppose the evil of which the suffering is but an expression. We do the latter by resisting the evil that stands *behind* suffering, while growing through the sorrow that comes *from* suffering. In this way, we turn evil back on itself by not wasting our sorrows.

<hr />

According to one tradition, Michelangelo claimed he envisioned the final outcome of each masterpiece: "In every block of marble I see a statue as plain as though it stood before me, shaped and perfect in attitude and action. I have only to hew away the rough walls that imprison the lovely apparition to reveal it to the other eyes as mine see it."[187]

God sees those who are "in Christ" as "shaped and perfect in attitude and action"—in fact, so much so that we who believe are *already* considered, not only justified, but glorified (Romans 8:30)! If we are *in Christ* (which is only by grace), we can be assured that God will faithfully complete his work of forming Christ *in us*—which, too, is only by grace. We were originally created as the likeness-image of God, and it is into the likeness-image of God that we, as Christ's family members, are being restored. Though this process involves suffering, it also brings with it a different kind of happiness.

CHAPTER 9

A Different Kind of Happiness

The people of God ought to be the happiest people in all the wide world! People should be coming to us constantly and asking the source of our joy and delight.
—A. W. Tozer

Happy is the one who endures testing.
—James the Just (James 1:12, NET)

Since the death of my firstborn son, I do not believe I have experienced a single day of happiness—at least not the *kind* of happiness I knew before. When Jonathan died, a part of me died. Now there is always an empty place at the table of our family and of our hearts. To the degree that empty place exists, happiness *as I once knew it* doesn't.

My wife and I often reflect on the few years just before Jonathan's death. We sensed that we were on the verge of a rich, new phase of deeper, more authentic relationship with our son who had moved from adolescence into young adulthood. This brought with it happiness.

Then suddenly, abruptly it was gone.

Such is true, of course, in so many experiences of life. Every loss, grief, pain, suffering, illness, or injustice indiscriminately and often irreparably rips from us another layer of happiness until we have nothing left but the harsh, dim realities of life in a damaged, sin-sick world. Dreams shatter, parents divorce, investments are lost, health dissipates, friends betray, children rebel, accidents happen, and life in general disappoints. Sooner or later, we discover that no earthly person or possession can ultimately satisfy the deeply inbred longing for happiness that pervades our inner being as those who are image bearers of our Creator.

Augustine once said: "God wants to give us something, but cannot, because our hands are full—there's nowhere for Him to put it."[188] The "something" God wants to give is happiness. This theme is repeated so frequently in the Bible that it's hard to miss! When the Queen of Sheba saw firsthand the blessing of God upon the people of Israel, she exclaimed, "How *happy* your people must be!" (1 Kings 10:8). The prophet Joel exhorts, "Be *happy* and full of joy, because the Lord has done a wonderful thing" (Joel 2:21, NCV). And the psalmist David declares, "But the godly are *happy*; they rejoice before God and are overcome with joy" (Psalm 68:3, NET). Although more than one third of the psalms are classified as laments, twenty-six times the descriptive word "happy" describes those who place their trust in the Lord.[189]

The New Testament only echoes and amplifies this theme of happiness. Jesus tells his disciples, "Now that you know this truth, how *happy* you will be if you put it into practice!" (John 13:17, GNT). In speaking of the benefits of justification, Paul declares, "This is what David meant when he spoke of the *happiness* of the person whom God accepts as righteous, apart from anything that person does" (Romans 4:6, GNT). Even martyrdom cannot extinguish the profound happiness of those who serve the Lord: "*Happy* are those who from now on die in the service of the Lord!" (Revelation 14:13, GNT).

Furthermore, the Scriptures make it clear that such happiness springs from God who himself is happy. Paul speaks of the "gospel concerning the glory of the *blessed* God" (1 Timothy 1:11). At the end of the same letter to Timothy, he describes God as "he who is *blessed* and only Sovereign, the King of kings and Lord of lords" (1 Timothy 6:15). As I will demonstrate below, the word "blessed" literally means "happy." A. W. Tozer once wrote, "God is happy if nobody else is."[190] God is not only good, he is also good natured. And it is out of his goodness that he longs to bring untold blessing into our lives. Larry Crabb is correct when he writes: "There's never a moment in all of our lives when God is not longing to bless us. At every moment, in every circumstance, God is doing us good. He never stops. It gives Him too much pleasure. God is not waiting to bless us after our troubles end. He is blessing us right now, in and through those troubles. At this exact moment, He is giving us what He thinks is good."[191]

Our problem is that we sometimes fail to discern what is signified by "good." We tenaciously cling to our good dreams more than to the One who can make our best dreams come true. Just as the first couple in Eden, we tend to live by *our* knowledge of good and evil rather than place childlike trust in our loving Father. In doing so, we often pursue what immediately *feels* good and shun what is in *fact* good. So we go through life attempting to grasp our own handful of happiness as we understand it. God's words through the suffering prophet are just as applicable today as they were in the seventh century BC: "My people have committed two sins: They have forsaken me, the spring of living water, and have dug their own cisterns, broken cisterns that cannot hold water" (Jeremiah 2:13).

To help us stop digging and searching in all the wrong places, God makes wise, good use of the inevitable pain of living in this fallen, disappointing world. Little by little, he helps our hands relinquish what can never ultimately satisfy so that we can earnestly grasp the One who can fully satisfy.

Yes, God longs to give us happiness! *But it's a different kind of happiness.* And that's why it is not easily recognized or often experienced. We keep digging in all the wrong places.

THE PATHWAY TO HAPPINESS

James the Just describes the biblical pathway to genuine happiness when he writes, "*Happy* is the one who endures testing . . ." (James 1:12, NET). To be sure we get the point, he begins and ends his letter with the same emphasis. James' opening words are, "Consider it *pure joy* . . . when you face trials of many kinds" (James 1:2). Then, toward the end of his epistle he writes, "We call those *happy* who were steadfast" (James 5:11, RSV). The biblical pathway to happiness is not around suffering, but through suffering. It is arduous and strewn with the afflictions of living in a physically and spiritually war-torn world. Suffering, however, need not be a deterrent to happiness; when viewed correctly, it is an essential step along the pathway to happiness (Figure 2, page 150).

How do we describe this happiness? Though the Hebrew (*asher*) and Greek (*makarios*) terms are often translated "blessed," the concept of profound happiness is predominate in both.[192] This is clear in my French Bible, which consistently translates the Greek term as *heureux* (happy). The idea of "bliss" or "inexpressible delight" conveys well the idea. That is why throughout this chapter I use various Bible translations in order to highlight the most appropriate translation of the Greek word for "happy." The British Bible commentator G. Campbell Morgan (1863-1945) writes, "I wish we were brave enough to write in our Bibles, 'Happy,' rather than 'Blessed,' for that is the right translation."[193] Nevertheless, the biblical writers speak of a different kind of bliss or delight. According to the Bible, happiness *is* an inward feeling, but one that is founded upon and governed by a state of being. This different kind of happiness is found uniquely in the gospel, the "good news of happiness" (Isaiah 52:7, NASB). It is a growing sense of bliss and inexpressible delight firmly founded, not upon the ever changing circumstances of life, but upon the never failing favor of God. It is a happiness that does not depend on what *happens*.

One Sunday, a lady in an electric wheelchair came to the worship service of the church of which I was pastor at the time. It was apparent she had little muscle control and possibly suffered from cerebral palsy. As the congregation was singing, she wheeled her way down the aisle toward the back of the auditorium. She clicked and moved her wheelchair a bit, then paused, re-aimed her chair, and began clicking and moving in a different direction, eventually reaching the open area in the back of the auditorium. As the congregation continued to sing—("Blessed be your name, when I'm found in a desert place, though I walk through the wilderness, blessed be your name")—she clicked and turned to the left a full 360 degrees, then stopped, then clicked again and turned to the right another full 360 degrees. It appeared she was looking for something or someone . . . but no, she wheeled right almost a full circle, then left almost a full circle, just clicking and spinning round and round. It then became clear—the song was playing, the congregation was singing, and she was dancing! Sure enough, when the song was over, she stopped turning. And during the closing prayer, she reverently bowed her head.

Hers, too, is a happiness that does not depend on what *happens*.

A HYMN TO HAPPINESS

The pathway to happiness as described by James echoes that of Jesus in his well-known Sermon on the Mount (Matthew 5-7). The most likely location of the Master Teacher's famous sermon is the Korazim Plateau in northern Israel. It over-looks the northwestern shore of the Sea of Galilee, offering an enchanting view of the cliffs of the Golan Heights. There, in typical rabbinic fashion, Jesus "sat down" to instruct his followers—a posture illustrative of the divine authority with which the Master Teacher would present his Kingdom Manifesto to the crowds.

The first eleven verses of Jesus' Sermon on the Mount are well-known as the Beatitudes. I like to call them a hymn to happiness. Again, G. Campbell Morgan writes, "'Happy' is the first word of the Manifesto. It is a word full of sunshine, thrilling with music, brimming over with just what man is seeking after in a thousand false ways."[194] On Mount Sinai, God gave the law for our holiness; from a mountain in northern Israel, the Son of God offered a new law for our happiness. The order is vital, for the one prepares for the next. While God's law shows us our need, God's grace satisfies our need. In Moses' day, the people were prohibited from approaching. In Jesus' day and today, all in this unhappy world are invited to draw near and taste the indescribable happiness we will experience in the next world.

How do we come to experience such biblical bliss? Part of the answer is found in the name given to these eight pronouncements: beatitudes. The name is appropriate. As *be-attitudes*, they focus more on *being* than on doing, on *attitude* more than action: "Happy *are* the . . . poor in spirit, those who mourn, the meek, etc." Happiness begins within, not without. The beatitudes are a snapshot of the mature Christian who, having been radically transformed, is profoundly happy—a happiness that springs from character more than circumstances. The more we grow in the character described by Jesus, the more we grow in happiness. In these eight profound declarations, Jesus cuts to the chase of the "under the water line" issues in our lives. In doing so, he perfectly describes the type of person who not only enters, but also is ready to rule in God's Kingdom. In James' words, this is the one who is "mature and complete, not lacking anything" (James 1:4).

In eight concise declarations, Jesus succinctly explains the progressive pathway to genuine happiness. He does so without redundancy or the slightest omission. Each pronouncement has its appropriate place, like rungs on a ladder, providing divine insight into what is humanly out-of-sight. There is movement that progressively takes us from poverty of spirit to purity of heart and then to the peacemaker. In the fourth beatitude—hungering and thirsting after righteousness—we reach the pinnacle toward which the first three ascend and from which the last four freely flow. In the original language, each quartet of four pronouncements has thirty-six words, a perfect balance.[195] Finally, the eighth—persecuted because of righteousness—is the privileged result of the previous seven. Throughout we find, as C. H. Spurgeon describes it, both "deepening humiliation and growing exaltation."[196]

This extraordinary pathway to the heights of such profound happiness is both progressive and strikingly paradoxical. Just before delivering these eight pronouncements of happiness, Jesus was ministering to the demon-possessed, the paralyzed, and those suffering from various diseases (Matthew 4:23-25). Fewer than forty years later, Matthew records Jesus' words with the express intent of encouraging the suffering church. Moreover, Jesus' select use of the word "happy"—repeated nine times in eight verses—only heightens the surprise among those who hear and would later read the Master Teacher's words. Does happiness really come from misery? Can one truly be happy when harassed? It's as if life is a display window in a department store where Jesus has crept in and changed all the price tags. But this is the upside-down world of the Kingdom of God in which the smallest are the greatest, the first are the last, the weak are the strong, and the humble are exalted.

Not only is this pathway progressive and paradoxical, it is also exclusive. Jesus' twice repeated declaration—"For *theirs* is the kingdom of heaven" (vv. 3, 10)—serves as bookends clearly delineating the uniqueness of Jesus' offer. What Jesus describes is not *a* pathway among others; it is the *only* pathway to genuine, lasting happiness. All other humanly concocted roadmaps to happiness lead only and ultimately to God's indictment: "What sorrow awaits you!" (Matthew 23:13-29, NLT).

To avoid that, let's listen to Jesus' words.

HAPPY ARE THE HELPLESS

The upside-down perspective of Christ's Kingdom is evident from the very start: "Happy are those who know they are spiritually poor; the Kingdom of heaven belongs to them!" (Matthew 5:3, GNT). Jesus' penetrating words turn prideful, status-seeking arrogance on its head. For Jews and Gentiles alike living under the sway of the Roman Empire, no words could be more paradoxical than these! Roman society was marked by a highly stratified social pecking order. Based on their particular social status, people wore different clothes, sat in different seats, and experienced different treatment in court. Everybody wanted to be somebody! But in Christ's kingdom, it is the nobodies who are truly somebody.

In contrast to the other beatitudes, Jesus' first pronouncement describes the lack of something rather than the presence of something: "Happy are those who know they are spiritually *poor*." Such spiritual poverty is a sign of dire neediness that highlights our utter helplessness. Paradoxically, it is not what I have, but what I don't have that provides the opportunity to embark on this most extraordinary journey. Only those who recognize their spiritual bankruptcy before God can enter and flourish in the kingdom of God. Roman citizenship could be purchased at a price; citizenship in the kingdom of God is given purely by grace.

To enter this upside-down kingdom, we must heed Jesus' words, "Truly I tell you, unless you change and become like little children, you will never enter the kingdom of heaven" (Matthew 18:3). Such radical change begins when we admit as Peter, "I am a sinful man" (Luke 5:8). Recognition of spiritual poverty is the first step to spiritual wealth: "For you know the grace of our Lord Jesus Christ, that though he was rich, yet for your sake he became poor, so that you through his poverty might become rich" (2 Corinthians 8:9).

Such recognition of our spiritual poverty empties us, enabling us to be filled. Just as water always flows toward and fills up the lowest places, so God's goodness and happiness fills to the brim those who are humble and empty and then flows over to fill others. That is why brokenness is the soil from which springs all the other virtues. But this soil has a constant tendency to harden. C. H. Spurgeon writes, "Our imaginary goodness is more hard to conquer than our actual sin." He further explains, "Till we are emptied of self we cannot be filled with God; stripping must be wrought upon us before we can be clothed with the righteousness which is from heaven. Christ is never precious till we are poor in spirit."[197]

Such humble helplessness is not simply the only way to enter the kingdom, it is the foundational virtue for spiritual growth once in the kingdom. That is why James reminds all believers facing suffering of another paradoxical principle: "Believers in humble circumstances ought to take pride in their high position" (James 1:9). Why? Because in God's economy, brokenness is the beginning of blessedness. Once Jacob was broken at his point of greatest strength, God right away "blessed him there" (Genesis 32:29). Happiness is something we gain in coming to Christ, not something we give up.

The Adversary of our souls knows that genuine happiness springs from deep humility. That is certainly why pride is our most vulnerable point of temptation. In his book, *The Screwtape Letters,* C. S. Lewis depicts the correspondence between two demons named Screwtape and Wormwood. On one occasion, Screwtape counsels his fellow demon to use the patient's humility to destroy him, making him proud of his humility:

I see only one thing to do at the moment. Your patient has become humble; have you drawn his attention to the fact? All virtues are less formidable to us once the man is aware that he has them, but this is specially true of humility. Catch him at the moment when he is really poor is spirit and smuggle into his mind the gratifying reflection, "By jove! I'm being humble," and almost immediately pride—pride at his own humility—will appear. If he awakes to the danger and tries to smother this new form of pride, make him proud of his attempt—and so on, through as many stages as you please.[198]

The word humble comes from the Latin word *humus*, meaning clay or dirt. God formed mankind out of the *humus*, the dust of the ground. That's really all we are . . . clay or dirt in the hands of the Master Potter. Just as it was the breath of God that originally gave mankind significance and meaning, so it is now only the breath of God that can replace what Adam erased—authentic happiness. Such happiness is not simply a promise for the future, but a guarantee in the present: "for theirs *is* the kingdom of heaven" (Matthew 5:3).

In possessing nothing, we possess everything!

HAPPY ARE THE UNHAPPY

Golda Meir (1898-1978), the fourth Prime Minister of Israel, once quipped, "Those who don't know how to weep with their whole heart, don't know how to laugh either." Her words merely echo those of Israel's true Messiah, Jesus Christ: "Happy are those who mourn; God will comfort them!" (Matthew 5:4, GNT).

Happy are the unhappy? On life's journey apart from Christ, it makes no sense to say that someone is feeling terrible but doing great. But on life's journey with Christ, there are seasons in our life when doing great *requires* that we feel terrible. Contemporary culture tells us that happiness depends on *feeling* good. God tells us that true happiness—a different kind of happiness—depends on *becoming* good. Contemporary culture shuns suffering, for suffering is not compatible with feeling good. God makes wise use of suffering, for he knows that it can serve to make us good, leading us to greater maturity and a different, better kind of happiness.[199]

Jesus' pronouncement uses the strongest of nine Greek words that describe grief. The same term describes the deep, inner agony of Jacob's grief over the supposed death of his son, Joseph: "Then Jacob tore his clothes, put on sackcloth and *mourned* for his son many days" (Genesis 37:34). Whatever the extent of our grief and sorrow, we can be assured that God takes our mourning very seriously. He is as mindful of our tears as he is of our trials.

Though deeply touched by all of our sorrow, Jesus speaks here to a specific expression of mourning that ultimately leads to a deeper experience of happiness. To know and grow in the happiness of which Jesus speaks, we must move from confession of sin to contrition over sin. James the Just once again interprets the significance of Jesus' words when he writes:

> Come near to God and he will come near to you. Wash your hands, you sinners, and purify your hearts, you double-minded. Grieve, mourn and wail. Change your laughter to mourning and your joy to gloom. Humble yourselves before the Lord, and he will lift you up. (James 4:8-10)

Both Jesus and James speak of the same thing—a profound mourning over sin that leads to repentance. Such mourning over sin often begins with regret. This is especially true when we lose a loved one. In looking at ways I failed in relating to my son, Jonathan, I've intensely struggled at times with regret. I have come to realize, however, that regret focuses more on myself (Why did *I* do such and such?), paralyzing me in the impossible attempt to rewrite history.

We must learn from the past, but never live in the past. And though we limp in the present, we must lean into the future. Nicholas Wolterstorff, author of *Lament for a Son*, writes, "I shall accept my regrets as part of my life, to be numbered among my self-inflicted wounds. But I will not endlessly gaze at them. I shall allow the memories to prod me into doing better with those still living. And I shall allow them to sharpen the vision and intensify the hope for that Great Day coming when we can all throw ourselves into each other's arms and say, "I'm sorry."[200]

The mourning of which Jesus speaks is not merely intellectual (regret), but also deeply emotional (remorse), leading to appropriate feelings of guilt. But how we handle such guilt is crucial. Judas experienced deep regret and remorse, leading not to repentance but to self-destruction (Matthew 27:5). On the other hand, godly sorrow moves us from regret to remorse and ultimately to repentance: "Godly sorrow brings repentance that leads to salvation and leaves no regret, but worldly sorrow brings death" (2 Corinthians 7:10). Biblical repentance is not merely intellectual and emotional; it is also volitional. Repentance means to turn and move in a different direction. It springs from being overwhelmed with the terrifying fact that we have sinned against a holy God and arrogantly turned away from the One who alone is the source of true happiness. In repentance, we become like the prophet Isaiah who, when he saw the holiness of God, said, "It's all over! I am doomed, for I am a sinful man. I have filthy lips and I live among a people of filthy lips" (Isaiah 6:5, NLT). When we repent, we turn from *all* the expressions of sin that put Jesus on the cross. We cannot hold Jesus in one hand and the sin that killed him in the other.

The same Spirit that convicts, also consoles. Author Llion T. Jones has written, "Repentance is not a fatal day when tears are shed, but a natal day when, as a result of tears, a new life begins."[201] This new life brings with it deep, inner comfort that finds its source in the Holy Spirit. In some of his last words to his disciples, Jesus said, "And I will pray the Father, and he shall give you another Comforter, that he may abide with you for ever" (John 14:16, KJV). The Holy Spirit is our Paraclete (*parakletos*), meaning the "one called alongside" to give supernatural comfort in our moment of deepest need.

As we are comforted, we in turn can comfort others. Paul speaks of this in his second letter to the Corinthian believers: "Praise be to the God and Father of our Lord Jesus Christ, the Father of compassion and the God of all comfort, who comforts us in all our troubles, so that we can comfort those in any trouble with the comfort we ourselves receive from God." (2 Corinthians 1:3-4). Sometimes God's comfort through others follows a circuitous route. On April 5, 1943, Dietrich Bonhoeffer was arrested by the Gestapo because of his affiliation with the resistance movement opposing Nazi ideology. Among his letters from prison during the air raids on Berlin is a beautiful poem written to his fiancée, Maria von Wedemever, entitled "New Year 1945." The third stanza reads:

> Should it be ours to drain the cup of grieving
> Even to the dregs of pain, at thy command,
> we will not falter, thankfully receiving
> all that is given by thy loving hand.[202]

Only three months later, on April 9, 1945, Bonhoeffer was executed by hanging in the Flossenbürg prison.

Fast forward eighteen years. On the other side of the Atlantic, another bride-to-be found much comfort in Bonhoeffer's poem as she grieved the death of her fiancé. She mailed Bonhoeffer's poem to her deceased fiancé's parents, Joseph and Mary Lou Bayly, hoping it would comfort their hearts as it had hers. A few years later, the Baylys received a letter from a pastor they knew in Massachusetts. The pastor told of visiting a terminally ill woman in a Boston hospital.

One day, the pastor gave this woman one of Joseph Bayly's books in which he recounts the suffering of his own loss as well as the sufficiency of God's grace and comfort. The woman stayed awake the entire night to read the book and the next day spoke of the comfort it had brought her. A few hours later, she died. That woman was Maria von Wedemever-Weller, the one engaged to be married to Dietrich Bonhoeffer three decades earlier! From Dietrich Bonhoeffer to Maria von Wedemer to Joseph Bayly, Jr's fiancée and then on to his grieving parents, and finally back to Bonhoeffer's one-time fiancé, God's comfort traveled through time and around the world to comfort those who mourn.

HAPPY ARE THE MEEK, NOT THE MIGHTY

Genuine contrition over and confession of sin leads to submission to God and humility before others. That is why Jesus pronounces his third *be-attitude*: "Happy the meek—because they shall inherit the land" (Matthew 5:3, YLT).

Meekness is not weakness. In his book, *The Art of Horsemanship*, the Ancient Greek soldier and writer Xenophon, describes the meticulous process of training war horses.[203] Only the most powerful and most submissive were chosen for such an elite status. These horses were called *praüs*, or "meek." These powerful, thoroughbred stallions were capable of courageously galloping into the heat of battle, but were always under the command of their rider. When a horse reached this level of training, it could be trusted in the heat of battle not to do something stupid or foolish. Meekness is power under authority or strength under control.

To be "poor in spirit" focuses on my sinfulness and leads to brokenness. To be "meek" focuses on God's holiness and leads to submission. Only those who are inwardly strong in Christ can be genuinely meek before others. To grow in meekness is to grow in Christlikeness, which begins with knowing what Christ is like. The meek, gentle King who spoke these beatitudes also modeled these virtues as he presented himself to the Jewish nation: "Say to Daughter Zion, 'See, your king comes to you, gentle and riding on a donkey, and on a colt, the foal of a donkey'" (Matthew 21:5). Little wonder he was rejected. The Zealots of the day were looking for a military messiah. The Pharisees were expecting a miraculous messiah. The Sadducees, who denied the supernatural, wanted a materialistic messiah. The Essenes were looking for a monastic messiah. But Jesus came as the meek Messiah.[204] As such, he invites each of us to journey along the same pathway of meekness—"Take my yoke upon you, and learn of me; for I am meek and lowly in heart: and ye shall find rest unto your souls" (Matthew 11:29, KJV).

Meekness is the blossom of which contentment and peace are the fruit. An attitude of meekness moves our eyes off our difficult circumstances and onto Christ, reminding us of his unfailing care. The meek are assured that if Jesus can bring peace in the midst of a storm, he can certainly bring peace to their hearts. Peter writes, "Cast all your anxiety on him because he cares for you" (1 Peter 5:7). The writer of the third gospel, Luke, uses the same word "cast" to describe the garments the disciples threw on the beast of burden that Jesus rode into Jerusalem (Luke 19:35). We are to do the same with our worries—throw them, unload them on the Lord (Philippians 4:6,7).

The pathway to meekness is the pathway of death to self, but it is also the pathway to happiness. Peter Kreeft states it well when he writes, "The way to perfect joy is incredibly simple. It is simply to die—to die to self-will and self-regard—to say to God, 'Thy will be done,' and mean it. To put God first, to consecrate everything—everything—to him."[205] For those who do, Jesus leaves a promise—*they shall inherit the land*" (Matthew 5:3, YLT). To enter a house is not the same as inheriting that house. So it is with the kingdom of heaven which will someday be established on this earth. Jesus is speaking not only of *entering* his kingdom, but also of the rich reward of *ruling* in his kingdom. Paradoxically, we inherit the promised kingdom not by might but by meekness. Those who will rule in Christ's kingdom are not the mighty, the proud, and the defiant, but the meek, the lowly, and the humble.

HAPPY ARE THE HUNGRY AND THIRSTY

A Christian is *someone* before he does *something*. Those who are helpless because of sin, repentant over sin, and submissive to the One who has conquered sin, are now in a position to hunger and thirst for the opposite of sin, which is righteousness. That is the focus of the fourth *be-attitude*: "Happy those hungering and thirsting for righteousness—because they shall be filled" (Matthew 5:6, YLT).

There are as many human pathways to happiness as there are religions and philosophies in the world. They are all, apart from Christianity, founded on one universal premise: *Happiness is compromised by suffering, and suffering exists to the degree that we have unfulfilled desires.* Since the Fall of mankind, the default pathway in the quest for happiness is the indulgence of self-centered desire. The Greek term for "pleasure" (*hēdonē*) is the source of our word "hedonism," which is the belief that personal pleasure is the highest good. At its core, sensual hedonism attempts to ease suffering by exploiting selfish desires. The Bible has much to say about the hedonistic pathway to happiness, describing it as nothing more than another expression of idolatry. The Apostle Paul speaks of those who are "lovers of pleasure (*hēdonē*) rather than lovers of God" (2 Timothy 3:4).

If hedonism seeks happiness by the indulgence of desire, Buddhism promises happiness by the elimination of desire. The primary quest of Siddhartha Gautama (ca. 600 BC), better known as the Buddha, was to find the answer to the problem of suffering. One day he sat down in full lotus posture under a fig tree, known from then on as the sacred Wisdom Tree, and determined not to rise until he had solved the riddle of suffering. This was the crowning moment of his life when he received the enlightenment for which he was searching. When he finally arose, he proclaimed, "I am Buddha," and enunciated his Four Noble Truths: (1) suffering is omnipresent and is inextricably bound up with individual existence; (2) suffering arises from attachment to desire—a deep, inner craving that ultimately cannot be satisfied; (3) suffering ceases when attachment to desire ceases; and (4) freedom from suffering is possible by practicing the Eightfold Path, a comprehensive course in disciplined self-improvement. This path is a gradual process of desire-reduction leading to the existential state of *Nirvana*, quintessential bliss through the elimination of suffering.[206]

Jesus Christ proposes a pathway to happiness that stands in stark contrast to both hedonism and Buddhism. In this fourth beatitude, he does not teach us to ease suffering by indiscriminately indulging our desires or to eliminate suffering by deadening desire. The Master Teacher instructs us rather to *endure* suffering by having our desires ("hungering" and "thirsting") transformed and reoriented toward the true source of happiness.

As we have seen, Jacob came to this crucial point of passionately *desiring* the Giver of all good gifts more than the gifts themselves. As his desire for lesser pleasures was frustrated, his desire for God increased. The same is true for us. While suffering may strip us of one kind of happiness, God uses it to prepare us for a different kind of happiness that he alone can provide.

Happiness is only as satisfying as its source. The good things of life are given to serve us, but never to ultimately satisfy us. Jesus speaks of the many worries of this life that can so easily occupy our minds in our relentless search for happiness: food, drink, clothes, possessions, and plans for the future (Matthew 6:25-32). Then he reminds us of where our focus should be: "But seek first his kingdom and his righteousness, and all these things will be given to you as well" (v. 33). Righteousness in Matthew's gospel always refers to living in harmony with God and his will (Matthew 3:15). Of course, we cannot do that on our own. That is why in his concluding remarks, Jesus declares himself to be the *only* source of righteousness as well as of happiness: "*Blessed* (happy) are you . . . *because of me*" (Matthew 5:11).

The fact is, happiness eludes those who pursue it as an end in itself. Our pursuit of happiness may put us on the pathway toward God, but it is ultimately the pursuit of the kingdom of God and his righteousness that bring us the happiness for which our souls long. According to Jesus, the degree of authentic happiness derived from certain blessings ("all these things") is determined by the far more noble quest of hungering and thirsting after the Giver of all blessings.

Those who follow this pathway to genuine happiness are called the "generation of Jacob." The psalmist David says, "Such is the generation of those who seek him, who seek your face, God of Jacob" (Psalm 24:6). Those of the generation of Jacob are not satisfied with spiritual snacks to temporarily calm the aching soul. No, they are passionate, like Jacob, who cried out, "I will not let you go until you bless me!" (Genesis 32:26).

We must do the same. As we do, Jesus promises that we will "be filled." But with what? God's righteousness, which alone brings the contentment of happiness. Paul writes, "Godliness with contentment is great gain" (1 Timothy 6:6). If covetousness is misdirected desire, contentment is fulfilled desire. Misdirected desire toward unrighteousness never ultimately gets what it wants. Directed desire toward righteousness ultimately does. To the degree that I drink of the wellspring of true happiness, I no longer desire the broken cisterns of false happiness that can never satisfy. That is why the German mystic Thomas à Kempis (1380-1471) prayed, "Come, O come, for without You there will be no happy day or hour, because You are my happiness and without You my table is empty."[207]

I, too, have found that as my desire for God's secondary blessings is frustrated, my desire for God increases, resulting in contentment and genuine happiness. And as my satisfaction in God increases, so does my enjoyment of his secondary blessings! When I desire to encounter the Blesser more than to experience his blessings, then and only then do the blessings become all the more delectable. This, I believe, is part of what it means to be filled. But it is not the only part. Augustine of Hippo wrote, "Thou hast made us for thyself, O Lord, and our heart is restless until it finds its rest in thee." The final rest of righteousness will be realized when God finally and fully answers our heartfelt cry, "Your kingdom come, your will be done, on earth as it is in heaven" (Matthew 6:10).

HAPPY ARE THE MERCIFUL

The fifth beatitude is the fruit of the first four. When we recognize our helplessness, mourn over our sinfulness, submit to Jesus' lordship in meekness, and hunger and thirst after righteousness, our most natural response is to demonstrate to others the same mercy we have received. Jesus says, "Happy are those who are merciful to others; God will be merciful to them!" (Matthew 5:7, GNT).

Both the Roman and Judaic legal systems were merciless. A Roman philosopher once said, "Mercy is the disease of the soul." The father of a Roman household had the right of *patria potestas*, which allowed him to take the life of a newborn if he didn't want the child. As for his slaves, he could kill them at will and face no legal accusation. This was not a society that favored the biblical concept of mercy.[208] However, the values of Christ's kingdom are quite the opposite. The litmus test of an obedient faith is a merciful heart. The prophet Micah reminds us, "He has shown you, O mortal, what is good. And what does the Lord require of you? To act justly and to love mercy and to walk humbly with your God" (Micah 6:8). Jesus, after telling his disciples to love their enemies and do good to those who hate them, adds, "Be merciful, just as your Father is merciful" (Luke 6:36). And James reminds us that "Mercy triumphs over judgment" (James 2:13). Nowhere do we imitate our Lord more than in showing mercy.

What does it mean to be merciful? The writer to the Hebrew Christians describes Christ as our merciful high priest who is able to help us in our suffering "since he himself has gone through suffering and testing" (Hebrews 2:18, NLT). Grace is God's response toward the guilty. Mercy is God's response toward the needy. Grace deals with the sin that lies behind suffering. Mercy responds to the suffering that ultimately comes from sin. Grace pardons, mercy pities. Mercy is not merely the feeling of sympathy, but the concrete demonstration of compassion. Mercy is meeting the need, not just feeling the need. It is seeing a person without food and providing food. It is encountering someone who is lonely and providing company. It is forgiving what is considered unforgivable. Mercy is the "religion" in which God delights: "Religion that God our Father accepts as pure and faultless is this: to look after orphans and widows in their distress . . ." (James 1:27).

We all want to receive mercy, but it is much harder to give mercy. However, the mercy we receive from God motivates us to identify with the misery and suffering of others. I have found that God can make wise use of my misery to increase my capacity for mercy. Suffering reminds me of the mercy that I have received from my faithful High Priest and that I now have the privilege of extending to others.

Though mercy can be expressed in multiple ways, it flows best through the channels carved in our lives through excruciating circumstances. Amy Carmichael, an Irish missionary to India, endured almost constant pain during the last twenty years of her life. During much of this time, she was confined to her bed. Yet it was during these years that she wrote more than twenty books that have impacted lives around the world. These works are the fruit of her suffering. One of them, *Rose from Brier*, is a compilation of letters to the ill. In the introduction, she writes: "Reading them through I am troubled to find them so personal and sometimes so intimate . . . If I had waited till the harrow had lifted, perhaps a less tired mind would have found a better way. But then the book would have been from the *well* to the ill, and not from the *ill* to the ill, which I think is what it is meant to be—a rose plucked straight from the brier."[209] For Amy, the "harrow" (distress) never lifted. Neither has the ministry of mercy she brought to so many through her compassionate writings.

Jesus promises that those who extend mercy will receive mercy—"for they will have mercy shown to them." In the kingdoms of this world, mercy does not necessarily carry its own reward. Jesus had mercy upon the sick and demon possessed, the blind and lame, the publicans and prostitutes. In return, what did he receive? Not mercy, but death! However, in the merciful kingdom of God, mercy engenders mercy. Jesus is not saying that mercy is based on merit. It is not "earned mercy," which would be a contradiction in terms. It is rather an enticing description of the happy state of the kingdom of heaven that offers what an unmerciful world never can—mercy upon mercy throughout eternity.[210]

HAPPY ARE THE HOLY

Inner righteousness always precedes outward righteousness. That is why Jesus reminds us, "Happy are the pure in heart; they will see God!" (Matthew 5:8, GNT). The sage Solomon reminds us, "Above all else, guard your heart, for everything you do flows from it" (Proverbs 4:23). As the seat of our deepest longings, the heart must be kept *pure*—a word derived from the Greek term *katharsis* (catharsis). The pure in heart experience an ongoing spiritual catharsis involving inner purification that results in outward transformation of life and character. Their lives are marked by singleness of purpose, a heart undivided in its devotion to God (Matthew 22:37). For this reason, any expression of idolatry always compromises purity of heart. The psalmist asks, "Who may ascend the mountain of the Lord? Who may stand in his holy place? The one who has clean hands and a pure heart, who does not trust in an idol or swear by a false god" (Psalm 24:3-4).

Saint Augustine defined idolatry as worshiping what should be used or using what should be worshiped.[211] We do the former when we take what is to be used—money, possessions, career, sports, family, music, etc.—and put it in the place of God. In doing so, we are "worshiping and serving created things rather than the Creator" (Romans 1:25). While God has given all things to enjoy, anything that displaces God's supremacy in our lives is a form of idolatry.

Worshiping what should be used focuses on material objects of God. Using what should be worshiped focuses on false mental images of God. Fallen humanity innately wants a god he can manipulate. Indeed, the word "idol" signifies "something to be seen." The idols of the Ancient Near East were normally chiseled into some likeness out of wood or stone and covered with a precious metal (Isaiah 44:9-20). The purpose was to make the intangible tangible and the invisible visible, bringing one's "god" or "gods" down to a manageable position. That's why the pagans had so many gods. No one god could provide all the benefits the adherent desired!

As we have seen in the life of Jacob, a subtle tendency exists in all of us to want to *use* God more than we want to *worship* God. This is because what we think we need so often blinds us to what we really need (Revelation 3:14-21). According to James, such subtle forms of idolatry can even affect the way we pray: "You do not have, because you do not ask God. When you ask, you do not receive, because you ask with wrong motives, that you may spend what you get on your pleasures" (James 4:2-3). Author Jill Briscoe captures well this tendency when she writes:

> When we pray for ourselves, our petitions usually center around what we think we need or what we are sure so-and-so needs. God sees needs in our lives that are far more urgent than those we have written on our heavenly supermarket list and daily present to our 'Need-Meeter' in the sky. Our need for changed attitudes, a new acceptance of someone we have been rejecting, our need to be 'cut down to size'—these are not things we pray for too readily. On the other hand, we do find we can pray these things for other people![212]

Idolatry is placing God at my disposal. Worship is placing myself at God's disposal. John Calvin once famously said, "The human heart is a perpetual idol factory."[213] Knowing this pernicious tendency of the human heart, the Apostle John writes, "Dear children, keep yourselves from idols" (1 John 5:21).

In the search for happiness, our idols will always betray us. But God never does. In his futile attempt to run from God, the prodigal prophet Jonah exclaimed from the belly of the whale, "Those who cling to worthless idols turn away from God's love for them" (Jonah 2:8)—the very love that alone can fully satisfy the deepest longings of the human heart. The well-known prodigal son did the same. When hungry, he fed on the leftover husks in the pig pen. But when he came to his senses and recognized that he was spiritually famished, he passionately pursued the path back to his loving father (Luke 15).

We must not miss the paradox of Jesus' promise. Though an idol is "something to be seen," it is *not* the idolaters who will see God, but rather the pure in heart. Jacob could not see the face of God without throwing off the idols of his heart (Genesis 31:19; 35:2). Neither can we. When responded to in the light of God's truth, suffering disappointment in life takes the mask off the idolatrous thought that ultimate happiness can be found apart from God. For this reason, suffering provides the opportunity to discover our deepest desire for the highest blessing God wants to give us—an encounter with himself.[214]

HAPPY ARE THE PEACEMAKERS

The God of the Bible is a God of peace. The prophet Isaiah tells us that the Messiah is the "Prince of peace" (Isaiah 9:6). Apostle Paul writes, "Now the God of peace be with you all" (Romans 15:33). And the author of Hebrews speaks of Christ as the "Lord of peace" (Hebrews 13:20). It's understandable, then, that those who make peace are called "children of God." In Jesus' sixth pronouncement of happiness, he says, "Happy are those who work for peace; God will call them his children!" (Matthew 5:9, GNT).

Peace is more than the absence of conflict; it is the presence of righteousness that results in right relationships. When a Jew says to another, "Shalom," he's not saying, "May you have no war." He means, "May you have all the righteousness and goodness God intends for you." For this reason, the peace of God must never be confused with the appeasement of man. Appeasement makes concessions to gloss over a relational problem. Christ went to the cross to resolve a relational problem, securing peace between God and mankind (2 Corinthians 5:19; Ephesians 2:14-16).

The Bible speaks of three kinds of peace: peace *with* God, peace *of* God, and peace *with* others. The latter—in any durable sense—is dependent upon the first two. Moreover, peace with God depends on being made right with God: "Therefore, since we have been made right in God's sight by faith, we have peace with God because of what Jesus Christ our Lord has done for us" (Romans 5:1).

The same grace that makes peace *with* God possible also makes the peace *of* God available as we walk and grow through suffering. Elsewhere, Paul reminds us: "Do not be anxious about anything, but in every situation, by prayer and petition, with thanksgiving, present your requests to God. And the peace of God, which transcends all understanding, will guard your hearts and minds in Christ Jesus" (Philippians 4:6-7). The result of not worrying about anything, praying about everything, and giving thanks in all things is peace. Like sentinels stationed on a city wall, peace protects our hearts and minds.

Those who know peace with God and the peace of God are best prepared to make peace with others, both believer and unbeliever alike (Colossians 3:15). Irenaeus (ca. 130-202 AD) was bishop of Lugdunum in Gaul (now Lyon, France). His name means "peacemaker," and he had several opportunities to live up to his name. One of these occurred when Pope Victor I, bishop of Rome (189-199 AD), threatened to excommunicate from the church the Christians from Asia Minor who used a different dating of Easter. Though strict in matters of essential doctrine, Irenaeus stood for tolerance in minor issues and convinced Victor to exercise a more conciliatory approach. It may be that the pre-reformer Erasmus referred to this occasion when, at the end of his introduction to his edition of *Against Heresies*, he prayed God would raise some new peacemakers like Irenaeus to bring peace to his troubled times.[215] His prayer is just as relevant today.

The legacy left to us by Jesus and the apostles is a pair of shoes that speak of peace. We make peace as we share the gospel of peace with those who are searching for peace. More than seven centuries before Christ, the prophet Isaiah wrote, "How beautiful on the mountains are the feet of those who bring good news, who proclaim peace" (Isaiah 52:17).

In speaking of our spiritual armor as defense against Satan's ferocious attacks, Paul makes the same connection between our feet and peace: "Stand your ground . . . For shoes, put on the peace that comes from the Good News so that you will be fully prepared" (Ephesians 6:14-15). Roman soldiers were equipped with a type of half boot made of leather and tied to the ankles with ornamental leather straps. The soles of these boots were studded with nails giving the soldier a firm, solid stand that kept him from sliding. The shoes of peace we have available provide firm footing and equip us to be agents of peace in a suffering world, knowing that "The God of peace will soon crush Satan under your [our] feet" (Romans 16:20).

In this world we have trouble, but in Jesus—who has overcome the world—we have peace (John 16:33). There is no better reason to be happy!

HAPPY ARE THE HARASSED

G. K. Chesterton (1874-1936) has been credited with saying, "Jesus promised His disciples three things—that they would be completely fearless, absurdly happy, and in constant trouble."[216] He was right. In this eighth and last beatitude Jesus says: "Happy are those who are persecuted because they do what God requires; the Kingdom of heaven belongs to them!" (Matthew 5:10, GNT).

How can peacemakers be such troublemakers? It only follows that those who hunger and thirst *after* righteousness will be persecuted *for* righteousness. Such expression of hatred is the natural result of the conflict of two irreconcilable value systems—the kingdom of Christ and the kingdom of this world. The puritan writer Thomas Watson (1620-1686) describes it this way: "Though they be ever so meek, merciful, pure in heart, their piety will never shield them from suffering . . . The way to heaven is by the way of thorns and blood . . . Set it down as a maxim, if you will follow Christ, you will see the swords and staves. Put the cross in your creed."[217]

Of course, Jesus had already alerted his disciples to this inevitability: "Then you will be handed over to be persecuted and put to death, and you will be hated by all nations because of me" (Matthew 24:9). What Jesus predicted proved true. According to the biblical account and reliable tradition, the majority of Jesus' inner band of disciples suffered martyrdom. Peter was crucified upside down. James (the Elder) was beheaded by Herod. Andrew was crucified on a cross in the form of an X. Philip died a martyr at Hierapolis. Bartholomew was beaten to death in Armenia. Thomas suffered martyrdom in India. Matthew died a martyr in Ethiopia. James (the Younger) was crucified in Egypt. Jude died a martyr in Persia. Simon (the Zealot) was crucified. Matthias preached and suffered martyrdom in Ethiopia. And the Apostle Paul was beheaded by Nero's order in Rome. Only the much loved disciple, John, died a natural death. The ensuing generation of disciples were also not exempt from such persecution. *Foxe's Book of Martyrs* gives us a graphic description of the suffering experienced by believers throughout the Roman world:

> This monarch [Nero] . . . gave way to the greatest extravagancy of temper, and to the most atrocious barbarities . . . In particular, he had some sewed up in skins of wild beasts, and then worried [strangled] by dogs until they expired; and others dressed in shirts made stiff with wax, fixed to axletrees, and set on fire in his gardens, in order to illuminate them. This persecution was general throughout the whole Roman Empire.[218]

The world of today is no exception. More than 340 million Christians live in places where they experience high levels of persecution and discrimination.[219]

Why should the harassed be so happy? Jesus underscores the answer to that question when he adds a double pronouncement of happiness over those persecuted: "Happy are you when people insult you and persecute you and tell all kinds of evil lies against you *because you are my followers*" (Matthew 5:11, GNT). This is indeed a *different* kind of happiness! It first looks back, identifying us with our Pioneer in suffering, Jesus Christ. "Suffering becomes the identifying mark of a follower of Christ . . ." writes Dietrich Bonhoeffer. "The disciple is not above his master."[220] But it also looks forward to the promised eternal reward. Jesus continues, "Be happy and glad, *for a great reward is kept for you in heaven*" (Matthew 5:12, GNT). The hope of eternal reward in the future brings unprecedented happiness in the present. As mentioned earlier, the beatitudes describe the type of person who—not only enters—but is ready to rule in God's Kingdom. We enter the kingdom by grace through faith; we rule and receive reward in the kingdom to the degree that we are willing to associate with the Pioneer of our faith, the model martyr, Jesus Christ.

Unfortunately, a misinterpretation of Jesus' words led some in the early history of the church to actively pursue persecution and even martyrdom. When Origen, the famous theologian of the third century, was only seventeen years old, his father was sentenced to death. Origen said, "Tomorrow when my father is burned at the stake, I will go there and provoke the governor to have me martyred too." To spare his life, his mother took all his clothes out of the house during the night so that the next morning Origen had nothing to put on![221] But this is not the intent of Jesus' words. We are not to pursue persecution anymore than we are to pursue happiness—*as an end in itself.* In this life, both coexist and are experienced to the degree that our ultimate satisfaction is found in one person, Jesus Christ (2 Timothy 3:12). Whatever our circumstances, if we are not living for Jesus in the present, we will never be ready to die for Jesus in the future.

Yes, since the loss of my firstborn, I have not experienced a day of happiness as I once knew it. But every day I am coming to experience more of a different kind of happiness as God intended it. This sort of happiness is upside down and from the inside out. It's profound, radical, surprisingly paradoxical, and ever-growing. It's offered to all, yet experienced by relatively few.

If our ultimate goal is maximum happiness with minimum difficulty *in this life*, then the promises of Jesus in the Beatitudes will ring hollow. Of the eight Beatitudes, six relate happiness to something yet to be fully experienced in the future. On the other hand, if our ultimate goal is the kind of happiness that glorifies our happy God and deeply satisfies the human soul, we'll keep our eyes on all that God promises for us in the next life.

CHAPTER 10

Homesick for Heaven

If you read history, you will find that the Christians
who did most for the present world were just those who thought
most of the next . . . It is since Christians have largely ceased
to think of the other world that they have become so ineffective
in this. Aim at Heaven and you'll get earth 'thrown in':
aim at earth and you will get neither.
—C. S. Lewis

That person will receive the crown of life
that the Lord has promised to those who love him.
—James the Just (James 1:12)

For centuries, the people of Spain proudly viewed their country and culture as the last frontier. Beyond them, so they thought, was nothing but the vast expanse of endless sea. They were so convinced of this that they imprinted their coins with a picture of the fabled Pillars of Hercules, those two stalwart sentries on either side of the Straits of Gibraltar. Underneath that image they inscribed in Latin *ne plus ultra*— nothing beyond. The dictum was even inscribed on their maps and eventually became Spain's national motto. From their perspective, Spain with her famed pillars proudly marked the end of the earth.

Of course, there was only one problem. "In 1492, Columbus sailed the ocean blue" and discovered the boastful claim—*ne plus ultra*—was an illusion. The discovery of worlds beyond humbled the Spaniards to the point where they took the little negative "*ne*" off their coinage. *Ne plus ultra* (nothing beyond) became *plus ultra* (more beyond).

When it comes to the subject of death, many live with the perspective of *ne plus ultra*—nothing beyond. For others, there is the impression that something lies beyond death's door, but just what that something is remains quite vague. The French physician and humanist Rabelais (1483-1553) once quipped: "I am going to the great perhaps." The poet Edgar Allen Poe (1809-1849), who was never at a loss for words, simply said, "Rest, shore, no more." (At least it rhymed!) The famed musician Beethoven (1770-1827) casually joked on his deathbed: "Clap now, my friends, the comedy is done!"[222]

Such statements stand in stark contrast to that of the well-known nineteenth-century evangelist, D. L. Moody, who on his deathbed said, "Earth recedes . . . Heaven opens before me! This is my crowning day!"[223] It is of that "crowning day" that James speaks when he writes, "Blessed [happy] is the one who perseveres under trial because, having stood the test, that person will receive the crown of life that the Lord has promised to those who love him" (James 1:12). James encourages us to patiently endure suffering because he knows that it will result in greater maturity leading to a different kind of happiness in this life as well as eternal reward in the next (Figure 2, page 150).

James' words immediately transport us beyond this life into the *plus ultra*. He wants to radically transform our myopic earth-bound perspective in the face of suffering into an expansive, expectant, faith-filled assurance of what lies beyond our limited, terrestrial existence. The Bible promises eternal life for those who believe in Christ. It also promises eternal reward for those who persevere with Christ. God has indeed "set eternity in the human heart" (Ecclesiastes 3:11). Therefore, we must learn to view the temporal in light of the eternal, the earthly in light of the heavenly, the present in light of the future.

The Apostle Paul views present suffering from this same futuristic perspective when he writes, "I consider that our present sufferings are not worth comparing with the glory that will be revealed in us" (Romans 8:18). Commenting on this verse, C. S. Lewis observes, "If this is so, a book on suffering which says nothing of heaven, is leaving out almost the whole of one side of the account. Scripture and tradition habitually put the joys of heaven into the scale against the sufferings of earth, and no solution of the problem of pain which does not do so can be called a Christian one."[224]

I, too, must not leave out the "whole of one side of the account." Just what does the Bible say about the joys of heaven in comparison to the sufferings of earth?

ABSENT FROM THE BODY, HOME WITH THE LORD

We must never minimize the awful tragedy of death. Author Joseph Bayly, who grieved the death of three of his seven children, writes: "Birth and death enclose man in a sort of parenthesis of the present. And the brackets at beginning and end of life are still impenetrable . . . We may postpone it, we may tame its violence, but death is still there waiting for us. Death always waits. The door of the hearse is never closed."[225]

Death is inevitable, but death is *not* invincible. Death is evil's trump card; only the supernatural can trump death. And it has! God stands appalled by death, is grieved by death, but has also determined to defeat the sting of death once and for all. Paul asks, "Where, O death, is your victory? Where, O death, is your sting?" (1 Corinthians 15:55). Once a honeybee stings, it no longer has the power to sting again. Having left its sting once for all in the God-Man, Jesus Christ, death can no longer eternally harm God's children. That is why, as I hesitantly reached out to touch Jonathan's cold, lifeless frame, I repeated to myself Paul's reassuring words: "Away from the body and at home with the Lord" (2 Corinthians 5:8). The body is but a shell, an "earthly tent" (2 Corinthians 5:1). In death, Jonathan was delivered from death by death . . . the death of another. And that One, Jesus Christ, now lives that death may die.

In light of these truths, I can sincerely affirm that *the day my son died was the best day he ever lived.* The same is true for all who place their faith in Jesus Christ. That is why Lutheran pastor and theologian Dietrich Bonhoeffer could pray just before he was hanged by the Nazis, "Oh, God, this is the end; but for me it is just the beginning." With this perspective, the New Testament writers describe the death of Christians as an "exodus," a "departure," or as "sleep." For unbelievers, death begins the night that has no sunrise; but for Christ followers, death begins the day that has no sunset.

DEATH IS AN "EXODUS"

Imagine being sentenced to death with others in a dark, damp dungeon with no hope of deliverance. Suddenly and unexpectedly, someone finds an escape hatch and he's gone! It appears at first that he *alone* has avoided the irreversible sentence of death. But then . . . he looks down through the hatch with a huge grin on his face, reaches out his hand, and says, "Trust me and come on up! I've provided the way of escape from inevitable doom!"

Jesus Christ, the "first fruits" and guarantee of our exodus from death, has done just that. "For in Adam all die, so in Christ all will be made alive. But each in turn: Christ, the first fruits; then, when he comes, those who belong to him" (1 Corinthians 15:22-23).

When Jesus was transfigured before his disciples, Moses and Elijah also appeared as they spoke "of His departure (*exodus*) which He was about to accomplish at Jerusalem" (Luke 9:31, NASB). Apparently, Jesus' death was going to accomplish something significant—the possibility for his followers to experience a similar "exodus" from the dungeon of sin and death. Peter also speaks of his impending death by martyrdom as an exodus from this earthly life: "And I will make every effort to see that after my departure (*exodus*) you will always be able to remember these things" (2 Peter 1:14). Just as the Israelites made their exodus from suffering in Egypt into a land flowing with milk and honey, death for the believer is a welcomed exit from the afflictions of this earthly pilgrimage into the promised delights of heaven. For as Paul writes, "We long for our bodies to be released from sin and suffering" (Romans 8:23, NLT).

Such an exodus from our painful earth-bound limp seems to be the emphasis of the prophet Isaiah's words, which brought great comfort to me and my wife following our son's "premature" death: "Good people pass away; the godly often die before their time. But no one seems to care or wonder why. No one seems to understand that God is protecting them from the evil to come. For those who follow godly paths will rest in peace when they die" (Isaiah 57:1-2, NLT).

Though the prophet is speaking in the context of impending judgment on Judah in the seventh century BC, the principle he describes is timeless and applicable today. The French reformer John Calvin (1509-1564) applies this verse to Martin Luther's (1483-1546) death when he writes:

> In our own times a remarkable instance of this was given in the death of Luther, who was snatched from the world a short time before that terrible calamity befell Germany, which he had foretold many years before, when he exclaimed loudly against that contempt of the Gospel, and that wickedness and licentiousness which everywhere prevailed. Frequently had he entreated the Lord to call him out of this life before he beheld that dreadful punishment, the anticipation of which filled him with trembling and horror. And he obtained it

from the Lord. Soon after his death, lo, a sudden and unforeseen war sprang up, by which Germany was terribly afflicted, when nothing was farther from her thoughts than the dread of such a calamity . . . We ought, therefore, to consider diligently the works of the Lord, both in the life and in the death of the "righteous," but especially in their death, by which the Lord calls them away to a better life.[226]

The "sudden and unforeseen war" to which Calvin referred was most likely the Schmalkaldic War (1546-1547) that was but a precursor to the Thirty Years' War (1618-1648), one of the longest and most brutal in human history resulting in famine and disease throughout much of Europe. Irrespective of the specific circumstances, death for a Christ follower is an exodus, a welcome release from this world of agony and grief.

DEATH IS A "DEPARTURE"
The Bible not only views the believer's death as an exodus from evil and suffering, but as a departure for heaven and happiness. Only months before his execution, Paul writes to Timothy, his protégé in the faith, "For I am already being poured out like a drink offering, and the time for my *departure* (*analusis*) is near" (2 Timothy 4:6).

Previous to the period of the New Testament, the word "departure" described the pulling up of stakes when breaking camp or the loosening of the ropes and cables when a ship weighed anchor and set out to sea. Though we are presently anchored to the hardships and heartaches of our earthly existence, death is but the loosening of the ropes and weighing anchor. With a mere blast of wind in the sails, the believer will be off to his heavenly home.

I have frequently cited at funerals a poem entitled "Gone From My Sight," which beautifully describes what it means for a Christian to die:

I'm standing on the seashore. A ship at my side spreads her white sails to the morning breeze and starts for the blue ocean. She's an object of beauty and strength and I stand and watch her until, at length, she hangs like a speck of white cloud just where the sea and the sky come down to mingle with each other. And then I hear someone at my side saying, "There, she's gone." Gone where? Gone from my sight, that is all. She is just as large in mast and hull and spar as she was when she left my side. And just as able to bear her load of freight to the place of destination. Her diminished size is in me, not in her. And just at that moment when someone at my side says, "There she's gone," there are other eyes watching her coming, and there are other voices ready to take up the glad shout, "Here she comes!" And that is— dying.[227]

DEATH IS "SLEEP"

For some, death is but an endless "sleep" in which body and soul are extinguished forever. The Latin poet Catullus (84 BC-AD 54) wrote, "The sun can set and rise again, but once our brief light sets, there is one unending night to be slept through."[228] Such a fatalistic perspective of the afterlife pervaded the first century world. An inscription from first century Greece reads, "I was not, I became, I am not, I care not."[229]

But God cares!

In writing to the Thessalonian believers, Paul speaks of those who "sleep in death" (1 Thessalonians 4:13). Some years later, he pens these words to the Corinthian believers: "We will not all sleep, but we will all be changed" (1 Corinthians 15:51). Some have concluded from these verses that at the moment of death one enters a state of unconscious existence described as "soul sleep." However, many passages of

Scripture confirm that a person's soul or spirit experiences *conscious* existence following physical death. For example:

- "The dust returns to the ground it came from, and the spirit returns to God who gave it" (Ecclesiastes 12:7);
- Lazarus and the rich man were fully conscious in the afterlife (Luke 16:22-31);
- Jesus told the dying thief on the cross, "Today you will be with me in paradise" (Luke 23:43);
- Paul said that to die was to be "with Christ" (Philippians 1:23);
- To be absent from the body is to be present with the Lord (2 Corinthians 5:8);
- The martyrs in heaven are described as praying to God, asking questions, feeling sorrow, and remembering their lives on earth (Revelation 6:9-11).

When speaking of those who "sleep in death," Paul is speaking figuratively of the temporary "sleep" of the body, *not* that of the soul. The imagery is telling—when a family member falls asleep at night, you expect that person to wake up in the morning! The grave is nothing more than a temporary dormitory in the ground for the *body* that "sleeps" now, but will awake in the day of resurrection. On the other hand, the soul never passes into an unconscious existence or "spiritual coma," whether for the believer or unbeliever (Luke 16:19-31). If, when Christ returns, God "brings with Jesus those who have fallen asleep in him" (1 Thessalonians 4:14), then it follows that between the moment of a believer's death and Christ's return, the believer is with Christ—alive, conscious, and enjoying the benefits of heaven.

Exodus. Departure. Sleep. That is why I didn't "lose" my son, for I know where he is! Calvin Miller, in his book *The Divine Symphony,* poetically describes the passage from death to life for the believer:

I once scorned ev'ry fearful thought of death,
When it was but the end of pulse and breath,
But now my eyes have seen that past the pain
There is a world that's waiting to be claimed.
Earthmaker, Holy, let me now depart,
For living's such a temporary art.
And dying is but getting dressed for God,
Our graves are merely doorways cut in sod.[230]

Unbelievers are living (somewhat) on the way to dying; believers in the resurrected Christ are dying on the way to truly living. When a believer passes into the presence of Christ, it is the happiest moment of his life. At that moment, Jesus says, "Come and share your Master's happiness" (Matthew 25:21).

With this conviction, the Puritan pastor Richard Baxter (1615-1691) wrote, "The day of death is to true believers a day of happiness and joy."[231] Centuries earlier the psalmist declared, "Precious in the sight of the Lord is the death of his faithful servants" (Psalm 116:15). Does this not explain why there are no birth dates—only *death* dates— inscribed on the graves of those buried in the Christian catacombs in Italy? The important date for those first century Christians was not their day of birth, but their day of death. The same is true for every believer in Jesus Christ. Death is our day of exodus and weighing anchor. It is merely the sleep of the body as we await the next best day of our lives—the day of resurrection. No wonder Paul can say, "I desire to depart and be with Christ, which is better by far" (Philippians 1:23).

A HEAVENLY WINK

On one occasion, the rationalistic Sadducees, who denied the resurrection as well as any sense of continued personal existence after death, posed to Jesus a trick question concerning the afterlife (Matthew 22:23-33). Though their thorny question concerned marriage in heaven, it revealed their ignorance

259

of the Old Testament teaching regarding life after the grave. Jesus' response cuts to the chase, pointing their (and our) attention to truth that brings comfort in the face of death: "But about the resurrection of the dead—have you not read what God said to you, 'I am the God of Abraham, the God of Isaac, and the God of Jacob'? He is not the God of the dead but of the living" (vv. 32-33).

I recently experienced what I consider to be a "heavenly wink," reminding me that God is indeed the God of the living, not the dead. During a visit to family in Tennessee, I was sharing with two of my grandchildren, Jonathan (named after his uncle, Jonathan) and Rachel, some of my experiences as a child of their age. Upon mentioning that I had attended a school called Brainerd (Chattanooga, Tennessee), Jonathan's eyes lit up with excitement: *"Grandad, several weeks ago I found a lost ring that apparently belonged to somebody from a school with that name!"*

Jonathan excitedly explained that he and his friends sometimes looked for crawfish in a nearby creek. One day, having displaced a rock with his handcrafted pole, he curiously spotted something shiny. Lifting it up by the end of his stick, he surprisingly discovered it was a well preserved girl's graduation ring. The inscription read: *Brainerd High School, 1963*.

The intrigue was captivating. *"Jonathan, this is absolutely amazing,"* I replied. *"My oldest sister, Jeanie Stevens, graduated from Brainerd High School in 1963. What a coincidence!"*

The intense surprise in his eyes told me there was yet more to the story. After informing me that he had done his research and had discovered that at that time there were no other schools in the country with the same name, he added: *"Grandad, get this . . . there are three letters inscribed on the inside of the ring, J.H.S. Could it be that?"*

By this time, my jaw had dropped and chills of incredulity swept through my body. My sister's maiden name is . . . *J*eanie *H*arrison *S*tevens.

How did my sister's ring travel 120 miles from Chattanooga, Tennessee to Mount Juliet (near Nashville, Tennessee) and end up fifty-eight years later under a rock in a creek in my grandson's neighborhood? I may never know. And what are the chances that my grandson would discover it as he hunted crawfish? Or that I would just happen to mention the word "Brainerd," evoking the connection with this most amazing scenario?

Coincidence? Divine providence? Loving reminder?

I favor the latter two. You see, seven years prior to this discovery Jeanie weighed anchor and made her exodus from this world of pain and suffering toward her heavenly home after a long battle with leukemia. While her body "sleeps" in the ground— awaiting the day of resurrection—her spirit lives in Christ's presence. Her ring, once lost now found, is a touching reminder that God cares—*really* cares—for each one of us with an eternal love. He's concerned about every detail of life on planet earth, like hungry crowds (John 6) and falling sparrows (Matthew 6). If He can provide the needed temple tax in a fish's mouth (Matthew 17:24-27), he can lovingly lead a twelve-year-old boy to discover a long lost ring under a rock in order to say, "*I am the God of the living, not the dead.*"

NEW HEAVENS, NEW EARTH

All of history is moving toward the ultimate goal of a restored and reconciled universe when all things will be "summed up" in Christ. What went down with mankind in the Fall will ultimately come back up in the resurrection of redeemed humanity destined to inhabit a restored and reconciled universe (Romans 8:18-21). The Apostle Paul describes it this way: "He thought of everything, provided for everything we could possibly need, letting us in on the plans he took such delight in making. He set it all out before us in Christ, a long-range plan in which everything would be brought together and summed up in him, everything in deepest heaven, everything on planet earth." (Ephesians 1:9-10, The Message).

When the Greeks added numbers, they would list them in a column as we do today. Then, rather than writing the sum of the numbers *under* the column, they would draw a line at the top of the column and above that line place the sum of the numbers. They "summed up" rather than "summed down." In Paul's words to the Ephesians, Jesus Christ is pictured at the *top* of the column, above the summation line of *all* things. When will this take place? "When the kingdom of this world has become the kingdom of our Lord and of his Messiah" (Revelation 11:15).

What will Christ's eternal kingdom look like? Is heaven some type of nebulous sphere of existence above the clouds? Will believers live eternally in a disembodied state, floating about in space or flitting from cloud to cloud? In answer to those questions, the Bible speaks of the future *restoration* of all things: "Heaven must receive him until the time comes for God to restore everything, as he promised long ago through his holy prophets" (Acts 3:21). Randy Alcorn writes, "This cosmic restoration is not God bringing disembodied people to fellowship with him in a spirit realm. Rather, it is God returning humankind to what we once were—what he designed us to be—and to something far greater. It means that the entire physical universe will not just go back to its pre-Fall glory but forward to something even more magnificent."[232] Such will entail a full restoration of the three integral aspects of who we are as the image of God: *resemblance, relationship*, and *rule*.

TRANSFORMED INTO HIS LIKENESS

Mankind was originally created as the likeness-image of God, and it is to the likeness-image of our Creator that the new humanity will be finally restored (Colossians 3:10). While never created to *be* gods, we were created to be *like* God. The template for our life both now and after death is that of the perfect man, Jesus Christ.

As we have seen, our contemplation of Christ in the present will ultimately result in our complete transformation into the image of Christ in the future (2 Corinthians 3:18). The Apostle Paul tells us, "And just as we have borne the image of the earthly man, so shall we bear the image of the heavenly man" (1 Corinthians 15:49). John adds, "Dear friends, now we are children of God, and what we will be has not yet been made known. But we know that when Christ appears, we shall be like him, for we shall see him as he is" (1 John 3:2).

The experience of seeing God is what theologians through the centuries have called the "beatific vision." The expression comes from three Latin words that together signify "A happy-making sight." To see God is to enter into his happiness. But it is also to be transformed into his likeness—*we shall be like him.* "The vision of God has a transforming power," writes F. J. Boudreaux. "Thus the soul, because she only sees God as He is, is filled to overflowing with all knowledge; she becomes beautiful with the beauty of God, rich with His wealth, holy with His holiness, and happy with His unutterable happiness."[233] As we have seen, in everything God is constantly and actively at work with those who love him and with one grand purpose in mind—*conformity to the image of Christ* (Romans 8:28-29). Though this takes place partially and progressively in this life, it will be achieved ultimately in the next.

Conformity to the image of the resurrected Christ necessitates the *physical* resurrection of his followers. Yes, the day my son died was the best day he ever lived, but it was not the best day he *will* ever live. That day will be when his earthly body is resurrected and transformed into a heavenly body. The same holds true for every Christ follower. As previously noted, the historical, bodily resurrection of Jesus Christ at daybreak on that first Easter morning is proof positive that "He has done it!" (Psalm 22:31). His bodily resurrection is the guarantee of the future bodily resurrection to life of those who believe.

There are multiple passages in the Bible that speak of the resurrection of the body for believer and unbeliever alike.[234] One day, God will resurrect from dust those who through death have returned to dust. Our earthly bodies are temporary and (for believers) will be replaced by an immortal, spiritual body suitable for our heavenly dwelling. No one is fully human without both body and spirit. The gospel is good news, and from the standpoint of the biblical writers, spending eternity in a disembodied state would not be good news at all!

What will our resurrected bodies look like?

Though the Bible doesn't tell us in specific terms, it's important to remember that the Scriptures speak of resurrection, *not* reconstruction. Though we have earthly tents today, we will have heavenly bodies tomorrow (2 Corinthians 5:1-5). Paul describes it this way: "But someone may ask, 'How will the dead be raised? What kind of bodies will they have?' What a foolish question . . . what you put in the ground is not the plant that will grow, but only a bare seed of wheat or whatever you are planting. Then God gives it the new body he wants it to have. A different plant grows from each kind of seed" (1 Corinthians 15:35-38, NLT).

The resurrection of the body is like a plant that grows from a seed. The dead body is the "seed," the resurrected body is the "flower" that comes from the seed. The flower is not identical to the seed that was planted. A believer's resurrected body will be a *spiritual* body, but a body nonetheless—a resurrected "upgrade!"

John G. Patton (1824-1907) was a Scottish missionary to the South Seas. Upon leaving his home to preach to the cannibalistic peoples of the New Hebrides Islands, a well-meaning church member tried to discourage him, saying, "The cannibals, the cannibals! You will be eaten by the cannibals!" Without hesitation, Patton replied, "I confess to you that if I can live and die serving the Lord Jesus Christ, it makes no difference to me whether I am eaten by cannibals or by worms; for in that Great Day of Resurrection, my body will rise as fair as yours in the likeness of our risen Redeemer!"[235]

A resurrected body is a healed body. Every healing Christ performed while on earth was a memorial to the Eden that was and a signpost to the New Eden that will be.[236] In describing the New Eden upon earth, the prophet-seer John writes, "On each side of the river stood the tree of life, bearing twelve crops of fruit, yielding its fruit every month. And the leaves of the tree are for the healing of the nations" (Revelation 22:2). The graphic imagery reminds us that God will bring lasting healing to every "limp" we have suffered in this life, whether physical or otherwise. In C. S. Lewis' *The Last Battle* Lord Digory says he and Lady Polly have been "unstiffened" upon entering heaven. That will describe every believer in heaven. The well-known author, Joni Eareckson Tada, a quadriplegic since the age of 17, writes,

> I still can hardly believe it. I, with shrivelled, bent fingers, atrophied muscles, gnarled knees, and no feeling from the shoulders down, will one day have a new body, light, bright, and clothed in righteous-ness—powerful and dazzling. Can you imagine the hope this gives someone spinal-cord injured like me? Or someone who is cerebral palsied, brain-injured, or who has multiple sclerosis? Imagine the hope this gives someone who is manic-depressive. No other religion, no other philosophy promises new bodies, hearts, and minds. Only in the Gospel of Christ do hurting people find such incredible hope.[237]

In heaven, every disabled body, wounded heart, and troubled mind will experience the healing touch of our loving Creator. While suffering exile on the island of Patmos, the Apostle

John writes: "He will wipe away every tear from their eyes. There will be no more death or mourning or crying or pain, for the old order of things has passed away" (Revelation 21:4). In heaven, all that defines our personhood as the image of God—our capacity to think, feel, desire, and choose—will be fully restored to their greatest and purest capacity and in perfect alignment with God's intentions! As a result, we will fully know in heaven the different kind of happiness we have only partially known on earth.

We will have healed *minds*. In the next world, many of our question marks concerning evil and suffering in the present world will be turned into exclamation points. As for our unanswered questions, we will continue to learn throughout the coming ages more and more of the incomparable riches of God's unfathomable grace (Ephesians 2:7). There will always be *plus ultra* when it comes to knowing God. Jonathan Edwards describes it as "a never-ending, ever-increasing discovery of more and more of God's glory with greater and greater joy in him."[238] However, God will *not* do a memory wipe of our minds. We will live in *truth,* which means literally "to stop forgetting."[239] The pierced hands and side of Christ's resurrected body will always remind us of the suffering that not only resulted from sin and evil, but ultimately conquered both (John 20:24-29). Could it not be that our future glory will so eclipse the evil and suffering of our present existence that in some unimaginable way even the memory of evil will not darken our hearts but only make us more satisfied and happy in our Savior?[240]

We will have healed *emotions*. Not only is there hope *in* the mourning of this life, there is sheer, pure happiness *after* the mourning of this life. The Zozias and Claires of this world will agonize no more over the demonically inspired abuse experienced in the wilderness of the old earth. As Isaiah prophesied long ago, "He will wipe away the tears from everyone's eyes and take away the disgrace his people have suffered throughout the world" (Isaiah 25:8, GNT). Heaven's happiness, however, will not depend on our ignorance. The eighteenth century evangelist George Whitefield (1714-1770) once said, "I believe it will be one part of our happiness in heaven, to take a view of, and look back upon, the various links of the golden chain which drew us there."[241] From that perspective the most miserable life on earth will simply look like one bad night in an inconvenient hotel.[242]

We will have healed *longings*. We will sincerely and unequivocally be able to say "God is the strength of my heart and my portion forever" (Psalm 73:26). We will realize that our previous search for happiness was actually our search for God. All of the contaminated cisterns from which we attempted to satisfy our deepest thirst within will be seen for what they were—*broken*. In their place we will drink incessantly and satisfyingly from the springs of living water and wonder how we could have ever wanted anything else (Revelation 7:17).

We will have healed *wills*. Not only will we not sin, we will not *want* to sin. We will be far removed, not only from the penalty and power of sin, but even from its presence. The pernicious downward spiral of evil desire, deception, disobedience—all leading to death—will have been definitively broken. Instead, "Love God and do as you please" (as Augustine famously said) will govern our very existence, for we will only desire that which pleases God and demonstrates our love for him.

GOD'S ETERNAL FAMILY

In the new heavens and the new earth, we will experience an intimate and satisfying relationship not only with our Creator and Savior, but also with fellow believers, Christ's "brothers and sisters" (Hebrews 2:12). John Calvin was certainly mistaken when he wrote: "To be in Paradise and live with God is not to speak to each other and be heard by each other, but is only to enjoy God, to feel his good will, and rest in him."[243] To the contrary, as the eternal Three-in-One enjoys intimate, loving communion between Father, Son, and Holy Spirit from eternity past to eternity future, so we as his image were created for loving relationship. This was true in the original Eden, it is true today, and it will be true throughout eternity.

Engraved on Jonathan's tombstone are these words: "When we see Christ, we will see you again." This, too, is an expression of our longing for heaven and has been the conviction of believers through the centuries. Puritan Pastor Richard Baxter (1615-1691) penned *The Saints' Everlasting Rest,* one of the most influential books on heaven ever written. Speaking of those who have lost loved ones, he writes, "I know that Christ is all in all; and that it is the presence of God that makes Heaven to be heaven. But yet it much sweetens the thoughts of that place to me that there are there such a multitude of most dear and precious friends in Christ."[244] About two hundred years later, Bishop J. C. Ryle (1816-1900) expressed the same thought, "Those whom you laid in the grave with many tears are in good keeping: you will yet see them again with joy. Believe it, think it, rest on it. It is all true."[245]

No longing grips the soul of one who grieves a loved one more than the desire to be together once again. But apart from Christ, such longings will never be fulfilled. An ancient papyrus from the first century contains the condolences from a parent whose child had died to another parent experiencing the same sense of loss: "I sorrowed and wept over your dear departed one as I wept over Didymas . . . but really, there is nothing one can do in the face of such things."[246] Archeologists have discovered a similar inscription in Thessalonica, Greece, which reads: "After death, no reviving, after the grave, no meeting again." That is why Paul wrote words of comfort to the believers in that city whose loved ones had died (1 Thessalonians 4:13-18). He reminds these grieving believers that they *will* meet their loved ones again!

For since we believe that Jesus died and was raised to life again, we also believe that when Jesus returns, God will bring back with him the believers who have died . . . First, the believers who have died will rise from their graves. Then, together with them, we who are still alive and remain on the earth will be caught up in the clouds to meet the Lord in the air. Then we will be with the Lord forever. So encourage each other with these words (vv. 14-18, NLT).

Paul's words in this passage are as much pastoral as they are theological. He is not as concerned about prophetic timelines as he is about instilling hope in those who grieve the death of loved ones. Grief over the death of a loved one should never be repressed, but expressed. But just as there is a different kind of happiness, there is also a different kind of grief. When a believer dies, the grief expressed by fellow Christians still alive is of another sort. In the face of death, we may be at our wit's end, but never at hope's end. We are "aching visionaries" who mourn and weep, but "not like the rest of mankind, who have no hope" (1 Thessalonians 4:13).[247]

I'll never forget my last goodbye to my son as he left on his third and final trip to South Korea. His characteristically timid wave remains indelibly imprinted on my mind and heart. Among loved ones, partings are painful. But among God's family members in heaven, such painful separations will exist no more. Father Boudreaux envisioned the eternal reunion of God's people in these terms: "What outbursts of gladness among the members of his family . . . No, no more separation! What delightful music there is in that short sentence! Death shall be no more, and therefore we shall never more be torn away from the society of our kindred and friends."[248]

REIGN OF THE SERVANT-KINGS

Every kingdom consists of three aspects—a ruler, a realm, and a reign. God's eternal kingdom is no exception. In his first coming, Christ came as a meek king to redeem. In his second coming, he will return as a mighty king to rule.

The Fall was a catastrophe of cosmic proportions; likewise, Christ's rule will extend to the entire cosmos including the demonic powers that have inspired so much evil and suffering throughout history (1 Corinthians 15:24-25). In Revelation 12:7-9, John describes the beginning of the end for Satan, the pseudo-king of this world, and his demons:

> And there was war in heaven. Michael and his angels fought against the dragon, and the dragon and his angels fought back. But he was not strong enough, and they lost their place in heaven. The great dragon was hurled down—that ancient serpent called the devil, or Satan, who leads the whole world astray. He was hurled to the earth, and his angels with him.

From heaven to earth and from earth to hell—that is the fate of Satan and his angels. After a moment of brief reprisal, the one who deceives the nations is ultimately "thrown into the lake of burning sulfur" and "tormented day and night for ever and ever" (Revelation 20:10). End of story for the powers that divide and destroy. The leash placed on Satan at the cross has led him straight to hell.

The final defeat of Satan, sin, and suffering will pave the way for establishing the realm of God's rule—*on earth*—a new earth on which God will live with his people. "Then I saw a new heaven and a new earth," John writes, "for the old heaven and the old earth had disappeared . . . I heard a loud shout from the throne, saying, 'Look, God's home is now among his people! . . . God himself will be with them'" (Revelation 21:1-3, NLT).

God's design for history is not just bringing people to heaven, but bringing heaven to earth—a world that is but the shadow of which heaven is the substance (Hebrews 8:5). Just as mankind was created as the image of God, so earth was created as the image of heaven. C. S. Lewis writes, "The hills and valleys of Heaven will be to those you now experience not as a copy is to an original, nor as a substitute is to the genuine article, but as the flower to the root, or the diamond to the coal."[249] That is why the Bible describes heaven as the "new earth," speaking of its fresh but familiar character (2 Peter 3:13; Revelation 21:1); as a "country," speaking of its vastness (Luke 19:12; Hebrews 11:14-16); as a "city," speaking of the large number of inhabitants (Hebrews 12:22; Revelation 21:2); as "paradise," speaking of its delights (Luke 23:43; Revelation 2:7); and as "my Father's house," speaking of the fact that once there, we will truly be home (John 14:2).

Resurrected bodies are designed for a resurrected earth. We are inseparably connected to this earth and it is on this earth that we will ultimately live and reign with Christ. Randy Alcorn describes it well when he writes,

> God doesn't throw away his handiwork and start from scratch—instead, he uses the same canvas to repair and make more beautiful the painting marred by the vandal. The vandal doesn't get the satisfaction of destroying his rival's masterpiece. On the contrary, God makes an even greater masterpiece out of what his enemy sought to destroy . . . Satan seeks to destroy the earth. God seeks to restore and renew the earth, rule it, and hand it back over to his children. God will win the battle for us and for the earth.[250]

This theme of our promised reign as servant kings with the Messiah is seen throughout the Bible (Revelation 22:5).[251] Moreover, the primary symbol of our rule in Christ's future kingdom will be a crown—one that will last forever (1 Corinthians 9:25). The New Testament mentions five different crowns given as a reward to faithful believers. Each of these rewards speak, not so much of the possession of eternal life shared by all believers, but rather of the richness and abundance of eternal life shared by those who overcome.[252] James the Just mentions a specific crown—sometimes referred to as the "martyr's crown"—promised to those who persevere through suffering as a demonstration of their love for Christ: "Blessed (happy) is the one who perseveres under trial because, having stood the test, that person will receive the crown of life that the Lord has promised to those who love him" (James 1:12). The same "crown of life" is also mentioned in the Lord's words to the church at Smyrna: "Don't be afraid of what you are about to suffer. The devil will throw some of you into prison to test you. You will suffer for ten days. But if you remain faithful even when facing death, I will give you the crown of life" (Revelation 2:10).

The Greeks called Smyrna the "crown of Asian Minor" because of its beauty. Every year, certain city officials would receive a crown of leaves for their faithfulness in performing their duties. The city was also famous for its games in which those who won would receive a garland.

The crown always follows the cross. The cross speaks not only of salvation, but also of a willingness to endure suffering and remain faithful for Jesus' sake. Eternal life is a gift by grace to all who believe in Christ (Ephesians 2:8-9). On the other hand, the "crown of life" is the high honor and special distinction given to those willing to suffer even to the point of losing their own life here on earth. It could be argued that the concept of reward in heaven for faithful service on earth encourages impure motives. But as C. S. Lewis reminds us, "Heaven offers nothing that a mercenary soul can desire. It is safe to tell the pure in heart that they shall see God, for only the pure in heart want to. There are rewards that do not sully the motives."[253]

Not only are resurrected bodies designed for a resurrected earth, they are also intended for resurrected cultures. Our biblical hope is not otherworldly. We are homesick for Eden, but not for a neo-Platonic sphere of celestial existence. Just as our mission on this present earth is to effectively steward creation and culture to the glory of God, so it will be throughout eternity on the yet future new earth. This, too, is part of reigning with Christ. Even in the eternal state, the diverse cultural riches of the world will be brought into the New Jerusalem. The Apostle John prophetically describes this heavenly city with all its majestic beauty when he writes, "The nations will walk by its light, and the kings of the earth will bring their splendor into it" (Revelation 21:24). Evidently, the redeemed magnificence of the world's varied peoples, cultures, customs, art forms, languages, music, and history will be offered up as an expression of pure, unadulterated praise to the Creator of it all. This truth also implies that work begun on this earth to the glory of God will continue on the new earth.

Only weeks before his death, Jonathan wrote from Soonchunhyang University in South Korea:

> This semester, I'm really hoping to be able to learn and advance in the Korean language, as I think this is key to almost any other objective and purpose for being in Korea. I'm also hoping to learn and improve in Taekwondo as this is one of my favorite pastimes and strong area of interest. The introduction to teaching this summer . . . has also been very helpful to me and has enabled me to discover new areas of interest as I didn't know I could enjoy this kind of work so well . . . After this semester, I'm hoping to stay longer in Korea, eventually learning the language and

possibly graduating here before continuing my studies in aviation in America.

Having left South Korea for his heavenly home, is Jonathan continuing to learn the Korean language? Is he enjoying his favorite pastime, Taekwondo? Or is he sharpening his teaching skills or learning more about aviation? It's quite possible, if not in the intermediate heaven,[254] most certainly in the new heavens and new earth. In reflecting on his lifelong literary investment, the famed French author Victor Hugo (1802-1885) describes what he anticipates in heaven:

> I feel within me the future life. I am like a forest that has been more than once cut down. The new shoots are stronger and livelier than ever. I am rising, I know, toward the sky . . . The earth gives me its generous sap, but heaven lights me with the reflection of unknown worlds . . . The nearer I approach the end the plainer I hear around me the immortal symphonies of the worlds which invite me . . . For half a century I have been writing my thoughts in prose, verse, history, philosophy, drama, romance, tradition, satire, ode, and song—I have tried all. But I feel that I have not said the thousandth part of what is in me. When I go down to the grave I can say, like so many others, "I have finished my day's work," but I cannot say, "I have finished my life." My day's work will begin again the next morning. The tomb is not a blind alley; it is a thoroughfare. It closes in the twilight to open with the dawn.[255]

LIVING IN LIGHT OF HEAVEN

In his well-known book *The Seven Habits of Highly Effective People,* Stephen R. Covey writes about seven key habits that characterize people of accomplishment. The second habit he addresses is this: *begin with the end in mind.*[256] Throughout the Bible, we are exhorted to do just that—to begin with the end in mind, to reflect on the world to come, to allow our final destiny and God's design for history to shape our life in the present. We cannot understand who we are or what we are called to do apart from understanding what we will ultimately be. As C. S. Lewis affirms, "It is since Christians have largely ceased to think of the other world that they have become so ineffective in this."[257]

Have you ever noticed how anticipation infuses into our being excitement, vitality, and even perseverance through the worst of circumstances? Some years ago I asked one of my daughters, Mary Lynne, how she was feeling about her upcoming wedding. She replied, "Well, just 312 hours and 30 minutes to go!" She was living each day in intense, excited anticipation of being united with her husband-to-be. Similarly, Christians—as the Bride of Christ—are to eagerly await our union with the Lord Jesus in the home he has prepared for us.

The biblical writers understood the transforming power of having our eyes fixed on our future hope. Their words betray the fact that they were homesick for heaven. The psalmist Asaph affirms, "You guide me with your counsel, and afterward you will take me into glory. Whom have I in heaven but you? And earth has nothing I desire besides you" (Psalm 73:24-25). The Apostle Paul writes, "But our citizenship is in heaven. And we eagerly await a Savior from there, the Lord Jesus Christ" (Philippians 3:20). Just before his martyrdom, Peter writes, "But in keeping with his promise we are looking forward to a new heaven and a new earth, where righteousness dwells" (2 Peter 3:13). Finally, the writer to the suffering Hebrew Christians describes the heroic faith that inspired the patriarchs and prophets of the Old Testament:

All these people were still living by faith when they died. They did not receive the things promised; they only saw them and welcomed them from a distance, admitting that they were foreigners and strangers on earth. People who say such things show that they are looking for a country of their own . . . They were longing for a better country—a heavenly one. (Hebrews 11:13-14, 16).

Though our Father refreshes us on our present journey with some pleasant inns, we must not mistake them for home.[258] But we do just that when we continue to dig in all the wrong places in misguided attempts to satisfy the deepest longings of the human heart. When faced with the tragedy of living in a fallen world with all of its pain and sorrow, we tend to numb our deepest longings by an idolatrous pursuit of our lesser longings. We demand in the present what only heaven can provide in the future. Essentially, we misdiagnose our home-sickness for heaven.

Randy Alcorn states it well when he writes, "We live between Eden and the New Earth, pulled toward what we once were and what we yet will be." He goes on to explain, "Desire is a signpost pointing to Heaven. Every longing for better health is a longing for the New Earth. Every longing for romance is a longing for the ultimate romance with Christ. Every desire for intimacy is a desire for Christ. Every thirst for beauty is a thirst for Christ. Every taste of joy is but a foretaste of a greater and more vibrant joy than can be found on Earth as it is now."[259]

Learning to wait for the complete transformation of our deepest longings in the future enables us to better overcome temptation in the present. Our insatiable drive to relieve the pain of living in a fallen world predisposes us to seek anesthetizing pleasure in the temporary delights of sin. Our misguided attempts to dull the pain of suffering in this life also diminish awareness of our deepest longings which can only and ultimately be fulfilled in the presence of Christ in the next life.

Martin Luther once said, "There are only two days on my calendar: Today and that Day!" Since my son's death, I've come to realize in a deeper way that the certainty of "that Day" must influence how I live today. Jonathan's premature death has made me more aware of my inevitable death, as well as of the promise of what lies beyond. Moreover, his present life in heaven with Christ inspires me to live my present life on earth for Christ.

God is preparing heaven for us. But he is also preparing us for heaven. As we endure the suffering of the present, we limp and lean into the future. We incessantly pray, "Thy kingdom come, thy will be done, on earth as it is in heaven." Such a perspective enables us to view all the suffering in the wilderness of this world in the splendid light of resurrection to life and the wonders of the world to come.

This life matters, not because it is the only life we have, but because it is the dress rehearsal for the next. That is why "It becomes us to spend this life only as a journey toward heaven . . . to which we should subordinate all other concerns of life. Why should we labor for or set our hearts on anything else, but that which is our proper end and true happiness?"[260] Such a perspective transforms our limp in this life into an opportunity to lean into God's precious promises concerning the next life. Peter encourages us to adopt such a perspective when he writes, "But the day of the Lord will come like a thief. The heavens will disappear with a roar; the elements will be destroyed by fire, and the earth and everything in it will be laid bare. Since everything will be destroyed in this way, what kind of people ought you to be? You ought to live holy and godly lives as you look forward to the day of God and speed its coming" (2 Peter 3:10-12).

This present life not only matters, *it is short*. Reflecting on the transient character of our earthly existence, Moses prays,

"Teach us to number our days, that we may gain a heart of wisdom" (Psalm 90:12). He even tells us *how* to number our days when he says to God, "For you, a thousand years are as a passing day, as brief as a few night hours" (v. 4). According to Peter, this fact must not escape our notice: "But do not forget this one thing, dear friends: With the Lord a day is like a thousand years, and a thousand years are like a day" (2 Peter 3:8). Presently, the average global life expectancy is 72.6 years. If a thousand years were a day, then one year would be a mere 86.4 seconds. Given this calculation, the average lifespan would be approximately one hour and forty-five minutes—the length of a soccer game or a movie at the theater.

Christ followers will have two opportunities to live on this earth. The first opportunity is now—this short, fleeting life. It's like the "dash" enclosed in the parenthesis of birth and death. It begins, it ends. It is brief. But the second opportunity will be in the future—in the promised new heavens and on the promised new earth that will have no end (Revelation 21:1). It's like the line, extending on forever. We all live *in* the parentheses, but if we're wise and learn to "number our days," we'll live *in light of* the line.[261]

Such a viewpoint radically transforms how we view suffering. In describing his own experience of suffering for the sake of the gospel, Paul writes, "For our light and momentary troubles are achieving for us an eternal glory that far outweighs them all" (2 Corinthians 4:17). That is why suffering is an integral part of our apprenticeship in view of heaven. The Bible commentator, G. Campbell Morgan, writes, "Affliction is not something to be endured in order to reach glory. It is the very process which creates the glory."[262]

This perspective enables us to "weigh" our sufferings in comparison to the promised glory of eternity, rather than "waste" our sufferings by complaining and refusing to grow through them. Once again, imagine an analytical balance with a weighing pan suspended from each arm of the scales. In one plate of the balance we place our "troubles." For Paul, these included such things as imprisonment, floggings, beatings, shipwrecks, danger from bandits, sleepless nights, hunger and thirst, and ultimately martyrdom (2 Corinthians 11:23-28; 2 Timothy 4:6). For you, they may include the tragic loss of a loved one, sexual abuse as a child, financial crisis, or persecution because of your faith. Previously in this letter, Paul described his afflictions as "weighing him down" (2 Corinthians 1:8, ASV). They were like a lethal weight on Paul's shoulders, and he was on the brink of losing heart. The same may be true for you. Given the heavy burden of these trials, the plate of the balance forcefully drops to the ground.

In the other plate, however, we place the "glory" of all that God promises to those who endure. Glory refers to the unimaginably brilliant, dazzling display of God's character reflected in his family members. In the Hebrew language, "weight" and "glory" come from the same term. Such glory is heavy in significance, whereas our afflictions are light in comparison. Such promised glory is eternal, whereas our present suffering is momentary. The promised glory does not merely "tip" the scales, it completely counterbalances the scales! All the passing burdens of this life that feel like a lethal weight will become weightless in comparison with the glory that will last forever!

Today, in Valladolid, Spain, is a monument commemorating the discoveries of Columbus. The most striking feature of this memorial is the statue of a lion devouring the first of the three Latin words, *"Ne plus ultra."* Jesus Christ, the Son of God, came into this suffering world in order that the *ne plus ultra* (nothing beyond) of our lives could become *plus ultra* (more beyond).

I previously mentioned that only months after my son's death, another young person of our church was killed in a tragic head-on collision while driving to the elementary school where she taught underprivileged children. Her body "sleeps" in the same cemetery only a short distance from where Jonathan's body also "sleeps." Hers was a relatively short existence, but a full life. Though not a martyr, she had the perspective of a martyr. Inscribed on her tombstone are her last words to a few friends whom she was encouraging along the pathway to a different kind of happiness both now and in the *plus ultra*:

> My prayer for you girls is that you would reach the end of your life with no regrets. Who knows when the end of life may be. As quoted in the Martyr's Prayer, "A long life is not necessarily a full life." I pray that your lives would be full and free of regret. Having no regrets does not require a perfect life. In other words, may you live your lives in such a way that you would learn from your mistakes and bless God in your trials. He can use anything and everything for His Glory and He will. Not even our suffering and downfalls are experienced in vain . . . May He always be your purpose for life on earth. If I never have the privilege of seeing you again, I will see you in Heaven where He is preparing a place for us beyond our wildest dreams! Thank you again! And God bless! Eva

That place of authentic happiness beyond our wildest dreams is available for all who believe in Jesus Christ, the One who lives in order that death may die. Once there, we will have no less days to sing God's praise than when we first began! Jonathan and Eva experience that now along with countless others who have placed their faith in God's final answer to all the sin and suffering in this world. At the end of the day our only hope is found in the death and resurrection of Jesus Christ, the Morning Star. He alone can help us discover the Father's purpose in our pain.

> *So we fix our eyes not on what is seen,*
> *but on what is unseen,*
> *since what is seen is temporary,*
> *but what is unseen is eternal.*
> —The Apostle Paul (2 Corinthians 4:18)

"... the growing good of the world is partly dependent on unhistoric acts; and that things are not so ill with you and me as they might have been, is half owing to the number who lived faithfully a hidden life, and rest in unvisited tombs."
—George Eliot (1819-1880), *Middlemarch*

Endnotes

Introduction

1 "Daisy" in *The Works of Francis Thompson, Poems*: Volume 1 (London: Burns Oastes & Washbourne, 1925), 5.

2 https://www.who.int/news-room/fact-sheets/detail/depression

3 Sermon on 1 Peter 1:7, "The Trial of Your Faith," December 2, 1888 at the Metropolitan Tabernacle.

Chapter 1 Out of the Depths

4 C.H. Spurgeon, *The Treasury of David*, vol. 6 (Marshal Brothers: London, nd), 124.

5 T. S. Eliot, *Four Quartets* (New York: Mariner Books, 1971).

6 See Job chapters 4-27 for the counsel given to Job by his three "friends."

7 Nicholas J. Wolterstorff, *Lament for a Son* (Grand Rapids: Eerdmans, 1987), 36.

8 Ibid., 106.

9 Martin Luther, *Luther's Works*, vol. 14, Selected Psalms III (Saint Louis: Concordia Publishing House, 1958), 145.

10 Ambrose of Milan, *On the Death of Satyrus*. https://www.newadvent.org/fathers/34031.htm

11 Gerald W. Peterman and Andrew J. Schmutzer, *Between Pain and Grace: A Biblical Theology of Suffering* (Chicago: Moody, 2016), 118.

12 Timothy Keller, *Walking with God through Pain and Suffering* (New York: Riverhead Books, 2013), 48-50.

13 Paul F. Boller, *Presidential Wives* (New York: Oxford University Press, 1998), 195.

14 Bernard Anderson, *Out of the Depths* (Philadelphia: Westminster Press, 1974), x.

15 Nicholas Wolterstorff, "If God Is Good and Sovereign, Why Lament?" *Calvin Theological Journal* 36 (2001), 42.

16 C.H. Spurgeon, *The Treasury of David*, vol. 2 (London: Marshall Brothers, nd), 272.

17 Brennan Manning, *All Is Grace: A Ragamuffin Memoir* (Colorado Springs: David C. Cook, 2011), 188.

18 For certain of these thoughts I'm indebted to Henry Drummond's "Dealing with Doubt" as found in Warren W. Wiersbe, *Listening to the Giants* (Grand Rapids: Baker Book House, 1980), 113-119.

19 Augustine, *De Vera Religione* cited by Os Guiness, *In Two Minds* (Downers Grove: Inter-Varsity Press, 1976), 48.

20 Ibid., 31.

[21] C. H. Spurgeon, *The Treasury of David*, vol. 6, 118.

[22] Kathryn Greene-McCreight, "Light When All is Dark," *Christianity Today* 53, no. 3 (2009): 30-31.

[23] Augustine, *Confessions*, 2.2.2.

[24] C. S. Lewis, *The Problem of Pain* (Québec: Samizdat University Press, 2016), 55.

[25] See Ezekiel 2:8; Lamentations 2:16.

Chapter 2 Why Does a Good God Allow Bad Things?

[26] Judges 6:13 (emphasis mine).

[27] C.S. Lewis, *A Grief Observed* (London: Faber and Faber, 1961), 26

[28] A conundrum lies somewhere between a mystery and a contradiction. A conundrum has not yet been demonstrated to be a contradiction, such as a round triangle or a married bachelor. On the other hand, a conundrum is not a mystery, like the biblical concept of the Trinity. While there are aspects of the doctrine of the Trinity that are beyond our understanding, there are no particular contradictions.

[29] See Henri Blocher, *Evil and the Cross*, trans. David G. Preston (Downers Grove: InterVarsity Press, 1994), 31.

[30] See Exodus 33:18-19; 34:6-7.

[31] I am indebted to two significant works on this topic by Gregory A. Boyd: *God at War: The Bible and Spiritual Conflict* (Downers Grove: InterVarsity Press, 1997) and *Satan and the Problem of Evil: Constructing a Trinitarian Warfare Theodicy* (Downers Grove: InterVarsity Press, 2001).

[32] *Martyrs and Fighters: The Epic of the Warsaw Ghetto*, ed. P. Friedman (New York: Frederick A. Praeger, 1954), 166-67.

[33] The name has been changed to protect confidentiality.

[34] Nerin E. Gun, *Eva Braun: Hitler's Mistress* (New York: Bantam Books, 1969), 209.

[35] Bart D. Ehrman, *God's Problem: How the Bible Fails to Answer Our Most Important Questions—Why We Suffer* (New York: HarperCollins Publishers, 2008), 3.

[36] Susan Neiman, *Evil in Modern Thought: An Alternative History of Philosophy* (Princeton University Press, 2002), ebook.

[37] Eckhart Tolle, *A New Earth* (New York: Penguin Books, 2005), 22.

[38] Mary Baker Eddy, *Science and Health* (Boston: The Christian Science Board of Directors, 2006), 71.

[39] Ibid. 447.

[40] A. W. Tozer, *The Knowledge of the Holy* (New York: Harper & Row, 1961), 9.

[41] The term "blueprint" as a description of a particular view of God's sovereignty comes from Gregory Boyd, *Satan and the Problem of Evil*, 418. Though I believe that the term "blueprint" appropriately describes the Augustinian-Calvinistic view of God's sovereignty, I do not subscribe to Boyd's view of "open theism."

[42] Philip Schaff, *St. Augustin's City of God and Christian Doctrine* (New York: The Christian Literature Publishing Co., 1890), 141. Available online at http://www.holybooks.com/augustins-city-god-christian-doctrine/.

[43] Jean Calvin, *Institutes of the Christian Religion,* 1.16.2.

[44] Wayne Grudem, *Systematic Theology: An Introduction to Biblical Doctrine* (Grand Rapids: Zondervan, 1994), 319. Emphasis mine.

[45] John Piper and Justin Taylor, *Suffering and the Sovereignty of God* (Wheaton, Ill.: Crossway, 2006), 42. Emphasis mine.

[46] R. C. Sproul writes, "God wills all things that come to pass . . . we can know that whatever comes to pass must be what God most wished to come to pass . . . I am not accusing God of sinning; I am suggesting that God created sin." R. C. Sproul, *Almighty Over All* (Grand Rapids, Mich.: Baker Book House, 1999), 53-54.

[47] During the first four centuries of church history, it was the heretics, not the orthodox defenders of the faith, who held tenaciously to a meticulously omni-controlling view of God's sovereignty. Much of the debate concerning how God exercises his sovereignty focuses upon the nature and mode of God's foreknowledge in relation to the nature of human freedom. Four major views are current today: (1) the Augustinian-Calvinist view; (2) the simple-foreknowledge view; (3) the middle-knowledge view; and (4) the open-theism view. I believe that the middle-knowledge viewpoint provides the best understanding of the biblical data. See William Lane Craig, *The Only Wise God* (Eugene Or.: Wipf and Stock Publishers, 200); *Divine Foreknowledge: Four Views*, ed. James K. Beilby & Paul R. Eddy (Downers Grove: InterVarsity Press, 2001).

[48] Psalm 34:9; Nahum 1:7; Romans 2:4.

[49] A. W. Tozer, *The Knowledge of the Holy*, 89.

[50] N.T. Wright, *Evil and the Justice of God* (Downers Grove, Il.: InterVarsity Press, 2006), 59.

[51] This is best represented by the NKJV which reads: "Neither this man nor his parents sinned, but that the works of God should be revealed in him. I must work the works of Him who sent Me while it is day." See Daniel B. Wallace, *Greek Grammar Beyond the Basics: an Exegetical syntax of the New Testament* (Zondervan, Grand Rapids, MI, 1996), 471-472, 476-477.

[52] Henri Blocher, *Evil and the Cross*, 103.

[53] A. W. Tozer, *The Knowledge of the Holy*, 118 (emphasis mine).

[54] C. S. Lewis, *Mere Christianity* (New York: HarperCollins, 2001), 48.

[55] C.S. Lewis, *The Problem of Pain*, 16.

[56] Sinclair B. Ferguson, *Deserted by God* (Grand Rapids: Baker Books, 1993), 19, 33. A similar account is found in Faith Cook, *Singing in the Fire: Christians in Adversity* (Edinburgh: Banner of Truth Trust, 1995), 149-162.

[57] Bruce R. Reichenbach, *Evil and a Good God* (New York: Fordham University Press, 1982), 64, 105.

[58] Randy Alcorn, *If God Is Good: Faith in the Midst of Suffering and Evil* (Colorado Springs: Multnomah Books, 2009), 329-330.

[59] Roméo Dallaire, *Shake Hands with the Devil: The Failure of Humanity in Rwanda* (New York: Carroll & Graf, 2004). Citation from book jacket.

Chapter 3 An Enemy Had Done This!

[60] Roméo Dallaire, *Shake Hands with the Devil: The Failure of Humanity in Rwanda* (New York: Carroll & Graf, 2004), xviii (preface).

[61] N.T. Wright, *Evil and the Justice of God* (Downers Grove: InterVarsity Press, 2006), 118.

[62] Cf. Leviticus 18:25, 28; 20:22; Isaiah 24:4; Jeremiah 4:28.

[63] Much of what follows in this chapter is adapted from the author's book, *God's New Humanity: A Biblical Theology of Multiethnicty for the Church* (Eugene, Oregon: Wipf & Stock, 2012), 35-56.

[64] F. R. Barry, *Recovery of Man* (New York: Charles Scribner's Sons, 1949), 61

[65] Augustus H. Strong, *Systematic Theology* (Philadelphia: American Baptist Publication Society, 1907), 347.

[66] *Against Heresies* 4.20.7.

[67] E. Kautzsch, *Gesenius' Hebrew Grammar,* trans. A.E. Cowley, 2nd ed. (Oxford: Clarendon, 1910): 320 §108.d. D. J. A. Clines, "Image of God in Man," *Tyndale Bulletin* 19 (1968), 76–77.

[68] Eric Sauer, *The King of the Earth* (Grand Rapids: Eerdmans, 1962), 80–81.

[69] C. S. Lewis, "The Efficacy of Prayer" in *The World's Last Night and Other Essays* (Harvest Books, 1960), 9.

[70] Lawrence J. Crabb, *Understanding People* (Grand Rapids: Zondervan, 1987), 94-95.

[71] C. S. Lewis, *The Screwtape Letters* (New York: HarperCollins, 2001), chapter 14.

[72] Cited by Peter Kreeft, *Making Sense Out of Suffering* (Ann Arbor: Servant Books, 1986), 14.

[73] Norman L. Geisler, *Chosen But Free: A Balanced View of Divine Election* (Minneapolis, Minn.: Bethany House Publishers, 1999), 23.

[74] Peter Kreeft, *Making Sense Out of Suffering,*176.

[75] Nancy R. Pearcey, *Total Truth: Liberating Christianity from Its Cultural Captivity* (Wheaton: Crossway, 2001), 87.

[76] Isaiah 14:4-20, Ezekiel 28:12-19, 2 Peter 2:4, Jude 6, and Revelation 12:7-9.

[77] J. R. R. Tolkien, *The Hobbit (*New York: Random House, 1982), 217.

[78] Exodus 14:14; 15:3; Deuteronomy 1:30, 3:22; 20:4.

[79] Walter Wink, *Naming the Powers: The Language of Power in the New Testament* (Philadelphia: Fortress, 1984), 4. For a helpful critique of Wink's presuppositions, see Clinton Arnold, *Powers of Darkness: Principalities and Powers in Paul's Letters* (Downers Grove: InterVarsity Press, 1992), 177–82.

[80] C.S. Lewis, The *Screwtape Letters* (New York: Macmillan, 1944), 9.

[81] John 12:31; 14:30; 16:11; Matthew 9:34; 12:14; Mark 3:22; Luke 11:15.

[82] Thomas G. Long, *What Shall We Say?* (Grand Rapids: Eerdmans, 2011), 121-22. I am indebted to Long for several of the helpful insights in this section.

[83] D. A. Carson, *How Long, O Lord?* (Grand Rapids, MI: Baker Academic, 2006), 161.

[84] So we have "this is what became of" the heavens and the earth (2:4-4:26), Adam (5:1-6:8), Noah (6:9-9:29), Shem, Ham and Japheth (10:1-11:26) and finally Terah (11:27-15:11).

[85] See also Hebrews 2:14-15; Revelation 7:17.

[86] Elie Wiesel, *Night* trans. Marion Wiesel (New York: Hill and Wang, 2006), 64-65.

Chapter 4 Hope in the Mourning

[87] For the imagery, I'm indebted to Peter Kreeft, *Making Sense Out of Suffering* (Ann Arbor: Servant Books, 1986), 33.

[88] C.H. Spurgeon, *The Treasury of David*, vol. 1 (Marshal Brothers: London, nd), 324. If the author is not directly prophesying the sufferings of Christ, at the very least he indirectly prefigures them in his descriptive language. See Matthew 27:35-46.

[89] Dietrich Bonhoeffer, *Letters and Papers from Prison*, ed. Eberhard Bethge (New York: Simon & Schuster, 1997), 361.

[90] See also Luke 9:22; 17:25; Mark 8:31.

[91] David Van Biema, "God vs. Science," *Time* (November 5, 2006); found online at http://content.time.com/time/magazine/article/0,9171,1555132-9,00.html

[92] https://www.apuritansmind.com/westminster-standards/chapter-2/; emphasis mine.

[93] William Barclay, *The Letter to the Hebrews* (Philadelphia: Westminster John Knox Press, 2002), 39-40.

[94] From the mournful chant of the Buddha in his famous Benares sermon as cited by John B. Noss, *Man's Religions.* 6th ed. (New York: Macmillan Publishing Co. 1980), 119.

[95] Ibid., 120. The citation is found in *Sacred Books of the East,* Vol. XVI.211, *The Dhammapada.* Translated by F. Max Müller (Oxford: Clarendon Press, 1881).

[96] Randy Alcorn, *If God Is Good: Faith in the Midst of Suffering and Evil* (Colorado Springs: Multnomah Books, 2009), 209.

[97] https://www.christianpost.com/news/jesus-crucifixion-described-graphic-de-tail-physician-lee-strobels-book-the-case-for-christ.html

[98] Marcus Tulius Cicero, *Pro Rabirio,* V, 16 as cited by Josh McDowell, *Evidence that Demands a Verdict* (San Bernardino, CA: Campus Crusade for Christ, 1972), 205.

[99] Lewis Sperry Chafer, *Systematic Theology,* vol. III *Soteriology* (Dallas: Dallas Theological Seminary Press, 1948), 48.

[100] The image is adapted from Henri Blocher, *Evil and the Cross* (Downers Grove: InterVarsity Press (UK), 1994), 103-4.

[101] N. T. Wright, *Evil and the Justice of God* (Downers Grove, Ill.: IVP Books, 2009), 82-83.

[102] Adapted from Philip Yancey, *Disappointment with God : Three Questions No One Asks Aloud* (Grand Rapids, Mich.: Zondervan Books, 1988), 185-186.

[103] Henri Blocher, *Evil and the Cross*, 133.

[104] Ibid. 130.

[105] Cornelius Plantinga, Jr., "A Love So Fierce," *The Reformed Journal* (November 1986): 6.

[106] Hebrews 11:35; 1 Corinthians 15:51-56.

[107] C. S. Lewis, *Reflections on the Psalms* (New York: Harcourt Brace Jovanovich, 1958), 96.

[108] Gerald W. Peterman and Andrew J. Schmutzer, *Between Pain and Grace: A Biblical Theology of Suffering* (Chicago: Moody Publishers, 2016), 124.

[109] https://www.goodreads.com/quotes/322727-if-we-have-never-sought-we-seek-thee-now-thine

[110] *The Message*.

[111] The first century Jewish historian Josephus understood the entire wrestling match to be nothing more than a dream. The philosopher Philo interpreted the account to depict the struggle of the soul against one's passions and vices. Many since the time of Jerome in the fourth century have understood the wrestling match to symbolize earnest and persevering prayer.

[112] For certain thoughts in this chapter I am indebted to the following excellent accounts of Jacob's life: Ron Dunn, *When Heaven is Silent* (Nashville: Thomas Nelson, 1994); Daniel R. Lockwood, *Unlikely Heroes* (Portland, Oregon: Multnomah University, 2012), 141-158; Allen Ross, *Creation and Blessing* (Grand Rapids: Baker Book House, 1988), 433-559; *Bibliotheca Sacra* 142 (October-December 1985), 339-40.

[113] Ross, *Creation and Blessing*, 449.

Chapter 5 Blessing from Brokenness

[114] Genesis 21:17; 27:4, 27-29; 28:4; Deuteronomy 21:17.

[115] *The Works of Francis Thompson, Poems*: Volume 1 (London: Burns Oastes & Washbourne, 1925), 107.

[116] J. F. X. O'Conor, *A Study of Francis Thompson's Hound of Heaven* (New York: John Lane Company, 1912), 7. Available at https://archive.org/details/studyoffrancisth00oconrich/page/6/mode/2up.

[117] Alexander Whyte, *Bible Characters* (London: Oliphants, 1952), 113.

[118] Adapted from Peter Kreeft, *Making Sense Out of Suffering* (Ann Arbor: Servant Books, 1986), 120.

[119] Whyte, *Bible Characters,* 116.

[120] C. S. Lewis, *The Problem of Pain* (Québec: Samizdat University Press, 2016), 59.

[121] William G. Heslop, *Gems from Genesis* (Grand Rapids: Kregel Publication, 1940), 97.

[122] Ron Dunn, *When Heaven is Silent* (Nashville: Thomas Nelson Publishers, 1994), 29.

[123] For a thorough discussion of the meaning of the name "Israel," see Allen P. Ross, *Creation and Blessing* (Grand Rapids: Baker Book House, 1988), 553-556.

[124] http://www.scripturezealot.com/sufferingchristians/2010/02/03/the-thorn/.

[125] Timothy Keller, *Walking with God through Pain and Suffering* (New York: Riverhead Books, 2013), 283.

[126] 1 Kings 15:13; 2 Kings 23:4-12; 2 Chronicles 29:16; 34:4,5; Jeremiah 26:23.

[127] http://www.earlychristianwritings.com/text/hegesippus.html. See also F. F. Bruce, *Peter, Stephen, James and John: Studies in Early Non-Pauline Christianity* (Grand Rapids: Eerdmans, 1979), 114-116; Josephus, *Antiquities* 20.9.1.

[128] Paul Brand and Philip Yancey, *The Gift of Pain* (Grand Rapids: Zondervan, 1997), 12.

[129] Ron Dunn, *When Heaven is Silent*, 77.

[130] Timothy Keller, *Walking with God through Pain and Suffering* (New York: Riverhead Books, 2013), 139.

Chapter 6 A Martyr's Advice on Suffering

[131] The word is *peirasmois* referring to the trial of one's integrity. The verbal form is used in verse 13 and translated "tempted."

[132] Jonathan Haidt, *The Happiness Hypothesis: Finding Modern Truth in Ancient Wisdom* (New York: Basic Books, 2006), 136.

[133] Timothy Keller, *Walking with God through Pain and Suffering,* 30 (emphasis mine).

[134] C. S. Lewis, *The Problem of Pain* (Québec: Samizdat University Press, 2016), 40–41.

[135] E. Stanley Jones, *A Song of Ascents* (Nashville: Abingdon Press, 1968), 180.

[136] For a detailed explanation of the various interpretations see Philip Edgcumbe Hughes, *Paul's Second Epistle to the Corinthians* (Wm. B. Eerdmans: Grand Rapids, 1966), 442-448.

[137] The "third heaven" is most likely a reference to the very presence of God, i.e. paradise (cf. Luke. 23:43; Revelation 2:7).

[138] Peter Kreeft, *Making Sense Out of Suffering* (Ann Arbor: Servant Books, 1986), 114.

[139] Ty Gibson, *A God Named Desire: What If You're the Object of an Unstoppable Love?* (Nampa, ID: Pacific Press, 2010), 117-118.

[140] Warren W. Wiersbe, *The Bible Exposition Commentary: Pentateuch* (Colorado Springs, Colo.: Cook Communications Ministries, 2001), 104.

[141] Cited by Stephen R. Covey, *The 7 Habits of Highly Effective People* (New York: Simon & Schuster, 2004), 309.

[142] Cited by Dave Goetz, "Suburban Spirituality," *Christianity Today* (July 2003): 3.

[143] https://www.fatherly.com/health-science/how-parents-experience-the-death-of-a-child/

[144] William Barclay, *The Letter to the Hebrews* in The Daily Study Bible series. 2nd ed. (Edinburgh: Saint Andrew Press, 1963), 143-144.

[145] Howard G. Hendricks, "The Other Side of the Mountain," *Bibliotheca Sacra* 157 (January-March 2000), 13.

[146] C. S. Lewis, *The Weight of Glory and Other Addresses*. Ed. W. Hooper (New York: Simon and Schuster), 25-26.

Chapter 7 Staying Under While Living Above

[147] For support of this translation see J. William Johnston, "James 4:5 and the Jealous Spirit," *Bibliotheca Sacra* 170 (July-September 2013), 344-60.

[148] Randy Alcorn, *Heaven* (Wheaton: Tyndale House Publishers, 2004), 54.

[149] See D. Edmond Hiebert, "Romans 8:28-29 and the Assurance of the Believer," *Bibliotheca Sacra* 148 (April-June 1991), 171.

[150] A detailed outline of the many exegetical concerns in this verse is found in C. E. B. Cranfield, *A Critical and Exegetical Commentary on the Epistle to the Romans*. Volume 1. The International Critical Commentary (Edinburgh: T & T. Clark, 1975), 424-430.

[151] https://www.desiringgod.org/articles/why-i-do-not-say-god-did-not-cause-the-calamity-but-he-can-use-it-for-good.

[152] In Islam, *kismet* refers to the will of Allah. But it is popularly used to refer to something that one believes was "meant to be"—or the reason why such a thing happened.

[153] See Roger T. Forster and V. Paul Marston, *God's Strategy in Human History* (Wheaton: Tyndale House, 1973), 14, note 25; James Denney, *St. Paul's Epistle to the Romans* in The Expositor's Greek Testament, ed. W. Robertson Nicoll, Vol. 2 (Grand Rapids: Eerdmans Publishing Company, n.d.), 652.

[154] The Greek word *theos* (God) was added in several early manuscripts (Papyrus 46 dating to about AD 200), uncials A (fifth century) and B (fourth century), and cursive 81 (ca. 1044). They also appear in two of five known quotations of this verse in the writings of Origen. See D. Edmond Hiebert, *op. cit.,* 175.

[155] F. F. Bruce, *The Epistle of Paul to the Romans* in the Tyndale New Testament Commentaries, ed., R. V. G. Tasker (Grand Rapids: Eerdmans, 1963), 175-176.

[156] Henri Blocher, *Evil and the Cross*, Trans. David G. Preston (Downers Grove: InterVarsity Press, 1994), 128.

[157] Ibid., 89.

[158] C. S. Lewis, *The Problem of Pain* (Québec: Samizdat University Press, 2016), 69-70.

[159] Alcorn, *Heaven*, 89.

[160] The expression is frequently used to contrast spiritual maturity and immaturity (Hebrews 5:13, 14; 1 Corinthians 2:6; 3:1; Ephesians 4:13, 14).

[161] Illustration taken from David E. Stevens, *God's New Humanity: A Biblical Theology of Multiethnicity for the Church* (Eugene, Oregon: Wipf & Stock, 2012), 156-7.

[162] "Self" defined as fallen humanity or the "body ruled by sin" (Romans 6:6).

[163] A similar version of this poem is attributed to John Bunyan (1628-1688). https://gracequotes.com/category/john-bunyan/

[164] L. E. Maxwell, *Born Crucified* in Moody Classics (Chicago: Moody Publishers, 2010), 15.

[165] Dietrich Bonhoeffer, *Discipleship*, Vol. 4 in Dietrich Bonhoeffer Works, trans. Barbara Green and Reinhard Krauss (Minneapolis: Fortress Press, 2003), 87.

[166] John Calvin, *Institutes of the Christian Religion* Vol. 2 trans. Ford Lewis Battles (Albany, OR: Books for the Ages, 1998), 267.

Chapter 8 The Image Restored

[167] Larry Crabb, *Understanding People* (Grand Rapids: Zondervan, 1987), 143.

[168] David Augsberger, *Caring Enough to Forgive* (Ventura California: Regal Books, 1981), 37

[169] Larry Crabb, *Understanding People*, 107.

[170] Larry Crabb, *Finding God* (Grand Rapids: Zondervan, 1993).

[171] See the excellent discussion of this topic in Peter Scazzero, *Emotionally Healthy Spirituality* (Nashville: Thomas Nelson, 2006), 26.

[172] Peter Kreeft, *Making Sense Out of Suffering* (Ann Arbor: Servant Books, 1986), 102.

[173] Nathaniel Hawthorne, *Great Stone Face* (Boston: The Riverside Press, 1935), 31.

[174] Cited by Kenneth Boa, *Conformed to His Image* (Grand Rapids: Zondervan, 2001), 154.

[175] L. E. Maxwell, *Born Crucified* (Chicago: Moody Publishers, 2010), 37.

[176] https://urbana.org/blog/helen-roseveare

[177] Timothy Keller, *Walking with God through Pain and Suffering* (New York: Riverhead Books, 2016), 163.

[178] The tradition is attributed to the theologian Jerome (c. 342-420 AD) in his commentary on Galatians.

[179] N.T. Wright, *Evil and the Justice of God* (Downers Grove, Il.: InterVarsity Press, 2006), 98.

[180] George MacDonald, *Unspoken Sermons, First Series* as cited by C. S. Lewis, *The Problem of Pain*, 5.

[181] Peter Kreeft, *Making Sense Out of Suffering*, 143.

[182] Source unknown.

[183] This date is according to the most probable chronology proposed by Harold W. Hoehner, *Chronological Aspects of the Life of Christ* (Grand Rapids: Zondervan, 1977), 143.

[184] R. H. Charles, *The Apocrypha and Pseudepigrapha of the Old Testament*, 2 vols. (Oxford), 1:298.

[185] Cited by Philip Yancey, *Prayer: Does It Make Any Difference* (London: Hodder & Stoughton, 2006), ebook.

[186] https://www.cslewisinstitute.org/webfm_send/231

[187] The citation is attributed to Michelangelo, but the original source and authenticity are not known. See https://www.michelangelo-gallery.com/michelangelo-quotes.aspx

[188] Cited by C. S. Lewis, *The Problem of Pain* (San Francisco: HarperCollins, 1996), 94.

[189] 1:1; 2:12; 32:1,2; 33:12; 34:8; 40:4; 41:1; 65:4; 84:4,5,12; 89:15; 94:12; 106:3; 112:1; 119:1,2; 127:5; 128:1,2; 137:8,9; 144:15,16; 146:5.

[190] Cited by Randy Alcorn, *Happiness* (Carol Stream, Ill.: Tyndale House Publishers, 2015), chapter 37, eBook.

[191] Larry Crabb, *Shattered Dreams* (Colorado Springs: Waterbrook Press, 2001), 1.

[192] Though Jesus probably spoke Aramaic, Greek was the common written language of the day. The Gospel writers selected *makarios* as the closest Greek equivalent. For a detailed study of these and other biblical terms related to happiness, see Randy Alcorn, *Happiness* (Carol Stream: Tyndale House Publishers, 2015).

[193] Cited by Randy Alcorn, *Happiness*, chapter 24.

[194] G. Campbell Morgan, *Studies in the Four Gospels* (Westwood, New Jersey: Fleming H. Revell, 1931), 42.

[195] Robert H. Gundry, *Matthew: A Commentary on His Handbook for a Mixed Church under Persecution* (Grand Rapids: Wm. B. Eerdmans, 1994), 73.

Chapter 9 A Different Kind of Happiness

[196] C. H. Spurgeon, "The Beatitudes," sermon published on Thursday, July 29, 1909, in *The Beatitudes,* e-book.

[197] C. H. Spurgeon, "The First Beatitude," sermon published on Thursday, August 5, 1909, No. 3156 in *The Beatitudes,* e-book.

[198] C. S. Lewis, *The Screwtape Letters* (New York: Macmillan, 1982), 56-67.

[199] Peter Kreeft, *Making Sense Out of Suffering* (Ann Arbor: Servant Books, 1986), 64-65.

[200] Nicholas Wolterstorff, *Lament for a Son* (Grand Rapids, Mich.: Eerdmans, 1987), 65.

[201] Ilion T. Jones, *Christian Reader*, Vol. 32, no. 5.

[202] Dietrich Bonhoeffer, *The Cost of Discipleship* trans. R. H. Fuller (New York: Macmillan, 1959), 16-17.

[203] Xenophon, *The Art of Horsemanship*, edited and translated by Morris H. Morgan (Mineola, New York: Dover Publications, 2006).

[204] John MacArther, *The Beatitudes: The Only Way to Happiness* (Chicago: Moody Bible Institute, 1980), e-book.

[205] Peter Kreeft, *Making Sense Out of Suffering,* 146.

[206] David Bentley-Tayler and Clark B. Offner, "Buddhism" in *The World's Religions*, edited by Sir Norman Anderson (Grand Rapids: William B. Eerdmans Publishing Co., 1980), 169-190.

[207] Thomas à Kempis, *The Imitation of Christ* (Milwaukee: Bruce, 1940), 68.

[208] John MacArthur, *The Beatitudes: The Only Way to Happiness*, e-book.

[209] Amy Carmichael, *Rose from Brier* (Fort Washington, PA: CLC Publications), 13.

[210] The same thought may be implied in John 1:16 "For we have all received from his fullness one gracious gift after another" (NET).

[211] Colin S. Smith, *The 10 Greatest Struggles of Your Life* (Chicago: Moody Publishers, 2006), 31-32.

[212] Jill Briscoe, "Before You Say 'Amen.'" *Christianity Today,* Vol. 38, no. 12.

[213] *Institutes* I.11.8.

[214] Larry Crabb, *Shattered Dreams: God's Unexpected Pathway to Joy*, (Colorado Springs: Waterbrook Press, 2001), 4.

[215] https://www.christianitytoday.com/history/people/evangelistsandapologists/irenaeus-gnosticism-gaul-erasmus-persecution.html

[216] Though credited to G. K. Chesterton, the citation appears to come from William Barclay, *The Gospel of Luke in The New Daily Study Bible* (Louisville: Westminster John Knox Press, 2001), 92.

[217] Thomas Watson, *The Beatitudes* (Edinburgh: Banner of Truth, 1975), 259.

[218] *Foxe's Book of Martyrs* ed., Marie Gentert King (Old Tappan, N.J.: Pyramid Publications, 1968), 13.

[219] https://www.opendoorsusa.org/christian-persecution/

[220] Dietrich Bonhoeffer, *Discipleship* (Minneapolis: Fortress Press, 2003), 89.

[221] Roger E. Olson, *The Story of Christian Theology: Twenty Centuries of Tradition and Reform* (Downers Grove, Illinois: InterVarsity Press, 1999).

[222] Herbert Lockyer, *Last Words of Saints and Sinners* (Grand Rapids: Kregel Publications, 1969), 108, 117.

[223] Michael P. Green, ed. *1500 Illustrations for Biblical Preaching* (Grand Rapids: Baker Books, 1989), 93.

[224] C. S. Lewis, *The Problem of Pain* (Québec: Samizdat University Press, 2016), 93.

[225] Joseph Bayly, "A Father's Afterthoughts on Death," *Moody Monthly* 1968: 35-36.

[226] John Calvin, *Commentary on the Book of the Prophet Isaiah* in Calvin's Commentaries, vol. 8 (Grand Rapids: Baker Books, 2009), 196-197.

[227] Presumably written by the Rev. Luther F. Beecher (1813-1903) but also attributed to Henry Van Dyke. Cited by Loraine Bettner, *Immortality* (Phillipsburg. N. J.: Pres. & Reformed, 1956), 29-20.

[228] Cited by F. F. Bruce, *1 & 2 Thessalonians* in Word Biblical Commentary (Waco, TX.: Word Books, 1982), 96.

[229] Warren Wiersbe, *Be Ready* (Wheaton: Victor Books, 1979), 83.

[230] Calvin Miller, *The Divine Symphony* as cited by Randy Alcorn, *Heaven* (Wheaton: Tyndale House Publishers, 2004), 447.

Chapter 10 Homesick for Heaven

[231] Cited by Randy Alcorn, *Happiness* (Tyndale House Publishers, 2015), ebook.

[232] Ibid.

[233] F. J. Boudreaux, *The Happiness of Heaven,* Chapter 2. https://www.gutenberg.org/cache/epub/25224/pg25224.html

[234] Daniel 12:2; 2 Corinthians 5:1-5; Philippians 3:21; 1 Thessalonians 4:15-18; Revelation 20:5-6.

[235] John G. Patton, *Missionary to the New Hebrides: An Autobiography,* ed. Rev. James Paton (London: Hodder and Stoughton, 1891), 56.

[236] Randy Alcorn, *Heaven* (Wheaton: Tyndale House Publishers, 2004), 240.

[237] Joni Eareckson Tada, *Heaven: Your Real Home* (Grand Rapids: Zonvervan, 1995), 53.

[238] Jonathan Edwards, "The End for Which God Created the Word," https://document.desiringgod.org/god-s-passion-for-his-glory-en.pdf?ts=1439242050

[239] The Greek term is *aletheia,* from the root *letho,* meaning "to forget" (the prefix "a" indicates a negative).

[240] Tim Keller, *Walking with God through Pain and Suffering* (New York: Riverhead Books, 2013), 118.

[241] George Whitefield, "Walking with God," *Selected Sermons of George Whitefield.* https://www.ccel.org/ccel/whitefield/sermons.iv.html

[242] The image comes from St. Teresa of Avila (1515-1582) as cited by Peter Kreeft, *Making Sense out of Suffering* (Ann Arbor, Mich.: Servant Books, 1986), 139.

[243] Cited by Colleen McDannell and Bernhard Lang, *Heaven: A History* (New York: Vintage, 1990), 155.

[244] Richard Baxter, *The Practical Works of Richard Baxter* (Grand Rapids: Baker, 1981) cited in Randy Alcorn, *Heaven,* 330.

[245] J. C. Ryle, *Heaven* (Ross-shire, UK: Christian Focus Publications, 2000) cited in Alcorn, *Heaven,* 359.

[246] John Luke Terveen, *Hope for the Brokenhearted* (Colorado Springs, Co.: Cook Communications Ministries, 2006), 141.

[247] The expression "aching visionaries" comes from Nicholas Wolterstorff, *Lament for a Son* (Grand Rapids: Eerdmans, 1987), 86.

[248] F. J. Boudreaux, *The Happiness of Heaven,* chapter 11. https://www.gutenberg.org/cache/epub/25224/pg25224.html

[249] C. S. Lewis, *Letters to Malcolm: Chiefly on Prayer* (London: Geoffrey Bles, 1964), 158.

[250] Alcorn, *Heaven,* 100.

[251] Daniel 7:18; Luke 19:17; 1 Corinthians 6:2-3; 2 Timothy 2:12; Revelation 22:5.

[252] Beyond the "crown of life," there is (1) the "crown of rejoicing," referring to people who have come to Christ through our influence (1 Thessalonians 2:19; Philippians 4:1); (2) the "crown of glory" that God promises to under-shepherds

who faithfully carry out their pastoral responsibilities (1 Peter 5:4); (3) the "crown of righteousness" as the reward for those who expectantly look forward to the Lord's return (2 Timothy 4:8); and (4) the "imperishable wreath" (NASB) that is given to those Christians who live a disciplined life (1 Corinthians 9:24-27). See Joseph C. Dillow, *The Reign of the Servant Kings* (Hayesville, NC: Schoettle Publishing Co. 1993), 574-583.

[253] C. S. Lewis, *The Problem of Pain*, 93.

[254] The Bible teaches that, upon death, the believer enters what theologians term the "intermediate heaven." It is intermediate in that it is the residence of the believer's spirit in the presence of God as he/she awaits the resurrection of the body. It is the dwelling place of believers who have died (Luke 23:43; 2 Corinthians 5:8) prior to the establishment of Christ's earthly reign (Revelation 20) and the new heavens and earth (Revelation 21).

[255] The original source of this citation is the *Sacramento Daily Union,* Volume 15, Number 20, 16 March 1882 found at the California Digital Newspaper Collection: https://cdnc.ucr.edu/?a=d&d=SDU18820316.2.18&e=-------en--20--1--txt-txIN--------1. It is also cited somewhat differently by Randy Alcorn, *Heaven*, 397.

[256] Stephen R. Covey, *The Seven Habits of Highly Effective People* (New York: Simon and Schuster, 1989), 96.

[257] C. S. Lewis, *Christian Behaviour* (New York: Macmillan, 1948), 55.

[258] C. S. Lewis, *Problem of Pain,* 72.

[259] Randy Alcorn, *Heaven*, 442.

[260] Ola Elizabeth Winslow, *Jonathan Edwards: Basic Writings* (New York: New American Library, 1966), 142.

[261] This concept is adapted from Alcorn, *Heaven*, 420.

[262] G. Campbell Morgan, *An Exposition of the Whole Bible.* (Westwood, N.J.: Fleming H. Revell, 1959), 480.

www.ingramcontent.com/pod-product-compliance
Lightning Source LLC
Chambersburg PA
CBHW020415150626
46554CB00014B/1238